Praying *with*
America

100 Years of Encountering God in Prayer with America *Magazine*

CONTRIBUTORS INCLUDE:
Thomas Keating, OCSO
Henri J. M. Nouwen
William O'Malley, SJ
Richard J. Hauser, SJ
Jane Redmont
Kaya Oakes
Daniel J. Harrington, SJ
William A. Barry, SJ
Evelyn Waugh

EDITED BY **JAMES MARTIN, SJ**

America | MEDIA
A JESUIT MINISTRY

D0684698

LOYOLA PRESS.
A JESUIT MINISTRY

3441 N. Ashland Avenue
Chicago, Illinois 60657
(800) 621-1008
www.loyolapress.com

America | MEDIA
A JESUIT MINISTRY

© 2015 AMERICA Press
All rights reserved.

Cover art credit: © iStock/Kaligraf

ISBN-13: 978-0-8294-4394-3
ISBN-10: 0-8294-4394-0
Library of Congress Control Number: 2015947674

Printed in the United States of America.

15 16 17 18 19 20 Bang 10 9 8 7 6 5 4 3 2 1

Contents

Introduction

James Martin, SJ

Since 1909, *America*, the "National Catholic Review," has been widely known as a place where readers can look in print and, more recently, online, for a smart Catholic take on events of the day. What is less well known is that during those same years *America* has regularly published a great many articles on more overtly spiritual matters. In other words, the editors and writers have turned their attention not simply to current events but also to timeless ones.

This new book brings together the very best of *America*'s writings on a particular topic: prayer.

Prayer can be difficult to write about, because trying to explain it is something like trying to pin down a butterfly. The more you seek to capture it, the more it wants to escape. In the end, what happens in prayer is incommunicable because it happens privately, between one person and God. Even the greatest and most articulate saints have struggled to communicate not only how they pray but also what happens when they do. Often they resort to metaphors that even they admit fail.

Then again, prayer is beyond no person. Everyone can pray. God desires to enter into relationship with each of us, and one need not be a cloistered mystic to enjoy the fruits of prayer.

And so, as the editors have realized since 1909, part of *America*'s mission is to help people encounter God. To help them encounter God, we are invited to help them to pray.

You'll notice right away how those efforts have changed over the years. Earlier articles are filled with language more flowery than what the modern reader is used to. Likewise, in the earlier work there is generally a more elevated way, as was the custom of the time, of referring to the object and source of our prayer: not "Jesus" but "Christ Our Lord," not "God" but "Almighty God." (And here's a warning for anyone allergic to noninclusive language: get ready for a lot of "Hims.") One can also see a gradual shift, after the Second Vatican Council, in favor of a greater degree of—for want of a better word—*relaxation* around the topic of prayer. Prayer becomes not so much something one *must* do as something one is *invited* to do.

Otherwise, not much has changed. The emphasis on trying one's best to pray no matter what the circumstances, the focus less on self and more on God, and the flexibility that has always marked Jesuits and their colleagues, are evident in almost every article.

Several authors take their cue from the Jesuit or "Ignatian" traditions of prayer—that is, those based on the writings, practices, and traditions of St. Ignatius of Loyola, the sixteenth-century founder of the Society of Jesus. Many authors make reference to the *Spiritual Exercises*, the now-classic manual for a four-week retreat written by St. Ignatius. In the *Exercises*, Ignatius frequently encourages the retreatant to imagine himself or herself within a Gospel scene, as one progresses through the life of Christ, with as much vividness as possible. So you will see frequent references to some aspects of the *Exercises*.

Several writers seem to be making a case for one form of prayer over another. So perhaps this is a good time to remind readers that there is no "best" way of prayer. Whatever works best for you is the best way of prayer. Some may enjoy Ignatian contemplation, others the Rosary, others centering prayer, others the examination of conscience. The Mass of course is the "source" and "summit" of Catholic prayer, as Vatican II reminded us, but in addition to the Mass it is important for believers to try a variety of ways to pray, in order to get a taste of a particular practice, and to try them at different points in one's life, because one's spiritual tastes may change. But any way that you choose to relate to God is worthwhile.

Think of prayer, as one of our writers, William A. Barry, SJ, likes to say, as a "personal relationship." Friends often relate to one another in different ways—some like to take long walks; some like to see movies together; some like to have cups of coffee in one another's home; some like to talk on the phone; and so on. At some point every relationship needs intimate, one-on-one time. This intimate, one-on-one time with God is called prayer. But there are many ways to pray.

Also, remember that prayer may not always seem "rich." As many writers admit in this collection, sometimes prayer seems "dry." This is simply part of the spiritual life. In the end, however, no time spent in the presence of God is ever wasted. Any time spent in the presence of God is transformative.

One final note: Much of this book—the preparation and the assembly of the articles—is the work of Joseph McAuley, an assistant editor at *America* magazine. His quiet, tireless, humble work on this manuscript was a kind of prayer itself. Thanks also to Tim Reidy, executive editor; and Ashley McKinless, associate editor; for all their help on this volume.

And to our co-publishers at Loyola Press, I would like to thank Joe Durepos for working so hard to help bring this book to completion; Vinita Wright and Yvonne Micheletti for their careful help in the editing; and Andrew Yankech for assisting with the final cover selection. We're so grateful to be working with such a wonderful Jesuit ministry.

On behalf of the editors of *America*, I would like to welcome you into this treasury of writings by authors who have graced our pages and our website. We hope that this little book helps you pray. We ask for your prayers. And we promise you ours.

James Martin, SJ, is a Jesuit priest, editor at large, of America and author of many books including Jesus: A Pilgrimage, The Jesuit Guide to (Almost) Everything, and My Life with the Saints.

1909

Official Prayer

The Editors

The presence in our waters of battleships from many nations, and especially of the Italian squadron, suggests the appositeness of reproducing "The Prayer of the Italian Mariner," composed by the bishop of Cremona. Admiral Mirabello, the Italian Minister of Marine, has pronounced it "fervently patriotic and thrilling with exalted poetic inspiration" and ordered that it be printed on sheets of parchment and posted on every warship of the Italian navy. We take it from *La Semaine Catholique* of Toulouse.

> To Thee, great God, Lord of the Heavens and the Deep, Whom winds and waves obey, we, men of the sea and of war, officers and soldiers of Italy, from the decks, of the armed fleet of our Fatherland raise up our hearts. Save and exalt in faith, Great God, our Nation; save and exalt our King; give power, give glory to our flag, where'er it waves; bid tempest and surge be subject, let the enemy be inspired with God-sent fear. May hearts of iron stronger than the armor of our fleet be ever beneath its folds to defend, and may it ever be victorious. Bless, Lord, our distant homes and those who dwell therein; bless, this coming night, the slumbers of our people. Thy blessing, too, for us who keep watch for them in arms upon the sea. Thy blessing!

This noble prayer expresses the sentiment of every Christian nation and might well be adopted by ours. It would fortunately involve no revolutionary change in our national customs. From the birth of our Republic, God's blessing has been invoked on congress, legislatures, soldiers and seamen. Every year our President sets a day apart and calls on all our people to give thanks to God. We have many faults and failings that fall short of the Christian ideal;

there are among us many sects and sectaries and people of no sect who take large liberties with Christian principles, and a few who deny them altogether. But the spirit that informs our Constitution and laws and directs the general conscience of government and people is such that in the broader sense we may be termed a Christian nation.

The Hudson-Fulton festivities[1] strengthen this impression, at least to a Catholic observer. Intended to signalize the material development initiated by explorers and inventors of whom Hudson and Fulton are types, the celebrations were equally suggestive of the growth of Catholicity. As the line of battleships moved up the Hudson, officers and men could not look shoreward without resting their eyes on a Catholic institution, nor their searchlights play long on either bank without lighting up a cross. Verily the Catholic Verrazzano would feel more at home on the stream today than Henry Hudson. He would marvel at the wondrous city that has grown on the barren isle he discovered in 1524, but were he here last Sunday, many familiar sounds and scenes would recall his native city. He would have heard as many Catholic bells call men to prayer as ever pealed from the towers of Florence; and he would find, with his countrymen who came officially to grace the occasion, that the prayer, composed by the Archbishop of New York and recited in all the churches of his diocese, was framed in the spirit of the Bishop of Cremona's:

> We pray Thee, O God of might and wisdom, that those entrusted with the guidance of the destinies of our beloved country may lead it in the paths of justice and mercy by encouraging due respect for justice and wisdom and restraining vice and immorality. . . . We recommend to Thy unbounded mercy the future welfare of our country. We pray that our brethren and fellow citizens may be blessed in the knowledge and sanctified in the observance of Thy most holy law, that they may be preserved in union and in that peace which the world cannot give; and after enjoying the blessings of this life be admitted to those which are eternal.

A prayer that fits our needs, and to which all our people will say, Amen.

October 2, 1909

---

1. Refers to Hudson-Fulton Celebration of 1909, which celebrated the 300th anniversary of Henry Hudson's discovery of the Hudson River and the 100th anniversary of Robert Fulton's "first successful application of steam to navigation" on that river. http://victoriansource.com/id24.html

1916

A Comprehensive Prayer

The Editors

"O God, make bad people good and good people nice" is the admirable prayer that a child in a recent novel used to offer every day. If that petition were granted without reserve, the earth would be an Eden, the Golden Age would return, sin would cease to be attractive and virtue would always be amiable. But now, alas!, so fallen is the world, that often a winning personality robs vice of ugliness, human imperfections obscure the beauty of holiness, and arrogant pretense triumphs over modest worth. This was the sad spectacle that made Shakespeare call for "restful death," so tired was he of beholding

> . . . .desert a beggar born.
> And needy nothing trimmed in jollity,
> And purest faith unhappily forsworn . . .
> And right perfection wrongfully disgraced,
> And strength by limping sway disabled,
> And art made tongue-tied by authority,
> And folly doctor-like controlling skill,
> And simple truth miscalled simplicity,
> And captive Good attending captain ill.

Without question, much could be done toward securing the desired answer to the first part of little Sally's prayer, and more "bad people" would become "good," if "good people" would only make greater efforts to be "nice." Piety should be amiable, and true Catholic piety, because it is so cheerful, sensible and practical, is always amiable. But the Novatian, the Jansenist, the Puritan, or whatever the rigorist of the age was called, invented a dour, inhuman and unworkable "virtue" which he misnamed piety, but which differs as widely from real piety as pinchbeck differs from gold. In the Ages of Faith, Christians were no less "merry" than pious; the Catholics of our day besides being "good" should also be "nice."

July 1, 1916

1918

The Holy Father's Day of Prayer

The Editors

On May 11, President Wilson, it will be recalled, issued a proclamation urging the people of the United States to observe Memorial Day this year as a day of "public humiliation, fasting and prayer," on which they should offer "fervent supplications to Almighty God for the safety and welfare of our cause, His blessings on our arms, and a speedy restoration of an honorable and lasting peace to the nations of the earth." Without question every Christian in the land rejoiced to see our Chief Executive officially attesting that "it has always been the reverent habit of the people of the United States to turn in humble appeal to Almighty God for His guidance in the affairs of their common life," and begging all his fellow citizens to beseech Almighty God to "forgive our sins and shortcomings as a people and purify our hearts to see and love the truth, to accept and defend all things that are just and right and to purpose only those righteous acts and judgments which are in conformity with His will." For that proclamation, being a humble acknowledgment of God's sovereignty and of our utter dependence on Him, presented a striking contrast to the absence of any similar official acknowledgments on the part of the European belligerents.

By a remarkable coincidence, on May 10, just a day before President Wilson issued his proclamation, Our Holy Father, Pope Benedict XV, by a *motu proprio* addressed to the Universal Church, named June 29, the Feast of Rome's chief Patrons, the great Apostles, Sts. Peter and Paul, as the day on which all the clergy and all the Faithful should unite with his Holiness in earnestly entreating Almighty God speedily to "give back His peace to the world and restore the reign of charity and justice among men."

After reminding his children that since he took up the burden of the Supreme Pontificate, almost four years ago, his Holiness has with anguish of heart shared in all the sorrows and sufferings of his children of every race and nation, he assures them that out of a burning desire to bring the war to an end he has "omitted nothing which consciousness of his Apostolic duty or the charity of Christ suggested" to him. He realizes, however, that Almighty God, "who rules the hearts of men and the course of events," and who "heals whilst punishing and forgiving saves," must first be appeased and made to forget the just anger which the world's iniquity has aroused in Him. "Humble and suppliant prayer," the Pope continues, "offered with perseverance and trust, will contribute much to this end; but more efficacious still in obtaining the Divine mercy is the Holy Sacrifice of the Mass in which we offer to our Heavenly Father Him 'who gave Himself in redemption for all,' and lives still to intercede for us."

The Holy Father ends his letter by expressing the hope that if every priest in the Church, with all the Faithful of course assisting, will celebrate Mass that day and unite their intentions to his, the restoration of peace to the world will not long be delayed. "Thus will the whole Catholic priesthood," his Holiness says in conclusion, "in union with the Vicar of Christ, offer on every altar in the world the Host of propitiation and of love and by doing violence together to the Heart of God will strengthen the hope that at length that for which all people long may be realized: 'Justice and peace have kissed.'"

The Pope's choice of the day and his selection of the means for propitiating Heaven and thus securing the return of peace could not be bettered. For the two great Apostles on whose feast the prayers of Catholic Christendom are to be offered up will effectively intercede with God to give the world that freedom from war's horrors which is so necessary a condition for the spread of the Faith among heathen peoples. St. Peter, the foundation stone of Christ's Church, will surely pray that the sheep and lambs committed to his keeping may no longer be scattered and ravened by the dogs of war, and the holy Apostle Paul, the preacher of truth and the doctor of the gentiles, will not cease to intercede for the beloved little ones, whom he brought forth in Christ, until God mercifully lays aside His anger and gives them peace. But far more efficacious even than the intercession of Sts. Peter and Paul is the clean oblation that will be made on all the altars of the world between the rising and the setting of June twenty-ninth's sun. For every priest in the Church will doubtless offer to God on that day for the Pope's intentions the unbloody sacrifice of propitiation which speaketh better than the blood of Abel, and will celebrate the mystical immolation of Our Divine Redeemer Himself, and by thus rendering God a satisfaction more than sufficient to atone, for the sins of ten thousand worlds, will hasten the coming of a just and permanent peace.

June 29, 1918

1925

The Secret of the Little Flower

C. M. de Heredia, SJ

"I will spend my heaven in doing good upon earth," said the Little Flower, and she fulfilled her promise. The favors granted through her intercession are counted by the thousands. She has been dead not yet thirty years and the "shower of roses" is so thick that the Holy See has decided to canonize her on May 17.

The Little Flower was not a theologian and, while living, made a statement that sounds theologically wrong if it is not well understood. "In heaven," she said, "the good God will do all I desire because I have never done my own will on earth."

Theology teaches us that the blessed in Heaven have no will of their own. They wish nothing else than what God wants. No saints will ask God any favor for us unless they see that such is the will of the Lord. Nevertheless Thérèse emphatically said that "in Heaven God was going to grant her all her desires," or in other words, that "in Heaven she was going to do her own will." She could not have meant that "in heaven God was going to do her will because her will there should be the will of God." In that way we may say that all blessed are doing their own will. She really meant what she said, that actually in Heaven the good God will do all she desires, and she gives the reason "because I have never done my will on earth." And the "shower of roses" proves to us that such is the real meaning of her words.

We practically see that "God is granting her all she wants."

Are the theologians wrong and the Little Flower right?

It seems to us that the theologians are right and little Thérèse is not wrong.

It is our common experience that when we pray to some saints it takes time to have our prayers answered and often we apparently receive no answer at all. But if we ask the same favor through the intercession of another saint, we receive a swift answer. Naturally we are curious to know the reason for it. We want to know why it is so.

There is no man on earth who knows the real reason for it. "For who hath known the mind of the Lord? Or who has been his counselor?" (Rom. ii, 34). Yet we are allowed to conjecture.

Theologians have excogitated several explanations for this fact. Some say that the nearer a saint is to Our Lord the easier it is for him to intercede on our behalf. Some claim that when the Almighty wishes to attract the attention of the Faithful towards one of the blessed, He grants favors more easily through his intercession. It may be so, but it seems to us that besides these and other reasons commonly adduced by Catholic writers to explain this fact, there is another explanation of it, which can be certainly applied to the special case of Thérèse. This is what we call the secret of the Little Flower.

> Give me a lever and a fulcrum on which to lean it, said Archimedes, and I will lift the world. But what this scientist could not obtain . . . the saints have obtained in all its fullness. The Almighty has given them as fulcrum to lean upon, Himself, Himself alone, and for a lever, the *prayer* that inflames with the fire of love. And thus they have uplifted the world. . . .
> (*A Little White Flower*, page 247).

These words of Little Thérèse show us what she thought of the power of prayer. And she was perfectly right. Prayer is all powerful. St. Augustine has defined prayer as "the strength of man and the weakness of God." But prayer being essentially an act of confidence in God, St. Augustine teaches us that if our confidence is weak, prayer expires; for "how then shall they call on him in whom they have not believed?" (Rom. x, 14). But where faith is strong, the power of prayer is boundless. "Amen, I say to you, if you shall have faith, and stagger not, not only this of the fig tree shall you do, but also if you shall say to this mountain, Take up and cast thyself into the sea, it shall be done. *And all things whatsoever you shall ask in prayer, believing, you shall receive*" (Matt. xxi, 21–22).

Now what was the "confidence" that the Little Flower had in God, how deep was her faith, can be easily found out by reading her autobiography. There is not a single page, we may say, on which her immense *trust in Christ* is not clearly expressed or implicitly understood. It is "the way of spiritual childhood, *the way of trust . . .*" her special "little way" that she taught and practiced constantly and faithfully during her whole life.

So we see that the Little Flower was fitted to pray for anything she wanted with certainty of having her prayer answered. But prayer can still be strengthened if it is supported by sacrifice and love. If the person who has an unbounded confidence in the Lord, loves Him tenderly, and is constantly offering sacrifices to show Him how much He is loved, prays for something, his prayer is omnipotent. No matter how great is the favor requested, God cannot but listen to that prayer. The Little Flower was doing this during all her life, and she could not be better fitted to have any of her prayers answered.

Now when Christ Our Lord said, "And all things *whatsoever* you shall ask in prayer, believing, you shall receive," He did not restrict in any way the field of prayer. We may ask for a spiritual as well as for a temporal favor, present or future, in time or in eternity. We must not forget either that while praying for a favor, it is not necessary to ask for it with a special formula or definite words; it is enough to manifest to our Lord in some way what we want, to have it granted. Let us suppose a girl, who is very anxious to have a doll, does not say a word to her father; she only tries to do her best to please him. But he knows well what his daughter wants, and seeing that she is good he makes up his mind to give her for Christmas the most beautiful doll in the market. When Christmas comes sure enough she gets a doll, but more beautiful than the one she had in her mind. Father knew much better. So with God, and as a father He is anxious to grant splendidly our inner desires.

Since Thérèse came to the use of reason she heard hundreds of times that her father and mother had been, all their married life, very anxious to have "a son who would be one day a missionary in the Far East." She knew too that at her birth they were somewhat disappointed because she was not a boy, and though they were perfectly resigned to the will of God, both went on praying that "in some way" their children would do a real apostolic work by praying for the souls of infidels and sinners. That is the reason why M. Martin so willingly made to God the sacrifice of separating himself from his daughters, glad to see them entering the Carmel, "an order of missionaries, by prayer."

So Thérèse since her childhood was accustomed to pray to God for the same intention, and when she grew up she entered the Carmel ready to sacrifice herself, "not doing her own will, but the will of God" to obtain from the Lord the grace to save, by praying, many souls. This was the "constant prayer of her lifetime." Then, little by little, this idea was crystallized in her mind: "Although I can be an apostle by praying during my life, I want besides to be a real missionary after my death and save many, many souls."

> One day one of the Mothers thought: How happy I should be if this little saint would only say, I will repay you in Heaven. Simultaneously Sister Thérèse turning to her said, "Mother, I will repay you in Heaven." And another time she said to her *Little Mother*: In Heaven I shall obtain many graces for those who have been kind to me. As for you, Mother, all I send will not suffice to repay you, but there will be much to make you rejoice (Epilogue).

From these words we can deduce two things: That her desire was to "repay" with benefits from Heaven those that had been good to her on earth. And that she had the "certainty" that she was going to do so. But "her little soul" had greater aspirations. She wanted to "repay love by love," and consequently she was exceedingly anxious to do for God all she could, not only in time but in eternity, hence:

> Another time she interrupted a Sister who was speaking of the happiness of Heaven. . . . It is not that which attracts me. What is it then asked the Sister. Oh, she said, it is Love! To love, to be loved, and *to return to earth to win love for our Love.*

So we see that her constant desire was "to become a missionary after her death." And to obtain this favor she *prayed* constantly, "*trusting* and loving" and, at the same time "sacrificing herself." That is what she meant when she said: "In Heaven the good God will do all I desire because I have never done my own will on earth." God is not obliged by any promise to do the will of any saint in heaven because they have never done their own will on earth, but He has certainly promised, and He is obliged to fulfill His word, that "all things whatsoever you shall ask in prayer, believing, you shall receive." It was not her self-sacrifice that obtained the Little Flower the grace to "return to earth to win love for Christ," *it was her prayer*, her trusting and loving prayer supported by her sacrifice what won her this uncommon privilege.

And she knew well while living that this grace "was *already* granted to her." That is the reason why she was so sure that "she was going to spend her Heaven in doing good upon earth." That is the reason why she added, "No, there cannot be any rest for me till the end of the world, till the Angel has said, 'Time is no more.' Then I shall take my rest. . . ." That is why she promised with an undoubting faith, "After my death I will let fall a shower of roses." She knew that her *prayer* was *already* answered and after her death she was going "to come down." She knew very well that "He has always given her what she desired, or rather He has made her desire what He wishes to give." This is "the *secret of the Little Flower*." God inspired her to pray that in Heaven the good God would do all she desired, and her constant, trustful and loving *prayer*, supported by her self-sacrifice, obtained it. Our Lord inspired her to pray "in that way" because "the will of God was to grant her in Heaven all her desires." And so by asking Him in Heaven all she wishes, she is doing the will of the Lord. The theologians are therefore right, and the Little Flower is not wrong; she is doing in Heaven her own will, because such is the will of God.

This may or may not be the ultimate reason why the Little Flower is letting fall such a wonderful "shower of roses upon earth," but one thing is perfectly true: that if we *pray with faith* we can obtain the same favor as the Little Flower has obtained. Because when Our Lord said, "All things whatsoever you shall ask in prayer, believing, you shall receive," He did not restrict the efficacy of prayer to time, past or present; we may as well ask, and obtain, favors in eternity.

In the meantime the mission of the Little Flower, to make the good God loved as she loved Him, has only begun, and the centuries shall bear their witness to the fruits of her trusting prayer and her loving trust in God's all-merciful Love.

May 16, 1925

1928

Thanksgiving Day

The Editors

The ancient and honorable festival which we call Thanksgiving Day is at hand. In the fact that in the United States alone does the civil power set aside a day on which the people are invited to return thanks to Almighty God, the religious-minded citizen will find cause for gratification. The custom undoubtedly had its origin in pioneer New England, where under an extreme of Puritan influence it usurped for many years the place of Christmas Day. Joel and little Deborah might gambol it, in the grave fashion befitting a Puritan festival, on Thanksgiving Day, but the poor little creatures knew nothing of the Friend of children in His crib at Bethlehem. Happily, however, even in New England we can now turn our minds to God in grateful remembrance on the last Thursday in November, and feel our hearts respond with deeper gratitude as we contemplate God's great Gift to the world on Christmas Day.

Christian folk will note with pleasure that within the last decade and a half Thanksgiving Day has assumed a more definitely religious tone than some of us knew in our childhood. Once it was a day for feasting merely, and without cakes, ale, and our national bird, the turkey, the festival was sadly incomplete. With these creature comforts at hand, the beginnings of a day of solid comfort were beyond hazard. But Mr. Volstead[2] has deprived us of ale, that creature baptized by centuries of Christian usage, and the food profiteers have made the once abundant turkey the peculiar comfort of the opulent gullet.

---

2. Refers to Andrew Volstead, chairman of the House Judiciary Committee when the 18th Amendment (National Prohibition Act) was passed; this was popularly known as the Volstead Act.

The rest of us must procure such meats as are in keeping with our lean purses, and season the dish liberally with thankfulness.

The custom of opening the churches for religious exercises is becoming common. There was a time when to throw open the doors on any morning save the Sabbath, savored of popery and the Gunpowder Plot. That era is passing as it should. Thanksgiving Day may be very properly celebrated with feasting, but its real purpose is lost unless we go down on our knees to return thanks to Almighty God for His countless blessings.

Governor Smith expressed one part of our duty admirably in his speech of November 13. "America cannot be unmindful of the blessings that have been showered upon her by an Almighty and Divine Providence," said the Governor. "No one can read our history and be unmindful of the proclamation of the President of the United States, asking that on Thanksgiving Day, in grateful appreciation, we offer thanks by prayer, and at the same time pray for a continuance of that benediction."

But we can go beyond this. For every Catholic the proper celebration of Thanksgiving Day will include, when possible, the bestowal of alms, attendance at the Holy Sacrifice of the Mass, and the reception of Our Lord in Holy Communion.

November 24, 1928

Praying Policemen

The Editors

It is related in the life of St. Alphonsus Liguori, prince of moralists and Founder of the Congregation of the Most Holy Redeemer, that on one occasion the holy old man received a visit from Mauro, architect of the King of Naples. Soon to behold the palaces of the Kingdom of God, the Saint was not greatly interested in earthly architecture, it may be supposed, but he was supremely interested in souls. "Are the churches frequented in Naples?" he asked. "Yes, yes, Monsignor, and you cannot imagine the good that results. We have Saints, even among the coachmen!" At these words—somewhat startling it must be confessed—the old man cried out, "Saintly coachmen at Naples! *Gloria Patri et Filio et Spiritui Sancto!* Saintly coachmen!" And that night he could not sleep but would frequently call for his attendant. "Did you hear what Don Mauro said?" he would inquire. "Saints among the coachmen in Naples! What do you think of that? Glory be to God!"

Now we have no testimony to the effect that saintly taxi drivers abound in New York, or anywhere else, but it is reasonable to suppose that the good Lord who two centuries ago drew Neapolitan coachmen in the way of perfection, still draws souls to Himself from all ranks of life. They are there. Only the beam in our eye keeps us from seeing them. But we feel quite certain that there are Saints among New York's policemen. At least one or two with whom we have come in contact (not officially, we hasten to add) indicated the possession of qualities which, in our inexpert eyes, appeared saintly. Once every year the members of the New York Police Department Holy Name Society gather at St. Patrick's Cathedral to receive Holy Communion in a body.

This year the day selected was Passion Sunday, and His Eminence, Cardinal Hayes, offered the Holy Sacrifice for them. Five thousand policemen on their knees is a sight not easily forgotten. Five thousand policemen approaching the Holy Table to receive their Saviour is enough to justify the cry, "Saintly policemen in New York! *Gloria Patri et Filio et Spiritui Sancto!* Saintly policemen in New York!"

It may well be. Only the Pharisee, doing good that all men may see and praise, would deny it. "You are not brought here by any order of a superior officer," said Mayor Walker, at the breakfast which followed. "It is your love of God that brings you. To find policemen on their knees before God will do more good than all the statutes on the books."

And there the Mayor touched upon an inescapable principle of good government. Teach the young to love God above all things, and their neighbor for His sake, and you lay, deep and unshakable, the foundations of stable government. Neglect that all-important duty, and you prepare for lawlessness. For unless the Lord keep the city, they labor in vain that guard it.

March 30, 1929

1937

The New Year

The Editors

Good things come to those who wait. So runs the ancient adage. But good things come more speedily to those who, while they wait, work and pray. It seems only yesterday that men high in authority assured us that prosperity was just around the corner, but six years have passed, and prosperity continues to lurk around an always distant corner. As we look back, we cannot understand how we have survived, but we still live and breathe. Yet since we have waited, and have prayed and worked, we may trust that in God's Providence, our expectations long-deferred will be fulfilled in 1937.

January 2, 1937

I Can't Pray

The Editors

Prayer has been described as the raising of the heart and mind to God. We pray when we think of Him with love, reverence, gratitude, or adoration. We pray when we talk with God, as a child might talk with its mother; when we tell Him of our needs of body and of soul.

All who believe in God and in Jesus Christ Whom He has given us, can pray. The complaint common among good people that they are unable to pray rests on a misconception of the nature of prayer. Prayer is not a matter of the emotions but of the will. In a very true sense it is correct to say that the sincere desire to know how to pray is itself a prayer. True, there are degrees in prayer, just as there are degrees in the facility and completeness with which we perform any good act, and they will learn to pray best who are faithful to regular practices of prayer. But no one can say with truth, "I can't pray." We can pray if only we wish to pray.

In tomorrow's Gospel, taken from the sixteenth chapter of the Gospel according to Saint John (xvi, 23–30), Our Lord gives us a brief but perfect sermon on prayer. It is most consoling to hear His solemn assurance "Amen, amen, I say to you, if you ask the Father anything in My Name, He will give it you." We ask in His Name, for the Son of God is our Elder Brother, and His merits give to our poor halting prayers an efficacy which in themselves they lack. But to ask in His Name means that we are to ask in His spirit, which is a spirit of abandonment to the will of God our Father. Of this abandonment He gave us a perfect example in His prayer in the Garden of Olives.

We are told in the *Imitation* that it is better to feel compunction than to know its definition. So too it is better to pray in the manner of a child talking to its mother than to trouble ourselves with learned disquisitions, useful and edifying as these may be, on the types and degrees of prayer of which the human soul is potentially capable. Before we can read Shakespeare with pleasure, we must learn the letters of the alphabet. We shall draw profit from tomorrow's Gospel if we end it with an examination of conscience. Do I give a certain time every day to prayer, just as I do to my meals, to my business, to my recreation? Do I pray in a purely routine manner, giving little or no thought to what I say? Or do I try to make my prayer a talk with God in which I adore Him, praise Him, thank Him for past benefits, and ask Him simply and with confidence to help me?

People who pray keep close to God. Those who habitually neglect prayer cut themselves off from many graces. Daily are we exposed to the assaults of the enemy of our soul, and daily must we through prayer draw nearer to Him Who is our secure refuge in every tribulation.

May 1, 1937

1938

The Dangerous Prayer

The Editors

Our grandmothers had more love of God than we, and more real faith in Him. Nothing but their faith and their love could have enabled them to treasure one of those voluminous old-fashioned prayer books, usually styled a "Manual," and use it, day by day, without losing a whit of their spirituality. We, more critical, wish our vocal prayers to be "practical."

We do not care to address Almighty God after the manner of a courtier humbly presenting a petition to Louis XIV. Very probably our pious grandmothers were eager to lay down their lives rather than commit the least sin, but if we were to put that in a prayer, we should be obliged to accuse ourselves of untruthfulness at our next confession.

But there is a prayer which most of us repeat every day; the prayer which Our Lord Himself taught to the Apostles. When we say it with the intention of pleasing Almighty God, we shall not lack our reward. But why not try to understand it? For this "Our Father" is really a very dangerous prayer.

To know why it is dangerous, we may turn to the Gospel according to Saint Mark and ponder on verses 23 to 25 of the eighteenth chapter. Here we have one of the most striking of Our Lord's parables, and it is striking because it is so very human. The story has been told again and again in the world's history, and it will be repeated as long as men bear in their hearts an unwillingness to forgive those who have offended them. The servant who owed his lord a great sum besought mercy and received it, when he could not pay the debt on demand. Immediately thereafter, he laid hold on a fellow-servant who owed him a small sum, and throttled him and threw him into prison because he could not pay. This ruthless servant at once met retribution at the hands of his master, and Our Lord warns us that eternal punishment will be our lot "if you forgive not everyone his brother from his heart."

Now let us return to the "Our Father." When we pray, "forgive us our trespasses, as we forgive those who trespass against us," we assuredly put ourselves in peril if our hearts are cold and unforgiving. We actually challenge God to deal with us as we deal with our offending brethren. Do we really wish God to take up that challenge?

When God forgives, He forgives and forgets. Our sin is as if it had never been. When we forgive, too often, alas, we remember! My sin ever rises up against me, mourned the Psalmist, but whatever rises up against us is our neighbor's sin. Outwardly we forgive, but not from our hearts. Of course, I'll speak to the fellow, we say; I won't cut him, but I haven't forgotten. And we await the day when we can repay evil, if evil it was, with evil.

One whose heart is filled with wrath, one who is unwilling to forgive and to forget, should sedulously avoid saying the "Our Father." As the words go, he calls down on himself God's wrath. What he should do, by the grace of God, is to put himself in a state in which he can say this dangerous prayer, and mean every word of it.

October 29, 1938

1941

What We Most Need

The Editors

We are assured by masters in the spiritual life that it is better to practice humility than to argue about what humility means. In the same way, it is more profitable to know how to pray than to be able to write a learned book about the nature of prayer. But these very masters have themselves given us definitions or descriptions of prayer which are very useful in helping us to learn how to pray. Thus the great Augustine has written that prayer is "the soul's affectionate quest of God," and Saint Gregory of Nyssa, that it is "familiar conversation with God." Both definitions stress the elements of simple love of God and confidence in Him, which are found in all true prayer.

Saint John Damascene comes nearer to the definition that has been very common since the time of that very practical Saint, Ignatius Loyola. Saint John teaches that prayer is "the elevation of the soul to God." This definition emphasizes our part in prayer by describing it as an act of the will, cooperating with Divine grace. By this prayer, possible to all of us, we raise ourselves above the limitations of sense to fix our minds and our hearts upon God. In prayer, we talk to God, as a child to his mother, as a friend to a friend; by prayer, we worship God, we glorify God, we praise God, and ask Him to give us, His children, all that we need to keep ourselves ever in conformity with His Holy will.

Prayer, then, can take many different forms. It can be expressed in words, or it can be borne to God by the unspoken aspiration of our souls. It can be a prayer by which, silent in His presence, we worship and glorify Him, or a prayer by which we put our needs before Him and beg Him to help us. In the Gospel for tomorrow (Saint John, xvi, 23–30) Our Lord speaks of this latter prayer, commonly called the prayer of petition. "If you ask the Father anything in my name, He will give it you." There is no limitation upon this promise, made by an infinitely truthful and loving Saviour, and in days when fears oppress the soul, we should find in it strength and consolation. We are as little children wandering in the night, weary, frightened children who have lost their way and fear they can never find the path back to the shelter of protecting love that they call home. Surely, surely, we must never forget that one sincere cry to God for His help will bring Him close to us. He is our loving Father, Who has solicitude for the least of His children, and He will not fail us.

But in our prayers of petition, do we not sometimes forget to ask Our Lord for the very things of which we stand in sorest need? We trouble ourselves about what we shall eat, and wherewith we shall be clothed, and too often think nothing of the greater needs of this poor soul of ours. It is sadly lacking in Faith, in Hope, in Charity, in humility; it is poor and naked in God's sight. Well is it to turn to God in simple childlike confidence in our temporal necessities, but better is it to beg Him for these heavenly graces which are food and raiment for our poor souls.

May 17, 1941

1943

The Great Prayer

The Editors

As the grip of war reaches closer into our lives, the mind of a Catholic who knows his Faith will turn more and more to "the Great Prayer," as the Sacrifice of the Mass is aptly called in a booklet recently issued by the Queen's Work Press in St. Louis (*The Great Prayer Now, in Time of War*).

The Mass is not only the prayer of Christ; it is Christ our Lord praying in person: offering the greatest of all prayers, that of the complete sacrifice of His own Body and Blood upon the Cross for the redemption and peace of the world.

How, then, can we take part in this Great Prayer? The Saviour does not wish to offer it alone but insists that we shall all pray with Him, join our thoughts and actions to His, one with Him, and thereby one with another.

So in order that there should be no doubt as to what He wants, He explained at the Last Supper, as Saint John relates, just how we should act.

The Great Prayer, as we see by our Lord's words, is directed not to the Person of Christ, the God-Man, but to the Person of God the Father. The Saviour prayed habitually to His Father; He taught His disciples to pray to His Father, and He asks us to do the same. There is a prayer of worship and a prayer of asking. In the Gospel of Saint John He speaks of the prayer of asking, but the idea is the same for both. The prayer is first and foremost to the Father, and our own prayer derives its power, its validity, from the fact that it is united with the prayer of the Risen Christ.

The Saviour in the Great Prayer does not just carry our prayers to His Father; He identifies Himself so closely with us that we speak "in His Name," in His own person, and so can put in an almost Divine claim on our own behalf. "In that day you shall ask in my name; and I do not say to you that I shall ask the Father for you, for the Father himself loves you because you have loved me, and have believed that I came forth from God" (St. John xvi, 26).

This is a new procedure. "Hitherto, you have not asked anything in my name. Ask, and you shall receive, that your joy shall be full." And in the preceding sentence the Saviour promises that no prayer thus uttered shall go unanswered; though the answer may not always occur as we expect. During the coming weeks the Church recalls the Saviour's urging that we pray "in His Name" for the Holy Spirit, as the great gift. We ask the Father, through the Son, for the gift of the Spirit of God.

When next you attend Mass, notice how every part—particularly where petition is expressed—conforms to this idea of our prayer-life as given us by Our Lord. (A quite natural exception is the celebrant's three prayers before Holy Communion.) If you have learned to live in the spirit of the Great Prayer during Mass, you will learn to live it during all your waking hours. If you have made the Great Prayer your prayer, you have mastered the secret of asking so that "your joy may be full."

May 29, 1943

1961

"Above All, Your Prayers"

Gerard F. Giblin, SJ

In a swift raid through the Shenandoah Valley in 1864, Confederate Lt. Gen. Jubal Early came within a hair's breadth of capturing Washington. For a few days the fate of the capital and its President was in doubt. A Union minister in a town occupied by Confederate forces approached Early and inquired if he might continue to offer prayers for Mr. Lincoln. Union commanders, when the situation was reversed, had forbidden prayers for President Davis. "Of course," said old Jube magnanimously, "he needs them."

The Yankee minister's custom of praying for the President was a laudable one. It might well lead Catholics of the present day to examine their own consciences. Do they pray for the man in the White House?

Time was long ago when prayer for the head of the state was an official part of the liturgy. Centuries back Catholics prayed on Good Friday for their "Most Christian Emperor N." (N. was for *Nomen*—whatever his name might be.) But things were simpler then: all of Christianity was, theoretically at least, united under one sovereign. The Holy Roman Empire, however, died officially in 1806; a century and a half later, in the 1955 revision of the liturgy, the prayer for the Emperor died too. Have Catholics stopped praying for their temporal rulers? Of course not. In the Archdiocese of Los Angeles, for instance, Cardinal McIntyre has directed the priests of his 295 parishes to add prayers for the President after all Masses. "Pray," the Cardinal directed his Flock, "that God will direct our President in the path of justice, truth and charity."

However, the lack of a generally approved prayer prompted Mary McLaughlin to write a letter recently to *America* (7/22). She complained that, although she had seen foreign missals which contained prayers for the English Queen, the Belgian King and the French government, there was no such prayer for the President of the United States.

A goodly number of readers seconded Miss McLaughlin's complaint. As a solution they proposed the prayer of John Carroll, first American bishop. The prayer is found in many current missals including the Lasance *Missal for Every Day* and the *St. Andrew Daily Missal.*

The Archbishop's prayer was composed in 1800, a troubled time, just a few short months after American frigates had ceased their undeclared war with France. "O God," runs a part of Carroll's petition, "assist . . . the President of these United States, that his administration may be conducted in righteousness and be eminently useful to Thy people over whom he presides."

This prayer is in use in many localities today. Msgr. Francis J. Jansen of Hammond, Indiana, wrote in his reply to Miss McLaughlin's letter that his congregation recites it every Thanksgiving Day after Mass. In the Archdiocese of San Francisco, Carroll's prayer is recited on the Feast of the Immaculate Conception, Patroness of the United States.

No one will deny that the President needs prayers. Mr. Lincoln needed them in 1864, and Mr. Kennedy needs them today. He openly confessed as much in his recent Berlin speech. "I could not realize," said the President, "nor could any man realize who does not bear the burden of this office, how heavy and constant would be these burdens." He concluded by asking his fellow Americans for "your good will, your support and above all, your prayers."

It is a modest and reasonable request, one that all Americans should be eager to fulfill.

August 26, 1961

1962

For Intellectuals: To the Wise Men

Evelyn Waugh

Like me you were late in coming. The shepherds were here long before; even the cattle. They had joined the chorus of angels before you were on your way. For you the primordial discipline of the heavens was relaxed and a new, defiant light blazed amid the disconcerted stars.

How laboriously you came, taking sights and calculating, where the shepherds had run barefoot! How odd you looked on the road, attended by what outlandish liveries, laden with such preposterous gifts!

You came at length to the final stage of your pilgrimage, and the great star stood still above you. What did you do? You stopped to call on King Herod. Deadly exchange of compliments in which there began that unended war of mobs and magistrates against the innocent!

Yet you came, and were not turned away. You, too, found room before the manger. Your gifts were not needed, but they were accepted and put carefully by, for they were brought with love. In that new order of charity that had just come to life, there was room for you, too. You were not lower in the eyes of the holy family than the ox or the ass.

You are our special patrons, and patrons of all latecomers, of all who have a tedious journey to make to the truth, of all who are confused with knowledge and speculation, of all who through politeness make themselves partners in guilt, of all who stand in danger by reason of their talents.

Pray for us. May we, too, before the end find kneeling space in the straw. For His sake who did not reject your curious gifts, pray always for all the learned, the oblique, the delicate. Let them not be quite forgotten at the Throne of God when the simple come into their kingdom.

Prayer put in the mouth of St. Helena, when she prays in Bethlehem, remembering "the three royal sages who had come from so far to adore Him."

From *Helena* by Evelyn Waugh (Chicago: Loyola Press, 1950), 208–210.

January 13, 1962

1963

Prayer for These Times

Rev. Terrence W. Halloran

Father in heaven, hear our prayer. Though we are different from each other in race, religion and culture, we are one in your family. You have made us all your children, brothers and sisters of one another.

Christ your Son has taught us by word and example what He means when He says, "Love your neighbor." He means "love everyone," not just those who are of our own race and nationality.

Father of us all, we thank you for making us live in "Freedom Summer 1963."[3] These are challenging times, and we can no longer be mediocre.

We thank you for the restlessness and impatience of those who want racial equality now. We thank you for the inspired leadership of the courageous men who are guiding the freedom movement.

Merciful God, forgive our past reluctance to involve ourselves in the fight for interracial justice. We have failed to practice the American virtue of directness. We have perhaps done more harm by our mediocrity than have the racists by their extremism.

We have seen our fellow citizens mistreated, and we have reacted with indifference, leaving them to work out their own problems. If their frustration erupts in violence, we can only blame ourselves. Pardon our failures, Lord, and strengthen our resolution to help secure freedom for all men.

Generous God and Father, give us a full outpouring of your Holy Spirit. Help us disregard the things that divide us, and make us one as members of your family.

---

3. Refers to a campaign to register African-Americans in Mississippi to vote in the 1964 presidential election and generally to participate in the political processes that so affected their lives.

Give us good leaders, who will teach us to be militant but not violent. Guard us from the temptation to be satisfied with tokenism or gradualism. Guide us into realistic discussion and effective action.

Make us see both the value of negotiation and the necessity for direct action against discrimination when negotiation has failed. Console us when we fail in breaking down racial barriers, or are criticized, or grow tired.

Continually disturb our consciences until we achieve a peace that is based on truth, justice, love and freedom for all.

Finally, Lord, be our reward in your everlasting kingdom, where people of every race and culture live in perfect unity. We ask these favors through Christ, your Son and our Brother. Amen.

August 17, 1963

1964

Subway Stations of the Cross

Cyril B. Egan

As a church, the subway is not much. In a pinch, a subway might pass for a church basement, maybe. But in general, not the place where you would expect to find God. Of course, you could make a smashing punch line out of such an upstairs in the downstairs. Just imagine: *I found God in the subway.* Sensational. But just a little bit absurd—or is it absurd?

I have seen a number of people reading prayer books in the subway. I have seen a priest reading his office in the subway. I have several times seen an old woman—at other times, a young woman—thumbing her rosary. And I am sure there are people who pray here or who devoutly meditate here without so much as moving their hands or their lips.

Prayer is the lifting of the mind and heart to God. God knows, a rider needs a lift in the subway. True, you can do crossword puzzles or read the ads, count beards and beatniks or the number of people who smile. But maybe what a man needs in the subway is to get away from people—to take off, imaginatively at least, in a flight to God.

But this is not religion. Religion must begin with people. These are the stubborn facts. Soulless as they appear, all these people have souls. I must face them—empathize, sympathize with my neighbor.

Who *is* my neighbor? My neighbor is an Irishman, an Irish-American. He is German, German-American. He is Negro, Puerto-Rican, Swedish, Chinese. My neighbor is the drunk across the aisle, the man who has squeezed into the half-foot of space between me and the next sitter. He is the swivel-hipped kid who is frazzling my ears with his transistor. Certainly I don't have to like these people, but I must love them.

If that's the case, I've got my task cut out for me here. All the sad, bored faces. The alien faces. Oh, to be back in the subway I first rode in 1904! Such a nice clean car, and so few people, and those mostly Irish-American and German-American. Today, if I saw an Italian in the subway, I, of Irish descent, would shout *Hurray, here's one of us!*

Why do I feel such a repulsion to these people? Do I dislike them because they are poor? Do I dislike them because they are bored? Because they do not smile? Because they are but cracked and dirty mirrors of exemplary me?

Who is my neighbor? "A certain Samaritan went down from Jerusalem to Jericho." Maybe he's only going from City Hall, at one end of town, to Fordham Road, at the other, but even a Samaritan moves warily here, worried lest the victim repudiate the rescue or, acceptant of the rescuer, snarl him in a web of litigious trouble.

I remember, after the lonely city streets of World War II, seeing at 34th and Broadway my first crowd of postwar people pouring into the subway. I felt overwhelmed. Some evil force seemed to be pelting people at me. I sighed with relief when I had moved off to the lonely end of the subway platform.

There is little physical aloneness, however, in this subway car where I now damply sit. . . . Enter through the center doors a man with a sign in bright heaven-blue letters: LOVE YOUR NEIGHBOR, JESUS DIED FOR YOU AND ME. . . . Isn't that ridiculous? In the middle of the subway! It's as if Christ walked in—in the rush hour—staggering under the weight of His cross. Would some Simon the Cyrenian help Him carry it? Would this Simon later get off with him to give him a hand? What an explanation Simon would have to make when he got home to his wife! Can you imagine the curtain lecture Simon's wife would give him?

"You're late. What's the reason? . . . You had to help someone out? A blonde? . . . Oh, a man. Did you *have* to help him? . . . An officer called on you to help him? Couldn't you have told him no? Well, you sure were a sucker to carry a cross all that way. What did *you* get out of it? . . . He said he was God? You really *are* crazy, aren't you? . . . So you want some liniment for your shoulder? Well, don't ask me to go get it for you. It's a long time since you went out of your way to carry anything for *me*."

On Good Friday I have seen at least one subway rider reading the Passion from the New Testament. Glancing over his shoulder at the page and the purple ribbon, I suddenly asked myself, *Why not the Subway Stations of the Cross?*

They're putting jazz in the liturgy, aren't they? I don't see why we can't put the Stations of the Cross in the subway. Maybe not *put* them, just *say* them. Does that sound blasphemous? Sometimes blasphemy and piety are separated by a hair's breadth. After all, I'm not taking God for a subway ride. God is everywhere, even in the dank air of the tomb, even in the subway, for that matter—as He was in the catacombs. The fact that I can conceive of His presence here as blasphemous indicates a certain unhealthiness in my own spiritual outlook.

Why *shouldn't* I make the Stations of the Cross in the subway? Why shouldn't I say, First Station, 14th Street?

The air is stale and stinking and a little sickening with pomade and cheap perfumes and the scent of tired bubble gum. The doors open to admit a surge of sticky, pushing people. Last man on has a bandaged head smelling of liniment. . . . "Hey, you, quit your shoving." "Get off my feet." . . . First Station, 14th Street: *Jesus is condemned to death.*

Identify, identify, identify. Well, if you can't identify, at least relate. Give me a rousing crisis, a big event, and I'll rise to it, finding not too much difficulty and not a little drama in relating to the sufferings of Christ. But the prosaic little difficulties that lie at the grass-roots level—at the subway level—are something else again.

What has my neighbor's kick in the shins—*my* shins—to do with the Passion of Christ? What have these sweating, stinking, aggressively scented, staring, glaring people to do with the Mystical Body? Who in this fifteen-cent hell is my neighbor? Maybe I can answer who is my neighbor—but not who are my neighbors, when there are seven and a half million of them, hundreds of whom have been packed hip to hip, sometimes almost eyeball to eyeball, in this mobile sardine can. How can I say, *Here Jesus is condemned to death*—where death has degenerated to a creeping claustrophobia for creatures whose life is already a part-time entombment?

We adore thee, O Christ, and we bless Thee, because by Thy holy cross Thou hast redeemed the world.

Second Station, 42nd Street. . . . At Times Square, five or six blocks west, my thoughts might readily escalate to the neighborhood aboveground—to the wantonness rampant on newsstand and movie billboard. That neighborhood bears a kind of cross. But here underground, at the drabber crossroads of 42nd Street and Lexington Avenue—how can I say, even under my breath, *Jesus is made to bear his cross?* Isn't it a bit melodramatic to call the hot, stale air a cross—the swastikas and sex symbols scrawled here a cross? How can I dignify as crosses the smell of dirty feet and oversweet perfume and humid humanity? Irritants, true. But what have they to do with God, or with me and religion?

We adore Thee, O Christ, and we bless Thee, because by Thy holy cross Thou hast redeemed the world. But to tell the truth, Lord, I find it pretty hard to relate these perspiring, prosaic experiences to myself and the Passion of Christ. You understand, Lord, don't You?

I think I have set myself too tough an exercise. I could of course make the Stations and ignore the people. But somehow this seems wrong. Somehow the people must come into this picture. But how? By stumbling over my feet? But I can't identify this sprawling somebody with the Saviour.

Jesus falls the first time, the second time, the third time; meets his mother, Veronica, the women of Jerusalem; is stripped of His garments, dies on the cross, is taken down and ensepulchered. . . . Where does any of this fit in the subway, unless it's the last stop at Woodlawn Cemetery? I know—that sounds like a ghastly joke. But it's no more than the honest hysteria of an overwhelmed imagination. Anyway, you can be sure there will be someone stopping off at Woodlawn, widow or widower, orphan or child-bereft, with the hope, if not of resurrection, at least of reunion in an eternal future—undistracted by frenetic subway noise.

A girl across the way opens a pocket book. The title reads *The Agony and the Ecstasy*. Very little ecstasy here in the subway. Change to the agony and the ugliness, and you have something more like it. A kind of small-time crucifixion. Creep, crawl, jolt, lurch.

Some people treasure the crucifix. Others hold it monstrous. Both are right. The crucifixion was monstrous, bloody and ugly. What could such a defacing be but ugly? But to the inner vision, the crucifix is God's love suffering and transforming ugliness—a bitterness that is but the prelude to beauty.

The train screeches to a halt. The motors stop; only the fans go whirling overhead, churning the stale air. Now the man standing to the right of my seat is arranging the pages of his newspaper so page one comes foremost; GANG LORD GETS CHAIR, reads the headline. Nineteen hundred and thirty years backward and forward, this could be—could have been—JESUS GETS THE CHAIR. And *Ecce Homo* could have been "Take a good look at this guy." . . . Is this too crude for you to stomach? So was the cross and the aching I.N.R.I. they tacked over the head of the Christ.

It looks, it feels, as if this subway will never run again. We are a carload of lost gaspers—a welter of suspended animation sidetracked in a corridor of eternity. Only the subway crusader, the holy guy with the inspirational signs, shows any evidence of being on the go. He has come back to our car and is passing through it with a new sign, which he has flipped over the old one.

WILL YOU NOT, says the sign, WATCH AND PRAY AN HOUR WITH ME? . . . The woman sitting on my right sees the sign bearer not. A luncheon tippler, she has been boozily dozing since she took her seat in the train. The passengers standing in front of me look beyond the sign bearer to the door. They are wondering if this car called claustrophobia is ever going to move again. "Watch and pray!" snorts the man on my left. He nudges me in the side. "Where the hell did that creep come from?"

"From the rear car," say I. "He was in this car a few minutes ago—with another sign. And I am beginning to think he may be the one sane man in the train. Maybe you and I are nuts."

Luckily, the sound of the motor stirring and the wheels rolling into action drown out my last sentence. In a minute we are moving into the streaming sunlight of the overground, on to my last station. Not to my last Station of the Cross (metaphor cannot stand so much strain), but to the end of my meditation—and a wheel-grinding *Amen*.

March 21, 1964

1972

The Credibility of Prayer

Doris Donnelly

There is a thirst among believers for prayer. Currently, it may be most obvious among the young whose yearning for interiority and evangelical fervor is closing the substantial credibility gap long associated with the idea of raising one's heart and mind to God. But the young are not alone. There are witnesses from disparate economic, generational and educational brackets who testify that they, too, are starved for a spiritual lifestyle centered on and nourished by the person and presence of Jesus Christ, who is master, mystery, conscience, inconvenience, friend and lover—who is God.

If we listen closely to the unequivocal and all-inclusive demands and response elicited by this personal spirituality, we learn that prayer at its core is a simple and direct "being with Christ." Only that and all that. It is a prayer that is long on experience and short on method, in touch with feelings and senses, alert mentally but unencumbered by cerebral machinations. Its interest is not in fitful startings and spurts of ardor, later abandoned and begun again, but rather in a constancy and permanency that is a way of life, embracing the whole person in ordinary as well as in its exquisitely intimate moments.

It is also filled, like the mystery it announces, with surprises, and the greatest of these may well be that men have rediscovered prayer in the first place. And not only rediscovered it, but also restored it to the center of the Christian experience, where it stands not merely as a diversionary or respectable activity, or even as a valid or necessary one, but as the heartbeat of the life of the follower of Christ who is called by name and in freedom to love as

Christ loves. Accepting the call will cost one's life, one's radical selfhood, but the simple fact is that for many, the experience of prayer is worth the price.

Not very long ago, the exercise of prayer was not regarded with the enthusiasm it is meeting at this time. To hear it told, there was a time when prayer was defined as group discussion and work in the ghetto. And there were those, believers among them, who argued with conviction that prayer was an excuse (help me, don't pray for me); that it made no difference (Divine Providence was unaffected by man); that it could not substitute for action (don't just stand there; *do* something); that it was, in varying degrees, frustrating, unnecessary and, most of the time (even for those committed to serving the will of God), a luxury.

Moreover, men who did not pray held that prayer was incompatible with psychology today: its passivity, it was felt, cultivated an inertia that stultified personal growth and debilitated the immediate and successful outcome of external events. It was argued that confidence in God fostered a type of psychological truncation and helped man revert to infantile stages of dependence. Prayer was suspect as a useless and unworthy enterprise that failed to involve man's creativity and imagination.

Eventually, those who did not pray confronted the disturbing first law of nonprayer dynamics—"a man cannot give what he does not have"—and learned that the God-as-father or Christ-as-brother experience they most urgently wanted to share in the ghetto, in the peace march and in the jail cell was the same personal experience they had meticulously sought to be without. Even the insight that God was found in all things, in work and in people, was short-circuited when it became impossible for the nonpraying man, by his own testimony, to recognize God in people and his work, unaccustomed as he was to discerning His presence in himself. The cult of nonprayer was a conviction and a way of life, but experience has changed these convictions and attitudes.

Renewed interest in prayer is a somewhat logical (if mysterious) consequence of the failure of those who tried to live without it and is their current testimony to the deeper level of engagement in other activities that is possible through prayer. Interestingly, this renewed enthusiasm for prayer is paralleled at the theological level by a series of insights that make God more accessible, hence knowable, hence lovable—insights that expose a gentle, personal, loving God, worthy of the risks and trust that are part of prayer. In particular, the process theology of Teilhard de Chardin, theologies of hope and the current theologies of Jesus Christ help reveal God as a person who grasps the imagination and heart of man, thereby making God and prayer credible once again.

These avenues of theologizing all point to a God of personality and presence who invites us to the intimacy of prayer. His credibility predicates the credibility of the effort and adventure of prayer. His presence explains the immediacy of His nearness even in His absence. His personality informs the mystery of transformation that occurs in prayer since prayer asks for nothing less than unconditional surrenders and change is implicit in the acceptance of these terms. This function of change, Hans Urs von Balthasar suggests, is "one of the main reasons why people so persistently avoid contemplative prayer, and, though admitting its necessity in principle, [they] evade any personal encounter with the Word."

Yet prayer remains the place where man deliberately situates himself in order to be changed, and theology today supports that situation. The sense of becoming, of changing, that is fundamental to process and hope theologies rests at the heart of prayer. If real prayer is going on, things will happen: man will listen, will follow, will die, will be born. He will never be the same. And this can happen because the God who leads and guides is at the same time fulfilling, uncompromising and believable.

Prayer, then, is credible when God is credible, and God is credible when He is approachable, loving, a father revealing His Son and His will. Prayer is a graced encounter with this personal God. It is an event characterized by peace, joy, praise, gratefulness, sorrow and, sometimes, terror—elicited not through a meeting with a God who punishes but rather through the wonder and awe spontaneously summoned by a God who saves.

If prayer is to be credible, there is no room for God's remoteness, inaccessibility and indifference, since these terms erode the mystery and corrode the vision; they posit a God devoid of personality and render the prayer enterprise incredible and idolatrous. The death of God is the death of prayer; distancing God is distancing prayer. And, in an effort to avoid this perennial problem of God's distance, contemporary theology, even on the pastoral level, has vigorously insisted on the immanence of God through the Incarnation, and the insistence has paid fruitful dividends.

For one thing, prayer is not insulated by the cumbersome abstract speculation about God's transcendence that tends to separate man from his God and to freeze prayer. Now, instead, God is seen as part of His own creation's history. He is present. He is now. He is, as Teilhard de Chardin explained, Someone "loving and lovable *at this very moment.*"

The personalization of God and theology, however, does not deny transcendence. The conviction that God transcends conventional categories of space and time is fundamental to Teilhard, but he approaches God in a way particularly supportive of prayer. For example, in answer to those who argue that prayer makes no difference and that God is the indifferent, unconcerned and nonparticipating programmer of human events, Teilhard's process thought suggests, without threatening His immutability, that God as creator is dependent on His creatures, and that the successful outcome of evolution holds the activity of man as necessary. Thus, man's free will is joined with the creative dynamics of a transcendent God in a way that encourages prayer.

The cosmos in process of becoming dispels any doubt that the final act has been done, or the last word uttered. On the contrary, even the fluidity of Teilhard's language informs us that without the positive, graced, love-motivated effort of man toward his goal, mankind, can, in fact, retard this becoming process and stultify the growth of the universe. Man and God must love and work together.

Current theologies of hope also suggest a rapprochement between prayer and theology. Theologies of hope provide access to miracle and mystery in a world where the constancy of evil seems to undermine any basis of belief in the future, and prayer appears to be an exercise in futility. The man who hopes is able to pierce through the now to a real future, to something new. His prayer is creative, indestructible, prophetic, visionary.

The man who hopes is not exempt from experiencing evil; alienation, poverty, misunderstanding, persecution are all part of his human experience. As a man who prays, however, the man who hopes is able to see these things infused with the vibrant, resurrected presence of Christ, who emptied Himself and who died in order to share our emptiness and death and to make them redemptive.

Process and hope theologies share an appreciation of the mystery of total and infinite Personality revealed in prayer and dramatically point to the wisdom of seeking and finding that Personality as it emerges through the Word of Scripture. Contemporary theologies of Christ also maintain two fundamental spiritual insights: the humanity of Jesus as the way to meet His divinity and full personhood, and the Word of Scripture as the place where this encounter will take place.

The first of these insights asserts that meeting the man Jesus will lead to a total decision that can be elicited not by any mere man but only by God. It is less concerned with doctrinal statements and more involved with existential commitment, holding that it is more likely for finite man to begin with an attraction to the teachings and personality of a human Jesus than with pronouncements of an infinite God. It is not difficult to see how prayer that is a "being with Jesus" as friend and lover would find this approach helpful and inviting.

The second insight is a little more complex. It maintains that the gospel is the norm and test of all spirituality and that a prayer life not supported by Scripture is a very weak one, indeed.

Contact with the Word of Scripture is indispensable if we are to experience Christ who is personal, who is God in our history and yet who is man, too. Contemporary Christologies vigorously acknowledge and accept the fruits of modern biblical scholarship with seriousness, but they also recognize that the prayerful use of Scripture is different from (though not incompatible with) a professional exegetical use. At their roots, current Christologies are in touch with the humanity as well as the divinity of Christ, accepting as determinative not who men say He is, but who we say He is. And the question is not simply calling for information; as a challenge, confrontation and invitation by Jesus, it calls for a commitment as well.

Response to such an invitation is characterized not by a cognitive rundown of the available data, but by a Christ-experience at once immediate, full, noncerebral and not threatened by the possibility of change, because a vision of living reality (and the Christ-experience is minimally that) accepts the inevitability of change and rests comfortably with the very idea of that inevitability.

To meet Christ in the simplicity of His word is an experience filled with paradox for the believer who is at once grasped and set free; conqueror and conquered; son and servant. Paradoxes confound the logical mind, but they are symptomatic of the real event of prayer where opposites are integrated and union with the beloved occurs. Self-conscious thought impedes and obstructs the contemplative frame of mind, and a current running through contemporary theology suggests a reliance on imaginative, nonabstract modes of thought that provide more direct access to oneness with self and oneness with God.

This is not an anti-intellectual stance. It seeks only to verify that factual data is inadmissible evidence for the credibility of prayer unless that information comes along with a profound sense of awe and reverence at the God (not man) who is at work drawing, revealing, loving—a discovery that touches the heart as well as the mind.

Theology can function by talking to a culture, about a culture, in a culture. But unless it's talking with a culture, with its concerns, preoccupations and hopes, then it profits nothing. Men of prayer have never asked theology to make its claim for relevance and authenticity by defining terms or solving problems of language analysis, but rather through an appreciation of mystery and human experience. What Karl Rahner calls "experiential mystery" lies at the heart of what his theological anthropology and much else of theology are about these days. And this angle of entry has enabled theology to establish the grounds of its credibility by talking with and not to the heart of our culture, to its experience of being, to its prayer life—a responsibility that theology has frequently abdicated in the past.

Many men who are rediscovering prayer have memories of a theology which chilled the emotions and drained their imaginations. But prayer and theology belong together as teachers and testers of one another. Theology today is ready for this encounter—particularly in the areas of hope, Teilhard's process and contemporary Christologies. This is good news for those who pray. Theology may now offer the deepening insights prayer always seeks and at the same time find itself nourished by prayer.

The possibility of rapport, dialogue and mutual support between prayer and theology is now present and palpable. This coincidence of the mind and heart of history could be a passing paradox, but more probably it is a mark of evolution brought about by grace and work and prayer. If so, it will continue to uncover new discoveries and new surprises.

July 22, 1972

1973

Jewish Prayer: A Share in Holiness

John C. Haughey, SJ

Jewish-Christian relations are improving only sputteringly. The reasons are complicated, no doubt. One of them is that the partners in the formal dialogues (admittedly only a small part of Jewish-Christian relations) act too often like brokers weighed down with heavy baggage rather than sons of the same Father and a common religious tradition.

Rabbi Heschel was an exception.[4] Anyone who knew him sensed the depth of his exposure to the Presence of God. He accorded prayer the highest priority in his daily routine, and when he spoke, a living faith shone through. This portion of our special issue will allow Heschel to say some things about prayer. The reader will find considerable simplicity in his words. Not surprisingly, of course, since pretentious statements about prayer come only from those who don't pray.

Hasidism had styled the piety of Heschel. Hasidism began in Poland in the mid-eighteenth century and has proved itself an effective form of renewal in orthodox Jewry up to the present. It stresses living one's tradition in distinction from simply learning it; it prizes wisdom and piety over speculation and scholarship; it values masters of prayer more than intellectuals.

Heschel's observations on prayer include all of these emphases as well as poetic variations on the favorite Hasidic theme of God's immanence. Prayer is rooted in life—one's own and that of other things. "To pray is to take notice of the wonder, to regain a sense of the mystery that animates all beings, the divine margin in all attainments." Man doesn't have to leave

---

4. Heschel died on December 23, 1972.

reality to contemplate God. "The world is always on the verge of becoming one in adoration," and it is through man, the cantor of the universe, that "the secret cosmic prayer is disclosed." The man who does not know prayer does not perceive the silent worship that rises from all living things in praise of their Creator. Reason alone will never "call upon the sun to praise the Lord." "Whose ear has heard how all trees sing to God?" Only the man whose prayer has become like the psalmist's: "All Thy works praise Thee, O Lord."

His desire for prayer did not come from an emotional need, Heschel explained, but from "an ontological necessity." More ponderously, he would say that "prayer is an act that constitutes the very essence of man." We can trace our dignity as men to our "being endowed with the gift of addressing God." A man who fails to pray is like a tree torn from the soil that nourishes it or a river separated from the source that feeds it.

While much of what Heschel has to say on a variety of subjects came from his prayer, he does not treat the explicit theme of prayer extensively in his writings. His primary piece of advice to would-be pray-ers: Know before whom you stand! Know—not in the sense of seeking to comprehend God's essence but rather yielding to His Presence. Know, too, that although God is personal in the way He deals with men, He cannot be reduced to the category of person since he transcends any of the connotations we attach to that category.

One should not expect, Heschel warns, that prayer will proceed the way a conversation between two people does. For while we express ourselves in prayer with complete confidence that we are being heard, God for his part does not speak to us. But if prayer is not dialogic, why pray? Heschel would respond (in a way that would bother many philosophers): because by prayer we became an object of God's thought and concern. Our prayer "makes the heart audible to God." And we, in turn, are changed by prayer because "His concerns become our own." By our willing exposure to His Presence, our concerns "bear the image of God's wishes and dreams."

There are some basic dispositions of soul, other than faith, that obstruct or facilitate prayer. A capacity for awe and a sense of the ineffable make prayer possible, even inevitable. Conversely, the illusion of total intelligibility, indifference to mystery and blind self-reliance make prayer difficult or unlikely. But even more subtly destructive is a vulgarity of spirit that is insensitive to the fittingness of things. By confusing the categories rightly employed in the political, economic or scientific realms with the things of God, a coarseness results. "Out-of-placeness generates vulgarity"; something, for example, that belongs to the sphere of the intimate is merchandized for public consumption.

But man's dismissal of prayer or his meager use of it is even more likely due to his loss of a reverence for words. Heschel complains that words have become slums rather than sacred "repositories of the spirit." The condition of a man's spirit stands forth in the words that come from his lips. They can spring from the depths of "the soil of the soul" or they can be waif and elusive, "a mouthful of dust." Since words for Heschel are the antecedents of a man's faith, he who would regain a spirit of praise must regain a taste for the sacredness of words.

Like Noah entering the Ark, so was a man to approach a holy word. It is not the word that enters a man, but man who enters the word. When the dignity of words has been perceived and their singularity confronted, they release their creative forces within us; their use rises from us "into the vast expanse of eternity." Words, then, are commitments. And when words are commitments a pray-er is born.

Not just any old words. Scriptural words have been "sanctified by ages of worship" and these are to be tasted in preference to those born in "the pitiful prison of the self." Heschel's love for the liturgy is evident in all his writings. The liturgy shaped his prayer while his prayer leavened all that he wrote. He likened liturgical prayer to an island. "Each time the island must be conquered as if we had never been there before . . . arriving on shore we face the same hazards, the same strain." Before us loom majestic utterances and lofty expressions that have to be, as it were, scaled anew.

At the same time, "prayer does not complete itself in an instant, nor does it move on a level plain. It thrusts itself forward through depths and heights, through detours and byways, advancing gradually only from word to word, from thought to thought, from feeling to feeling." The sacred words of the liturgy are like "mountain peaks pointing to the unfathomable; ascending their trails we arrive at prayer."

The Bible was, for Heschel, "holiness in words." Our neglect of it or our abusive use of it was never more evident than in the selection of the names we chose for God. Thus, Revealer and Redeemer have become so commonplace that we have failed to perceive His demanding Presence as Judge or Transcendent Creator.

But, Heschel would warn, there is also a danger of reposing upon the word, becoming dependent upon the text, however hallowed by the ages, letting it substitute for "the outburst of the heart." Prayer, in the last analysis, does not consist only in words nor even primarily in words. "Prayer begins where expression ends," Heschel insists. He often shows his exasperation with the inadequacy of words for prayer. "Where is the tree that can utter fully the silent passion of the soil?" Like the Hasidic masters before him, he accords silence a higher place than words in the many levels of worship.

But there is a level of prayer that goes beyond even silence. It is song. *Niggun*, as it is called, arises from the heart without words attaching to it. At times it will be a song with a familiar melody, at other times one that is spontaneous, as if it came to, rather than from, the pray-ers. This was a frequent occurrence with the Hasidim. (The phenomenon could be profitably explored for its connection with the "singing in tongues" of many Christian Pentecostals, or with the "groaning in the Spirit" that St. Paul sees beneath all our prayer.)

To Heschel, each Sabbath was a kind of tutor of prayer. Just as the Bible was holiness in words, so the Sabbath was "holiness in time." It was a time for him to rest beside the still waters that lay between him and eternity. In his volume *The Sabbath*, he contrasts time not to eternity, as one would expect, but with space. Things that are in space can be controlled and manipulated, but in the face of time all we can do is submit. Like God's own glory, time is not reversible nor manipulable, and hence it is the medium in which we can learn to submit to His inbreaking Presence. Man's whole relationship with

God was formed by every Sabbath! It was a fasting for a feasting, a separation from created things for a fuller appreciation of them, a resting from labor for more labor. It was a day for sensing the holiness of eternity in and through time.

Heschel stressed the interdependence between personal prayer and community worship. A personal piety that was not nourished by a praying community would become "a kind of impiety" sooner or later. And a community made of individuals who were innocent of personal prayer would never become a praying community. But Heschel's concern was that the individual's prayer be taught by the praying community. "Our relationship to Him is not as an I to a Thou, but as a We to a Thou." The echoes of Martin Buber can be heard here, but he also criticized Buber, who, he felt, had overstressed the personal relationship of the individual to God.

"Our share in holiness we acquire by living in the community." The stuff of Judaism is not a quality of soul that individuals possess but a covenant that the Living God keeps with a people chosen by Him. "Consequently, what we do as individuals is a trivial episode; what we attain as Israel causes us to become a part of eternity." One becomes the recipient of the Lord's bountifulness by fidelity to prayer, personal and communal.

Heschel never addressed himself systematically to the subject of prayer. His writings on the subject were always occasional pieces. What he did write, however, revealed him as typically Hasidic in dealing with prayer; he is not anxious to say new things, but instead he points to the treasures he has found in the old, neglected things and encourages others to avail themselves of what has been accessible for centuries. Heschel leaves one with a taste for God, not for more of Heschel.

His prayerfulness made him an extremely effective partner in the encounter with Christianity. He did not, in fact, trust a spirit of dialogue that did not emerge from a personal interiorization of one's own faith. "At a time of paucity of faith, interfaith may become a substitute for faith."

Nor, at the same time, did he have any patience with religious isolationism. "No religion is an island" any longer. There are only two choices before us, "interfaith or internihilism." He chose interfaith, knowing full well that "Judaism is sooner or later affected by the intellectual, moral and spiritual events within Christian society, and vice versa." One event in the 20th century that Christians were very happily affected by was Abraham Joshua Heschel.

March 10, 1973

1978

Contemplative Prayer in the Christian Tradition

Thomas Keating, OCSO

In the Christian tradition a positive attitude toward contemplation characterized the teaching of the church for the first 15 centuries, while a negative attitude has prevailed with growing intensity from the 16th century to the present. An overview of the history of the teaching of the church on contemplative prayer may help toward an understanding of this change of attitude and the present situation of the church in regard to religious experience.

The word *contemplation* is ambiguous in our day, because over the centuries it has acquired many meanings and connotations, and it is essential to know its history in order to renew and hand on the Christian tradition. To speak of the experiential knowledge of God, the Greek Bible used the word *gnosis* to translate the Hebrew word *da'ath*, a much stronger term, which implies possession of the thing known.

St. Paul used the word *gnosis* in his epistles to refer to the intimate knowledge of God, proper to those who love Him. He constantly asked this knowledge for his disciples, and he prayed for it as if it were an indispensable element for the complete development of Christian life. The Greek Fathers, especially Clement of Alexandria, Origen and Gregory of Nyssa, borrowed the term *theoria* from the Neoplatonists. In the vocabulary of the Neoplatonists this meant the intellectual vision of the truth, which they regarded as the supreme activity of the wise man. To this technical term the Fathers added the meaning of *da'ath*, that is, the kind of experiential knowledge that comes through love. It was with this expanded meaning that *theoria* was translated into the Latin *contemplatio* and handed down to us by Christian tradition.

This tradition is summed up by Gregory the Great at the end of the sixth century. He described contemplation as a knowledge of God that is impregnated with love. For Gregory, contemplation is the fruit of reflection of the Word of God in Scripture and at the same time a gift of God. It is a resting in God. In this resting, or stillness, the mind and heart are not actively seeking Him, but are beginning to experience, to taste, what they have been seeking. This places them in a state of repose, tranquility and profound interior peace. It is not the suspension of all action, but a mingling of very simplified thought and the loving experience of God.

This meaning of contemplation, as the knowledge of God based on the intimate and loving experience of His presence, remained the same until the end of the Middle Ages. Ascetical practices, as they were developed in various forms of monastic life, were always directed toward contemplation as the normal term of spiritual activity. Indeed, everything in monastic life was designed to foster and sustain this movement toward experiential union with Christ and, through Him, with the Father.

The method of prayer for these monks, compared with later developments, might be called methodless. They engaged in *lectio divina*, literally "divine reading," a practice that involved reading Scripture, or more exactly, listening to it. They would repeat the words of the sacred text with their lips so that the body itself entered into the process. The modern term "spiritual reading," though derived from *lectio divina*, is much broader in scope.

In those days before the invention of printing, monks were expected to learn the psalms and many other passages of Scripture by heart. When they were free from other occupations and gave themselves to *lectio*, it was primarily an exercise of listening and attention. The monks sought to cultivate through *lectio divina* the capacity to listen at ever deepening levels of inward attention. Prayer was their response to the God they were listening to in Scripture and celebrating in the liturgy.

The reflective part, the pondering upon the words of the sacred text, was what the monks called *meditatio*, meditation. The spontaneous movement of the will in response to these reflections they called *oratio*, or affective prayer. When these reflections and acts of will were very simple, they often moved on to a kind of resting in God, and that is what they meant by *contemplatio*, contemplation.

These three acts—meditation, affective prayer and contemplation—could all take place during the same period of prayer. They were interwoven one into the other. Like the angels ascending and descending Jacob's ladder, the monks' attention would go up and down the steps of the ladder of consciousness. Sometimes they would praise the Lord with their tongues, sometimes with their thoughts, sometimes with acts of will and sometimes with their silence, with their rapt attention—with their contemplation. They regarded contemplation as the normal development of listening to the Word of God. The approach to God was not compartmentalized into discursive meditation, affective prayer and mystical contemplation, as it came to be from the 16th century onward. The term "mental prayer" did not exist in Christianity prior to that time.

Around the 12th century a marked development in religious thought took place. The great schools of theology were founded. It was the birth of precise analysis in regard to concepts, division into genera and species, definitions and classifications. This growing capacity for analysis was a significant development of the human mind. Later this passion for analysis in theology was to be transferred to the life and practice of prayer and bring to an end the simple, spontaneous prayer of the Middle Ages based on *lectio divina* with its opening to contemplation. Meanwhile the spiritual masters of the 12th century, like St. Bernard, Hugh and Richard of St. Victor and William of St. Thierry, were developing a theological understanding of prayer and contemplation. The 13th century saw methods of meditation based on the life of Christ popularized by the Franciscans.

During the 14th and 15th centuries, events with great consequences for Christendom took place. The Black Death and the Hundred Years' War decimated cities, towns and religious communities, while nominalism and the Great Schism brought on a general decadence in morals and spirituality. *Devotio Moderna* arose in the Low Countries toward 1380 and spread to Italy,

France and Spain in response to the widespread need for reform. Its purpose was to use the moral powers issuing from prayer as a means of self-discipline in an age when institutions and structures of all kinds were crumbling. By the end of the 15th century, methods of mental prayer properly so called were elaborated, becoming more and more complicated and systematized as time went on. But even while this proliferation of systematic methods of prayer was taking place, contemplation was still presented as the ultimate goal.

As the 16th century progressed, mental prayer came to be divided into "discursive meditation," if thoughts predominated; "affective prayer," if the emphasis was on acts of the will; and "mystical contemplation," if graces infused by God were the prominent factor. Discursive meditation, affective prayer and contemplation were no longer different acts found in a single period of prayer, but distinct forms of prayer, each with its own proper aim, method and purpose. The possibility of prayer opening out into contemplation tended to be regarded as very unlikely. Contemplation did not fit into the approved categories and therefore was discouraged.

This division of the ongoing development of prayer into compartmentalized units entirely separated from one another was a disaster for the church's traditional teaching. It helped to further the wrong notion that contemplation is an extraordinary grace reserved for the very few.

At the same time that the living tradition of Christian spirituality was diminishing, the Renaissance came on the scene bringing new challenges for the spiritual life to contend with. No longer were the social milieu and religious institutions supportive of the individual. There was need to reconquer the world for Christ in the face of the pagan elements that were taking over Christendom. It was not surprising that new forms of prayer should appear that were almost entirely ordered to an apostolic ministry. Obviously the new emphasis on apostolic life, especially as it was instituted by St. Ignatius, required a transformation of the forms of spirituality hitherto transmitted by the monks and mendicants. It was Ignatius whose genius and mystical experience led him to channel the living tradition of spirituality, which was in danger of being lost, into a form appropriate to the new age.

The Spiritual Exercises of St. Ignatius, composed between 1522 and 1526, are extremely important, both in themselves and in the way that history treated them, in order to understand the present state of spirituality in the Roman Catholic Church. Three methods of prayer are proposed in the *Exercises*. The meditations prescribed for the first week are made according to the method of the three powers: memory, intellect and will. The memory is to recall the point chosen beforehand as the subject of the meditation. The intellect is to reflect on the lessons one wants to get from that point. The will is to make resolutions based on that point in order to put the lessons into practice. Thus, one is led to conversion and reformation of life.

The word "contemplation" in the *Spiritual Exercises* has a meaning different from its traditional one. It consists in gazing upon a concrete object of the imagination: seeing, for example, the persons in the Gospel as if they were present, hearing what they are saying, relating and responding to their words and actions. This is the method of contemplation prescribed for the Second Week and is aimed at developing affective prayer.

The third method of prayer in the *Exercises* is called application of the five senses. It consists of successively applying in spirit the five senses to the subject of the meditation. This method is designed to dispose beginners to infused contemplation and to develop the spiritual senses in those who are already advanced in prayer.

Thus Ignatius did not propose just one method of prayer. The unfortunate tendency to reduce the *Exercises* to a method of discursive meditation seems to stem from the Jesuits themselves. In 1574 Everard Mercurian, the Father General of the Jesuits, in a directive to the whole Society, forbade the practice of affective prayer and the application of the five senses. This prohibition was repeated in 1578. Thus the spiritual life of a whole congregation of apostolic men was forcibly limited to a single method of prayer, namely, meditation according to the three powers. The discursive character of this meditation continued to grow in importance during the course of the 18th and 19th centuries. Most modern manuals of spirituality until well into this century presented only schemas of discursive meditation.

To comprehend the impact of the latter development on the church's recent history, we should keep in mind the great influence the Jesuits exercised in the church as the outstanding representatives of the Counter-Reformation. Many congregations of men and women that were founded in the following centuries adopted the Constitutions of the Society of Jesus. They received at the same time the spirituality taught and practiced by the Society. Hence, they also received its limitations, which were imposed not by St. Ignatius, but by his less enlightened successors.

St. Ignatius wished to provide a form of contemplative prayer adapted to the apostolic needs of the church of his time. The *Exercises* are designed to form contemplatives in action. Taking into account its immense influence for good, if the Society had been allowed to follow the *Exercises* according to their original intent and had given more prominence to its own contemplative spiritual masters, like Fathers Lallemant, Surin, Grou, de Caussade, the present state of spirituality in the church might be quite different.

Other events occurred to increase the hesitation of church authorities toward contemplative prayer. One of these was the controversy regarding quietism, which was condemned as a kind of false mysticism by Innocent XII in 1687. A milder form of this doctrine flourished in France in the latter part of the 17th century and became known as semi-quietism. The condemned teaching was ingenious. It consisted in making once and for all an act of love for God by which you gave yourself entirely to Him with the intention never to recall the surrender. As long as you never withdrew the intention to belong to God, divine union was assured. No further need for effort either in prayer or outside it was required.

Obviously there is an important difference between making a good intention and achieving it as a permanent disposition. A number of people are said to have fallen into excesses. Bishop Bossuet, chaplain to the court of Louis XIV, was one of the chief enemies of this doctrine and, along with others, succeeded in getting it condemned in France. How much he exaggerated the real faults of the teaching is hard to reconstruct at this distance in time. In any case, the controversy brought mysticism into greater disrepute than it had already suffered. From then on, reading about mysticism was frowned upon in seminaries and religious communities. According to Henri Bremond in his book *The Literary History of Religious Thought in France*, no mystical writing of any significance appeared during the next several hundred years. The great mystical writers of the past were ignored. Even the writings of St. John of the Cross were thought to be suggestive of quietism, thus forcing his editors to tone down his statements lest they be misunderstood and condemned. The authentic, unexpurgated text only appeared in our own century, 400 years after its composition.

Another disaster for Christian spirituality was the heresy of Jansenism, which gained momentum during the 17th century. Although it was eventually condemned, it left behind a pervasive, antihuman attitude that perdured in many parts of the church throughout the 19th century and on into our own time. Jansenism strongly questioned the universality of Christ's saving power as well as the intrinsic goodness of human nature. The pessimistic form of piety that it fostered spread with the émigrés from France at the time of the French Revolution to many English-speaking regions, including Ireland. Since it is largely from French and Irish stock that priests and religious in this country have come, the Jansenistic spirit of narrowness and exaggerated asceticism has deeply affected the psychological climate of our seminaries and training centers. It is really only recently that priests and religious are shaking off the last remains of the negative attitudes produced by Jansenism.

Another trend in the modern church is an excessive emphasis on private devotions, apparitions and private revelations. One also finds confusion as to what true mysticism is. People tend to regard mystics as saints or wonder workers. But true mysticism is primarily an interior grace leading to holiness, though it does not guarantee it. Phenomena such as levitation, the stigmata and visions are strictly accidental to it.

During the 19th century there were many saints, but they did not speak or write of the mystical life. There was a renewal of spirituality in Eastern Orthodoxy, but the main stream of Roman Catholic development seemed to be legalistic in character, with a kind of nostalgia for the Middle Ages and for the kind of political influence that the church exercised in France before the Revolution.

Abbot Cuthbert Butler sums up the generally accepted teaching of the 18th and 19th centuries in his book *Western Mysticism*. Except for very unusual vocations, he writes, the normal prayer for everyone including contemplative monks and nuns, bishops, priests and lay people, was systematic meditation following a fixed method, which could be one of four: the meditation according to the three powers as laid down in the *Spiritual Exercises of St. Ignatius*, the method of St. Alphonsus (which was a slight reworking of the *Exercises*), St. Francis de Sales's method of meditation as described in *An Introduction to the Devout Life* or the method of St. Sulpice. These are all methods of discursive meditation only. Contemplation was regarded as extraordinary and identified with extraordinary phenomena, in other words, something miraculous to be admired from a safe distance, but left alone as dangerous, full of pitfalls and not something to which the ordinary Christian, layman, priest or religious, should aspire.

The final nail that was hammered into the coffin of the traditional teaching of the church was the obvious corollary that it was against humility to aspire to contemplation. Young religious and seminarians were thus presented with a highly truncated view of the spiritual life, one that did not accord with either Scripture or tradition. How could they possibly teach the art of prayer to the faithful? If one attempts to persevere in discursive meditation after the Holy Spirit has called one beyond it, as He ordinarily does, one is bound to end in a state of utter frustration. It is normal for the mind to move through many reflections on the same theme to a single comprehensive view of the whole, and then to rest with a simple gaze upon the truth. As devout people moved spontaneously into this development in their prayer, they were up against this very negative attitude. They hesitated to go beyond discursive meditation because of the instructions or warnings they were given about the dangers of mysticism. They either gave up mental prayer altogether or, through the mercy of God, found some way of persevering in spite of the obstacles.

In any case, the post-Reformation teaching opposed to mysticism was the direct opposite to the previous teaching of the church. The genuine Christian tradition, taught uninterruptedly for the first 15 centuries, is that contemplation is the normal evolution of a genuine spiritual life and hence open to all Christians. All these historical and cultural factors help to explain why the traditional spirituality of the Western church has gradually been lost in recent centuries, and why Vatican II had to address itself to the acute problem of spiritual renewal.

The main reason that the contemplative dimension of prayer is receiving attention in recent years is twofold. One is that historical and theological studies have rediscovered the true teaching of St. John of the Cross and other great masters of the spiritual life. The other is the challenge coming from the East, especially since World War II. Methods of meditation similar to contemplative prayer in the Christian tradition have proliferated, produced good results and received much publicity.

It is important for us to appreciate the values that are present in the genuine teachings of the great religions of the world. Since the spiritual traditions of the East possess a highly developed psychological wisdom, we need to know something about them in order to meet people where they are today. Many serious seekers of truth study the Eastern religions, take courses in them in college or practice forms of meditation inspired and taught by them.

When did the interest in mystical theology begin to revive? It seems to have begun with the publication of *The Degrees of the Spiritual Life* by the Abbé Saudreau in 1896, who based himself on the teaching of St. John of the Cross. In *The Living Flame of Love*, there is a long digression in which St. John speaks of the transition from sensible devotion to a truly spiritual relationship with God. All who seek to give themselves completely to God, he says, will "very quickly" enter this transitional period, which is the beginning of contemplative prayer. But how quick is "very quickly"? Is it a few months or a few weeks? He does not say. But the idea that one has to undergo years of superhuman trials, be walled up behind convent walls or kill oneself with various ascetical practices before one can aspire to contemplation, reflects the attitude of a Jansenistic world view or, at the very least, is an inadequate presentation of the Christian tradition.

The church finds itself at this moment in an embarrassing situation. There are many sincere people in our day anxious to learn contemplative prayer, and its official ministers are too often unable to say anything about it with the kind of conviction that comes from experience. For the various historical reasons outlined above, the road to the full development of the gifts of the Holy Spirit, leading to contemplative prayer in the Christian tradition, has been generally disregarded in seminaries, religious life and on the parish level. What is desperately needed is a widespread renewal of the church's traditional teaching and the actual experience of the mystical life, especially among its ministers.

The church is renewing its theology on all levels; it would be a serious omission if theologians neglected to renew its mystical theology. Unless scientific theology and Scripture studies are integrated into a deep understanding of the Christian mystery, based in some degree on an ongoing experience of it, preaching and the other ministries are not going to impress anybody. Among the many challenges the church faces today, the greatest challenge, without which the others cannot be met, is the challenge of spiritual renewal.

April 8, 1978

1978

Lectionary, Prayer, and Community

Jacqueline McMakin

Practical questions concerning the liturgy are often posed to our lay ministry team: How to become more formed in Scripture and enhance individual participation in the Sunday liturgy? How to develop an appreciation of Sunday worship in our families and build community in a large parish? How to engage in ecumenical prayer?

Two years ago our team stumbled on a practice which, we began to realize, does all these things. We decided to use the Sunday Scripture readings from the Sunday lectionary as a basis for our individual and group prayer and formation. A simple, almost obvious, practice, it has had some exciting ramifications.

First of all, we have become more formed in Scripture through this procedure. It may be helpful to describe in some detail how this happens. Each week, one of our team members prepares a few sentences suggesting a focus for prayer or a question to ponder from the readings for the coming Sunday. This is distributed at our Monday staff meetings. Each member then works with the suggestions and the Sunday readings daily for a week. The first portion of the following meeting is devoted to shared silence, meditation and prayer enlightened by our own Sunday liturgical experience in church, as well as by our individual reading and meditation during the preceding week. We focus on the concerns that seem given at the time, either for one another, our work or other needs that come to our attention.

There are several reasons why we have found the lectionary so nourishing. The present lectionary, prepared by the Roman Catholic Church and issued in 1969, is an exceptionally fine piece of work. A three-year cycle adopted in place of the formerly used one-year cycle made possible the selection of a more complete set of readings. It is designed, over the three-year period, to expose the reader to "the full sweep of God's revelation, not avoiding the hard words," according to one author. It is comprehensive. Moreover, it is the product of liturgists and Scripture scholars who worked closely together to include the best contributions of both disciplines in the new lectionary. It thus puts readers in touch with each liturgical season. In addition, the selections (usually from the Old Testament, Psalms, Letters and Gospels) are of reasonable length so that one is not overloaded with too much material to digest. Concentrating on the same four passages all week in private prayer, in the Sunday liturgy and in our small community has been enriching for our prayer. With so many exposures to the same Word, it comes to life in us, to inform our decisions, to guide our lives, to enlighten and enliven our work.

The use of the lectionary in this way has enhanced our participation in the Sunday liturgy. We begin to study the coming Sunday readings on Tuesday and thus have several days to meditate privately on the theme of the liturgy. If we are faithful, we can prepare ourselves and intercede for others (the pastors and people in our congregation) as they, too, prepare for common worship on Sunday. Not only can we contribute to the preparing of Sunday worship; we can receive more from it because we are prepared. There is no doubt about it: Since we have engaged in this practice, we have felt much more tied into the Sunday liturgy.

We have found some local Christians who see in the lectionary a way to develop in their families an appreciation of Sunday worship. Some parents are discovering that as they share their appreciation of one of the readings with a child, the child then becomes quite excited on hearing the reading read and talked about in church. Most notable is the work of Carol Poltorak (at St. Andrew the Apostle Church in Wheaton, Md.), who each month prepares written material for families to explore and experience the meaning of the Sunday Gospel readings. A typical booklet includes reflections on the theme for the month, a section relating the theme to the family and one on applying it to family experience. Additional reading and a bibliography are provided for adults.

Those who are sensitive about which version of the readings to share with their children could investigate the *Lectionary for Children's Mass*, edited by Aldo J. Tos and produced by Pueblo Publishing Company. The two volumes contain selected Scripture texts from the "A" and "B" cycles of lectionary readings assigned for these years. A recent review commented that this work's "sturdiness and graphic beauty offer us a solid symbol with which to celebrate and upon which to lavish attention and reverence."

Our team is often asked how to build a sense of community in a large parish. In those parishes where the Sunday readings are read not only in the weekly liturgy but also in homes and in small groups within the parish, an awareness of community is heightened. Indeed, study and meditation on a common reading is a time-honored way of building community among people whose residence and place of work are "out from" the faith community. The Daily Office, a way to pray the Psalms, has served this purpose among those who have been dedicated to saying it. By way of contrast, the Sunday readings encompass the whole Bible, provide a more concentrated focus each week and seem to appeal to a broader range of readers than does the Office.

One final ramification of using the Sunday readings as a basis for individual and parish prayer must be mentioned. That is the exciting ecumenical possibilities it affords. The Roman Catholic lectionary, finished in 1969, was of such quality that it had a tremendous influence on Protestant denominations. Many of the major Protestant groups revised their lectionaries based upon the Catholic version. The net effect is that in many Protestant churches across the land, the same readings (with some minor variations) are used each week as are used in Catholic congregations. Use of the lectionary in some denominations is suggested but left to the discretion of the local pastor. In this area, we are noticing that Protestant pastors, previously uncommitted to the use of the lectionary, are now finding such richness in the revised version that they are using it with more consistency than ever before.

During the years when ecumenical contact, dialogue and interest were high, many Catholics and Protestants came to believe with Yves Congar that "we can pass through the door of ecumenism only on our knees." Groups were formed to pray together for the unity for which our Lord prayed. In the ensuing years, the movement seemed to be back to the denominations to "get our own house in order." The need and in some cases the desire for ecumenical prayer did not die, but the opportunities did. The new common lectionaries seem to provide an ideal basis and opportunity to pray together.

Dr. Reginald Fuller of the Virginia Theological Seminary was among the first to realize the ecumenical possibilities of the lectionary as a basis for greater unity. An Episcopalian, Dr. Fuller wrote commentaries for preachers on the 1969 Catholic lectionary, which have been printed monthly by *Worship* magazine, a publication of the Benedictines. These have now been published in book form: *Preaching the New Lectionary: The Word of God for the Church Today*.

Several decades ago, Evelyn Underhill described a vision that is still gripping: "The basis of union [of the churches] must be interior, secret, out of reach of all ecclesiastical controversies. . . . For the development of unity in and through the Praying Christ, I do agree that a widespread group of praying souls, orders, and individuals is necessary; still more that these should belong to all Christian Communions."

Using the Sunday readings as a basis for individual and corporate prayer might be just the kind of practical tool needed to implement this vision. It is available and accessible, and takes no special expertise to get started. Perhaps the most practical benefit is that it need not take extra time and would not require a special group for those of us who already gather to pray, meditate and reflect on spiritual readings. How exciting to contemplate the impact this would have across the land in Christian Family Movement gatherings, in Cursillo reunion groups, in Protestant women's circles and Catholic Sodality meetings, in parish councils, church staff meetings, in families and homes. All Christians from the most liturgical backgrounds to the simplest silent Quaker worship could allow themselves to be fed and formed by this common Word. This would give us fresh common experience to draw on that could mitigate the effects of centuries of separate experiences. It would put into practice the wisdom, learned in many small groups, of sharing present lived experience rather than past learnings or opinions. It could unleash a new Spirit in us all, for did not the Lord promise in Isaiah 55 that "my word . . . shall not return to me void, but shall do my will, achieving the end for which I sent it"?

June 10, 1978

1978

Unceasing Prayer

Henri J. M. Nouwen

When we think about prayer, we usually regard it as one of the many things we do to live a full and mature Christian life. We say to ourselves or to each other, "We should not forget to pray, because prayer is important; without it, our life becomes shallow. We need to give our time not only to people, but to God as well." If we are fervent in our conviction that prayer is important, we might even be willing to give a whole hour to prayer each day, or a whole day every month, or a whole week every year. Thus, prayer becomes a part, indeed a very important part, of our life.

But when the apostle Paul speaks about prayer, he uses a very different language. He does not speak about prayer as a part of life, but says it is all of life. He does not mention prayer as something we should not forget, but claims it is our ongoing concern. He does not exhort his readers to pray once in a while, regularly or often, but without hesitation admonishes them to pray constantly, unceasingly, without interruption. Paul does not ask us to spend some of every day in prayer. No, Paul is much more radical. He asks us to pray day and night, in joy and in sorrow, at work and at play, without intermission or breaks. For Paul, praying is like breathing. It cannot be interrupted without mortal danger.

To the Christians in Thessalonica, Paul writes: "Pray constantly, and for all things give thanks to God, because this is what God expects you to do in Christ Jesus" (1 Thess. 5:17–18). Paul not only demands unceasing prayer but also practices it. "We constantly thank God for you" (1 Thess. 2:13), he says to his community in Greece. "We feel we must be continually thanking God for you" (2 Thess. 1:3). "We pray continually that our God will make you worthy of His call" (2 Thess. 1:11). To the Romans, he writes: "I never fail to mention you in my prayers" (Rom. 1:9), and he comforts his friend Timothy with the words "Always I remember you in my prayers" (2 Tim. 1:3).

The two Greek terms that appear repeatedly in Paul's letters are *pantote* and *adialeiptos*, which mean "always" and "without interruption." These words make it clear that for Paul, prayer is not a part of living but all of living, not a part of his thought but all of his thought, not a part of his emotions and feelings but all of them. Paul's fervor allows no place for partial commitments, piecemeal giving or hesitant generosity. He gives all and asks all.

This radicalism obviously raises some difficult questions. What does it mean to pray without ceasing? How can we live our life, with its many demands and obligations, as an uninterrupted prayer? What about the endless row of distractions that intrude on us day after day? Moreover, how can our sleep, our needed moments of diversion and the few hours in which we try to escape from the tensions and conflicts of life be lifted up into unceasing prayer? These questions are real, and have puzzled many Christians who wanted to take seriously Paul's exhortation to pray without ceasing.

One of the best-known examples of this search is the 19th-century Russian peasant who desired so much to be obedient to Paul's call for uninterrupted prayer that he went from staretz to staretz looking for an answer, until he finally found a holy man who taught him the Jesus Prayer. He told the peasant to say thousands of times each day: "Lord Jesus Christ, have mercy on me." In this way, the Jesus Prayer slowly became united with his breathing and heartbeat so that he could travel through Russia carrying in his knapsack the Bible, the *Philokalia*, some bread and salt, and living a life of unceasing prayer (*The Way of a Pilgrim*, trans. R. M. French. Seabury Press, 1965). Although we are not 19th-century Russian peasants with a similar "wanderlust," we still share the question of this simple peasant: How do we pray without ceasing?

I would like to respond to this question not in the context of the wide, silent Russian prairies of the 19th century, but in the context of the restlessness of our contemporary Western society. I propose to look at unceasing prayer as the conversion of our unceasing thought processes. My central question, therefore, is: "How can we turn our perpetual mental activities into perpetual prayer?" Or, to put it more simply: "How can thinking become praying?"

First, I want to discuss how our unceasing thinking is the source of our joy as well as our pain. Then I want to show how this unceasing thinking can be turned into an uninterrupted conversation with God. Finally, I would like to explore how we can develop a discipline that will promote this ongoing conversion from thought to prayer. In this way, I hope that unceasing prayer can be removed from the sphere of romantic sentimentalism and become a realistic possibility for our demanding lives in the 20th century.

Unceasing Thoughts

Lately I have been wondering if we ever do *not* think. It seems to me that we are always involved in some kind of thought process and that being without thoughts is not a real human option. When Blaise Pascal calls a human being a "roseau pensant," a thinking reed, he indicates that our ability to think constitutes our humanity and that it is our thinking that sets us apart from all other created beings. All our emotions, passions and feelings are intimately connected with our thoughts. We could even say that our thoughts form the cradle in which our joys as well as our sorrows are born. The words "thoughts" and "thinking" are obviously used here in a very broad sense and include different mental processes. When we look at these different mental processes, it would appear that whether we like it or not, we are involved in, or subjected to, unceasing thoughts.

One of the forms of thinking with which we are most familiar, but which represents only a small part of our mental processes, is reflective thinking. Reflection is a consciously bending back over events or the ideas, images or emotions connected with these events. It requires the application of our willpower in a concentrated effort; it calls for discipline, endurance, patience and much mental energy. Those who study a great deal know how hard systematic reflection is and how it can tire us and even exhaust us. Reflection is real work and does not come easily.

But not reflecting does not mean not thinking. In fact, we quite often find ourselves thinking without even realizing it. Suddenly we become aware of the fact that our minds have drifted off into thoughts about family, friends, future ambitions or past failures. We neither desired nor planned to think about these things, but simply discover ourselves being led into a complex network of ideas, images and feelings.

This passive, nonreflective thinking is often disturbing and can make us anxious or even apprehensive. We realize that our mind thinks things that we cannot control, that sneak up on us and interfere with our best intentions. During the most solemn moments, we may find ourselves thinking the most banal thoughts. While listening to a sermon about God's love, we find ourselves wondering about the haircut of the preacher. While reading a spiritual book, we suddenly realize that our mind is busy with the question of how much peanut butter and how much jam to put on our next sandwich. While watching a beautiful ceremony at St. Peter's, we notice ourselves trying to figure out where in the Vatican the laundromat is located, in which those thousands of surplices will be cleaned after the service. Indeed, not infrequently we catch ourselves thinking very low things during very high moments. The problem, however, is that we cannot think about nothing. We have to think and we often feel betrayed by our own uncontrolled or uncontrollable thoughts.

Our thought processes reach even deeper than our reflective moments and our uncontrolled mental wanderings. They also reach into our sleeping hours. We might wake up in the middle of the night and find ourselves part of a frightening car race, a delicious banquet or a heavenly choir. Sometimes we are able to give a detailed account of all the things that happened to us in our dreams. Sometimes we remember only the final moment of our dream and sometimes we are left with only a vague fear or an undefined joy. We know that much is going on during our sleep and that occasionally we catch only bits and pieces of it. Careful encephalographic studies have shown that our mind is always active during sleep; we are always dreaming even when we have no recollection of its occurrence or its content. And although we might tend to discard our thought processes during our night's sleep as insignificant in comparison with our reflections or our undirected mental wanderings, we should not forget that for many people, dreams proved to be the main source of knowing. The patriarch Jacob heard God's call when he saw angels going up and down a ladder. The first Joseph was deported to Egypt because he irritated his brothers with his visions of sheaves, sun, moon and stars bowing to him, and the second Joseph fled to Egypt after he had seen an angel warning him of Herod. And in our century, apparently so far from biblical times, we find Sigmund Freud and Carl Jung informing us that our dreams will tell us the truth.

Thus, we are indeed involved in unceasing thought day and night, willingly or unwillingly, during our most alert moments and during our deepest sleep, while working and while resting. This is our human predicament, a predicament that causes us great joy as well as immense pain. Our ceaseless thought is our burden as well as our gift. We wish that we could stop thinking for a while. Perhaps then we would not be haunted by the memories of lost friends, by the awareness of past sins, by the knowledge of hunger and oppression in our world.

These thoughts can impose themselves on us at the most unwelcome hours or keep us awake when we are most in need of sleep. So we wish that we could just be without thoughts, that we could simply erase this disturbing graffiti of the mind. But then, without thought there can be no smile, no laughter, no quiet joy. How can we be glad to see friends again when we are unable to think of them? How can we celebrate a birthday, a national holiday or a great religious feast if our mind is not aware of the meaning of the event? How can we be grateful if we cannot remember the gifts we have received? How can we lift up our heart and sing and dance without the thousands of thoughts that nurture our mind constantly?

Our thoughts are indeed the cradle where sorrow and joy are born. With an empty mind our heart cannot mourn or feast, our eyes cannot cry or laugh, our hands cannot wring or clap, our tongue cannot curse or praise. Thus, as "thinking reeds," we are able to feel deeply and experience life to the full with all its sorrows and joys. This unceasing thinking, which lies at the core of our humanity, needs to be converted slowly but persistently into unceasing prayer.

Unceasing Prayer

To pray unceasingly, as Paul asks us to do, would be completely impossible if it would mean to think constantly about God. Not only for people who have many different concerns to occupy their minds, but also for monks who spend many hours a day in prayer, thinking about God all the time is an unrealistic goal, which, if sought too vigorously, could lead to a mental breakdown.

To pray, I think, does not primarily mean to think about God in contrast to thinking about other things, or to spend time with God instead of spending time with other people. Rather, it means to think and live in the presence of God. As soon as we begin to divide our thoughts into thoughts about God and thoughts about people and events, we remove God from our daily life and put Him in a pious little niche where we can think pious thoughts and experience pious feelings. Although it is important and even indispensable for the spiritual life to set apart time for God and God alone, prayer can eventually become unceasing prayer when all our thoughts—beautiful and ugly, high and low, prideful and shameful, sorrowful and joyful—can be thought in the presence of God. What I mean is that we convert our unceasing thinking into unceasing prayer when we move from a self-centered monologue to a God-centered dialogue. This requires that we turn all our thoughts into conversation. The main question, therefore, is not so much what we think, but to whom we present our thoughts.

It is not hard to see how a real change takes place in our daily life when we find the courage to keep our thoughts to ourselves no longer, to speak out, confess them, share them, bring them into conversation. As soon as an embarrassing or exhilarating idea is taken out of its isolation and brought into a relationship with someone, something totally new happens. This obviously requires much courage and trust, precisely because we are not always sure how our thoughts will be received. But as soon as we have taken the risk and experienced acceptance, our thoughts themselves receive a new quality.

To pray unceasingly is to lead all our thoughts out of their fearful isolation into a fearless conversation with God. Jesus' life was a life lived in the presence of God His Father. He kept nothing, absolutely nothing, hidden from His face. His joys, His fears, His hopes and His despairs were always shared with His Father. Therefore, He could indeed say to His disciples: "you will be scattered . . . leaving me alone. And yet I am not alone, because the Father is with me" (Jn. 16:32). Thus, prayer asks us to break out of our monologue with ourselves and to follow Jesus by turning our life into an unceasing conversation with our heavenly Father.

Prayer, therefore, is not introspection. Introspection means to look inward, to enter into the complex network of our mental processes in search of some inner logic or some elucidating connections. Introspection results from the desire to know ourselves better and to become more familiar with our own interiority. Although introspection has a positive role in our thought processes, the danger is that it can entangle us in the labyrinth of our own ideas, feelings and emotions, and lead us to an increasing self-preoccupation. Introspection can cause paralyzing worries or unproductive self-gratification. Introspection can also create "moodiness." This "moodiness" is a very widespread phenomenon in our society. It reveals our great concern with ourselves and our undue sensitivity to how we feel or think. It makes us experience life as a constant fluctuation between "feeling high" and "feeling low," between "bad days" and "good days," and thus becomes a form of narcissism.

Prayer is not introspection. It does not look inward but outward. It is not a scrupulous analysis of our own thoughts and feelings, but a careful attentiveness to Him who invites us to an unceasing conversation. Prayer is the presentation of all thoughts—our intentional thoughts as well as our day and night dreams—to our loving Father so that He can see them and respond to them with His divine compassion. Prayer is the joyful affirmation of Psalm 139 that God knows our mind and heart and that nothing is hidden from Him:

You know me through and through
from having watched my bones take shape
when I was being formed in secret
knitted together in the limbo of the womb (14–15).

God, examine me and know my heart
probe me and know my thoughts
make sure I do not follow pernicious ways
and guide me in the way that is everlasting (23–24).

Prayer indeed is a radical conversion of all our mental processes because in prayer we move away from ourselves—our worries, preoccupations and self-gratifications—by directing all that we recognize as ours to God in the simple trust that through His love all will be made new.

But this conversion from unceasing thought to unceasing prayer is far from easy. There is a deep resistance to making ourselves so vulnerable, so naked, so totally unprotected. Naturally, we want to love God and worship Him, but we also want to keep a little corner of our inner life for ourselves, where we can hide and think our own secret thoughts, dream our own dreams and play with our own mental fabrications. We are always tempted to select carefully the thoughts that we bring into our conversation with God.

What makes us so stingy? Maybe we wonder if God can take all that goes on in our mind and heart. Can He accept our hateful thoughts, our cruel fantasies and our bizarre dreams? Can He handle our primitive images, our inflated illusions and our exotic mental castles? Or maybe we simply want to hold on to our own pleasurable imaginings and stimulating reveries, afraid that in showing them to our Lord, we may have to give them up. Thus, we are constantly tempted to fall back into introspection out of fear or out of greed, and to keep from our God what often is most in need of His healing touch.

This withholding from God of a large number of our thoughts leads us onto a road that we probably would never consciously want to take. It is the road of idolatry. Idolatry means to worship false images, and that is precisely what happens when we keep our fantasies, worries and joys to ourselves and do not present them to Him who is our Lord. By refusing to share these thoughts, we limit His lordship and erect little altars to the mental images that we do not want to submit to a divine conversation.

I remember how I once visited a psychiatrist complaining of my difficulty in controlling my fantasy life. I told him that disturbing images kept coming up and that I found it hard to detach myself from them. When he had listened to my story, he smiled and said: "Well, Father, as a priest you should know that this is idolatry, because your God is saying that you should not worship false images.". Only then did I realize fully what it means to confess having sinned not only in word and action, but also in thought. It is to confess idolatry, one of the oldest and most pervasive temptations.

Unceasing prayer is extremely difficult, then, precisely because we like to keep parts of ourselves to ourselves and experience real resistance to subjecting all that we are to God's lordship. Unceasing prayer is indeed an ongoing struggle against idolatry. When all our thoughts, those of our days as well as those of our nights, have been brought into a loving conversation with God, then we can speak about obedience in the full sense. Since this is obviously never a task that is completed, we need to raise the question of discipline. What disciplines are there to help us in becoming disciples of Christ and living in obedience to our heavenly Father?

Disciplines

Since there are so many resistances to the conversion of our unceasing thinking into unceasing prayer, we need discipline. Without discipline, unceasing prayer remains a vague ideal, something that has a certain romantic appeal but which is not very realistic in our contemporary world. Discipline means that something specific and concrete needs to be done to create the context in which a life of uninterrupted prayer can develop. Unceasing prayer requires the discipline of prayer exercises. Those who do not set aside a certain place and time each day to do nothing else but pray can never expect their unceasing thought to become unceasing prayer. Why is this planned prayer practice so important? It is important because through this practice God can become fully present to us as a real partner in our conversation.

This discipline of prayer embraces many forms of prayer—communal as well as individual prayer, oral as well as mental prayer. It is of first importance that we strive for prayer with the understanding that it is an explicit way of being with God. We often say: "All of life should be lived in gratitude," but this is only possible if at certain times we give thanks in a very concrete and visible way. We often say: "All our days should be lived for the glory of God," but this is only possible if a day is regularly set apart to give glory to God. We often say: "We should love one another always," but this is only a possibility when we regularly perform concrete and unambiguous acts of love. It is likewise true that we can only say, "All our thoughts should be prayer," if there are times in which we make God our only thought.

Common to all disciplined prayer, whether it be liturgical, devotional or contemplative, is that in it we try to direct all our attention to God and God alone. With this in mind, I would like to discuss in some detail the importance of the discipline of contemplation as one of the roads to unceasing prayer. Although many good things have been written about contemplation and contemplative prayer, many people still have the impression that contemplative prayer is something very special, very "high" or very difficult, and really not for ordinary people with ordinary jobs and ordinary problems. This is unfortunate, because the discipline of contemplative prayer is particularly valuable for those who have so much on their minds that they suffer from fragmentation. If it is true that all Christians are called to bring all their thoughts into an ongoing conversation with their Lord, then contemplative prayer can be a discipline that is especially important for those who are deeply involved in the many affairs of this world.

Contemplative prayer is prayer in which we attentively look at God. How is this possible, since nobody can see God and live? The mystery of the Incarnation is that it has become possible to see God in and through Jesus Christ. Christ is the image of God. In and through Christ, we know that God is a loving Father whom we can see by looking at His Son. When Jesus spoke to His disciples about His Father, Philip said impatiently, "Lord, let us see the Father, and then we shall be satisfied." Then Jesus answered, "To have seen me is to have seen the Father, so how can you say, 'Let us see the Father'?

Do you not believe that I am in the Father and the Father is in me?" (Jn. 14:8–10). Contemplative prayer, therefore, means to see Christ as the image of God the Father. All the images consciously or unconsciously created by our mind should be made subject to Him who is the only image of God. Contemplative prayer can be described as an act of seeing Christ in the imagination, of letting Him enter fully into our consciousness so that He becomes the icon always present in our inner room. By looking at Christ with loving attention, we learn with our mind and heart what it means to say that He is the way to the Father. Jesus is the only one who has seen the Father. He says: "Not that anybody has seen the Father, except the one who comes from God" (Jn. 6:46). Jesus' entire being is a perpetual seeing of the Father. His life and works are an uninterrupted contemplation of His Father. For us, therefore, contemplation means an always increasing imaginative vision of Jesus, so that in, through and with Him, we can see the Father and live in His presence.

How, then, do we imagine Christ so that we can indeed enter into dialogue with Him and allow our unceasing thought to be transformed into unceasing prayer? There is no single answer to this question, because every Christian must develop a personal discipline according to his or her task in life, work schedule, cultural heritage and personality. It belongs to the nature of a discipline that it conforms to the needs of the individual man or woman who wants to live a life with Christ. Therefore, rather than present a general account of contemplative prayer, I will describe one example of a contemplative discipline in the hope that it might suggest different ways of prayer to different people.

This very simple discipline for contemplative prayer is to read, every evening before going to sleep, the readings of the next day's Eucharist with special attention to the Gospel. It is often helpful to take one sentence or word that offers special comfort and repeat it a few times so that with that sentence or word, the whole content can be brought to mind and allowed slowly to descend from the mind into the heart.

I have found this practice to be a powerful support in times of crisis. It is especially helpful during the night, when worries or anxieties may keep me awake and seduce me into idolatry. By remembering the Gospel story or any of the sayings of the Old or New Testament authors, I can create a safe mental home into which I can lead all my preoccupations and let them be transformed into quiet prayer.

During the following day, a certain time must be set apart for explicit contemplation. This is a time in which to look at Christ as He appears in the reading. Obviously, the best way to do this is to reread the Gospel of the day and to imagine the Lord as He speaks or acts with His people. In this hour, we can see Him, hear Him, touch Him and make Him present to our whole being. We can see Christ as our healer, our teacher and our guide. We can see Him in His indignation, His compassion, His suffering and His glory. We can look at Him, listen to Him and enter into conversation with Him. Often, the other readings from the Old and New Testaments help to intensify our image of Christ, because, as Vincent van Gogh once said, the Gospels are the top of the mountain of which the other biblical writings form the slopes.

For me, this discipline of having an "empty time" to be with Christ as He speaks to me in the readings of the day has proved very powerful. I found that wherever I was or whatever I did during the rest of the day, the image of Christ that I had contemplated during that "empty time" stayed with me as a beautiful icon. Sometimes it was the conscious center of all my thoughts, but more often it was a quiet presence of which I was only indirectly aware. In the beginning, I hardly noticed the difference. Slowly, however, I realized that I could indeed carry Christ, the image of God, with me and let Him affect not only my reflective thoughts but my daydreams as well. I am convinced that this simple form of daily contemplation will eventually steal my dreams out of the hands of the Evil One and allow them once more to be gateways of God's ongoing revelation.

Finally, this discipline puts the celebration of the Eucharist into a totally new perspective. Especially when it is celebrated in the evening, the Eucharist becomes a real climax in which the Lord, with whom we have journeyed during the day, speaks to us again in the context of the whole community and invites us with our friends to the intimacy of His table. It is there that the transformation of all images into the image of Christ finds its fullest realization. It is there that the unity with Christ experienced through contemplation finds its perfection. Daily contemplation makes the daily Eucharist a transforming celebration. When we live the whole day with Christ in mind and heart, the Eucharist can never be merely a routine or an obligation. Instead, it becomes the center of daily life toward which everything else is directed.

This simple discipline of prayer can do much to provide a strong framework in which our unceasing thought can become unceasing prayer. In contemplative prayer, Christ cannot remain a stranger who lived long ago in a foreign world. Rather, He becomes a living presence with whom we can enter into dialogue here and now.

The contemplative practice I have described is only one of many possible examples, and I offer it merely as a suggestion that points in the direction of a disciplined prayer life. The important thing is not that we use this or that prayer technique, but that we realize that the Christian ideal of making all our life into prayer remains nothing but an ideal unless we are willing to discipline our body, mind and heart with a daily practice of entering directly, consciously and explicitly into the presence of our loving Father through His Son Jesus Christ.

Conclusion

I have tried to show that unceasing prayer is not the unusual feat of simple Russian peasants but a realistic vocation for all Christians. It certainly is not a way of living that comes either automatically by simply desiring it or easily by just praying once in a while. But when we give it serious attention and develop an appropriate discipline, we will see a real transformation in our life that will lead us closer and closer to God. Unceasing prayer as a permanent state of mind obviously will never be reached. It will always require our attention and discipline. Nevertheless, we will discover that many of the disturbing thoughts that seemed to distract us are being transformed into the ongoing praise of God. When we see with increasing clarity the beauty of the Father through His Son, we will discover that created things no longer distract us. On the contrary, they will speak in many ways about Him. Then we will realize that prayer is neither more nor less than the constant practice of attending to God's presence at all times and in all places.

Paul's words to the Christians of Thessalonica about unceasing prayer might at first have seemed demanding and unrealistic. Perhaps, we can now see that they can be the source of an ever increasing joy. After all, it is not just a man, but God Himself, who invites us to let our whole lives be transformed. That is why Paul could write: "Pray constantly and for all things give thanks to God, because this is what God expects you to do in Christ Jesus" (1 Thess. 5:17).

August 5, 1978

1981

Prayer and Liberation

M. Basil Pennington, OCSO

That our world is in something of a mess at the moment there can be little argument. There may be little all can agree upon, but on this we do, differing in opinion only as to how bad the mess is. More than a quarter of the globe's inhabitants profess to be Christians, disciples of Jesus Christ. It is significant, then, to find out what is the Christian response to this tragic situation. If God did indeed create man to share his life and happiness, if Christ's mission is one of re-creation, renewal even unto a new fullness, then how is this going to come about? How are life and order and a Garden of Eden going to rise again out of chaos? What is the Christian response to the chosen offspring of divine creative love whose very existence, not to speak of his full development, seems to be increasingly obstructed by all sorts of manipulation, by an unreasoned or misguided use of power and even by brutal force? Or is there a Christian response?

Christ Himself is the response. Christianity is following Christ, listening to Christ, being Christ. "Let this mind—this heart, this soul, this Spirit—be in you which was in Christ Jesus."

Christ Jesus was wholly free from interior oppression. And so will the Christian be, if he takes on the mind of Christ, if he lives what he has become by baptism, if he allows his Christ-nature to breathe, to catch up his whole being in the movement of Love for the Father, which is the Holy Spirit.

Jesus did know and experience exterior oppression. We might even be tempted to say that in the end it killed Him. But that is the point. In the end, though it had killed Him, he triumphed over it and lives. What was His response to the oppressive situation, His way to freedom? Union, communion with the Father, a communion that necessarily included obedience, for there can be union with the Father on no other terms: "Yes. Amen." And this is the Christian's response to all the oppression that rises out of the world's chaos, and to that chaos itself. For prayer is liberating, and the truly liberated person lives prayer.

To understand this we need to understand the two terms of our title: prayer and liberation.

The penny catechism—if there is anyone who can remember back to those far-off times when a penny could actually buy something, even a whole booklet—defined prayer for us as "lifting up the mind and heart to God." This is, of course, very figurative. God is not up or down, nor in any other direction for that matter. Nor is the heart the sort of thing one starts lifting up. Prayer is, rather, a happening. Or, better, a being present to. With the knowledge that comes from faith and the desire that is love, the Christian attends to the reality: God, actively present to him in the effectiveness of His creative love.

God does not just make things, toss them out and let them be. Everything, in all its being and activity, is at every moment coming forth from, being sustained by, and, indeed, participating in the goodness of the Divine Being. And so, if we truly see something, say this page on which these words are set, we do not see only paper. We also see God sustaining this paper, bringing it back into being, sharing with it in some mysterious way something of the fullness of His very own Being.

This is true of all created being, of all that we perceive about us. Yet when it comes to the human person, the one who has been baptized into Christ, we find something even more wonderful. Not only does this particular creature participate in the Divine Being from the outside, as it were. He certainly does that, like every other creature. Indeed, he does it most fully, being made to God's image and likeness, able to know and to love, a creature radically free. But as one baptized, he has been brought into the very inner life and being of the Godhead.

Christians are sons and daughters of the Book. God, in His awful goodness, and it is something to inspire awe, has revealed to us His own inner life, His personal relationships. And in baptism, God, Father, Son and Holy Spirit, taking up His abode in us, brings us into union with the Son. Sonship is the Christian's, not by some merely extrinsic legal fiction, but by some kind of intrinsic participation. "I live, now not I, but Christ lives in me."

This prayer is not going up or out or even really in. But it is a being present to the reality of what is here, and who we are. *Here* is God, in His creative goodness at this very moment and at every moment bringing each one forth into existence, sharing with us His being. We are creatures whose whole being is constantly, receptively in contact with God, coming forth from Him, and wholly orientated to Him as an end and meaning, the One who alone can fulfill the thirsting capacities to know and love that He has created in His creature. Even more, the baptized are in some most wonderful way, Christ, the Son, coming forth from the Father, and returning to Him in the personal response of love that is the Holy Spirit. Of its very nature our whole being is to the Father. The Spirit cries out, in groans that lace every fiber of our being together in an ardent movement of love, "Abba, Father." This is the reality of our being. And prayer is only letting it be. We simply stop distracting ourselves from this movement of love that we actually are.

Thus prayer is, in its essence, liberation: making the self free to be what it really is. When we enter into prayer, and simply let ourselves be, we enjoy the freedom of the Son of God. Interiorly Jesus could be subject to no form of oppression. There He was essentially free. So, too, is the Christian when, in prayer, he comes into his deepest self and simply is what he is, one with God in a deepest union of subjects. At this level of being nothing can ever enslave; he is radically free. Apart from those impairments of human nature that render the person functionally something less than human, the human person remains forever free. Once he has received the precious gift of divine filiation, only he can renounce it, and that he must do freely, taking on the slavery of sin.

Passion, psychological pressures, the construct of a false identity, while these cannot take away that radical freedom nor the basic orientation towards

God, they can limit and impede its use and enjoyment. This is a form of oppression and calls for liberation. The imperious demands of the loins and the pocketbook, of lust and greed, can really enslave a person. But it is easy to free oneself from these, compared to the socioeconomic shackles that bind with demands to keep up with the Joneses and indeed to outdo them. The shackles of our Americanism, our professionalism, our class, are made of weightier metal. We need to free our self, our own true self, our deepest self, from the false, superficial self that is created and shaped, and in the end totally dictated by these extrinsic forces. But how can we escape them? Go off to a monastery? That is a solution more and more are embracing, but even the monastery is in many ways, willy-nilly, involved in the society and economy that surround it, and in part sustain it. The commune in the woods is even less of a solution.

The Christian response is mortification, dying to self—the superficial, controlled self—so that the true self can live in the light of Truth. Know the Truth and the Truth will make you free.

But how do we die? Something of dying is found even in the very knowledge that we need to die, but do not know how. It is at best a slow process. If we would find the way, the Way that is the freeing Truth: "Be my disciple, take up your cross daily (I can remember my novice master saying: 'That's daily, young man, not weekly or monthly, but daily') and follow me." It is much in the pain of dying and not being able to die. Christ hung on the cross three eternal hours. It is a long, slow process, and prayer is at the heart of it; daily prayer, that reveals the freeing Truth, gains the needed help, gives the motivation.

We will not go on praying if we are not finding something in prayer. But we do find something there: that Truth whose searching light brings forth with inescapable clarity the truth of all other things. We then see how false are the claims of so much of the social mores and Madison Avenue brainwashing that have been fabricating the meaning of our lives. We see true values, so we can let go of many of the mirages, and we can use the good things of creation as if we used them not. Christ loved the poor with a special love, but He did not preach material poverty, rather, poverty of spirit: the freedom to get along with and without. In prayer human relations come alive. In the depths of our being we find unity with God in Christ and every other human being. The rest, all the wonderful trinkets of creation, become so much more precious when they are shared and undesirable when they are had at the cost of sharing.

Prayer—and the call to sharing—does not necessarily require that we go out from our land and our people, from our class and our station in life. But it may. It has sent a Lutheran minister to the crumbling inners of Chicago to share what he has and what he is. It has called a Baptist professor to sell his piece of suburbia to buy an apartment house in a burnt-out neighborhood and to fill it with an extended family of students and elderly persons. But we might stay with our own middle class, perhaps even stay in suburbia. But our values will necessarily change. And with the critical and creative insight that emerges from contact with Truth, we will seek and find new ways.

I think here of Packard Manse, an ecumenical community in the Boston suburbs. It is a cluster of family units, which includes also a monastic unit where a monk goes about his prayerful thing, fulfilling the prophetic and priestly role that no community can afford to be without. The houses and setting are typical suburbia, though the large interracial families tell of a difference. But through co-ops, extended hospitality, conscientization, this community is freeing itself from many of the conforming pressures of its class and environs, and indeed invites those environs to share in its freedom.

But let us not think that it is only suburbia or the middle class or the "have's" that need to be liberated. Perhaps even more do the "have not's." For their very need can be the fertile seminary of enslaving greed. It is easier to tell the rich they are better off and must share, than to tell those in ghettos that they have 20 or 50 times more than their sisters and brothers in Bangladesh and so must open their grasping hands and give up one of the widow's two mites.

Prayer does not unite us with the rich or the poor; it unites us with humankind. Let me quote that most beautiful word of Thomas Kelly's which sums up so well what God does to us in prayer:

> He plucks the world out of our hearts,
> loosening the chains of attachment.
> And he hurls the world into our hearts,
> where we and he together carry it in
> infinitely tender love.

The kind of prayer we speak of here, essential prayer, is quite different from the kind of prayer that some might be most accustomed to, a constant litany of petitions. I do not want to downgrade, in any way, petitionary prayer. Jesus Himself taught it in that most perfect prayer: Our Father, who art in heaven. . . . But prayer cannot end with petition. Nor should it begin with it. Indeed, such prayer may be feeding our greed and increasing our enslavement to our needs, real or imaginary.

If prayer is communion, union, then as pray-ers we know in whom we believe. And this knowledge must break forth in praise and worship as we realize who that is. We are filled with joy, satisfaction and pleasure at being able to communicate with Him, to praise Him, to be one with Him. How this diminishes needs and frees from false needs. There are no television sets in charismatic households where prayer is the satisfying pastime.

When we realize who God is and who we ourselves are, and the utter gratuity of creation, a total thanksgiving wells up from the very depths of a grateful, receiving being. All is gift and gratefully received. Greed is gone. Nothing is taken for granted. All is reverenced: "I thank you, God, for the wonder of my being." Ecological well-being is the necessary consequence. There is a loving care for every person and every thing. Sufficiency is more than enough, for it is more than is deserved. It is what is wanted for all. And what one has is shared with all, with that end in view.

At this point enters penitence, forgiveness and being forgiven, healing resentments, greed, selfishness. This whole mystery of forgiving and being forgiven involves freeing experiences we all very much need. Even the one oppressed can never be truly liberated until he forgives his oppressor.

But does the role of prayer end here: freeing the individual pray-er and others insofar as we are moved to share and to forgive? No. There is the role of prayer in political thought, political passion and political action. We do not want to deny the continuing validity of Paul's analogy of the Body. Not all are called to promote Christ's redemptive mission by political or social activism. Not all pray-ers are called to be social activists, even though all Christian activists must be pray-ers. But prayer addressed to and in contact with the authority of the power of God and enlivening one's bonds with all humankind increasingly stimulates, deepens, and enriches political thought and calls for supportive solidarity with those who are expressing Christ's healing presence on the political and social fronts.

And this support, this universal concern can, and must, for us Christians who have entered into true prayer, express itself in the power of intercession. As we enter more freely into and realize more fully our identity with Christ, all Christ's concerns become our own concerns, even as all our concerns are Christ's. As we take on the mind of Christ, the one Mediator, we come to understand the meaningfulness of intercessory prayer. For we understand that at the very moment, as He is creating and re-creating, God hears our prayer. Christ said it would be so. It is something quite staggering to realize that the very God has so disposed things that the unfolding of His creative sharing of His own infinite goodness, being and joy should be shaped in some way by a human petitioner's good will or lack of it. But such is His will. And hence with compassion and sensitivity born of true love we must constantly make intercession.

What does this realization not say of our true significance and dignity? Is this not a liberating realization: That God so esteems the human person? Need we then be unduly concerned about how our fellows value us? With all the creative power of God at our call—"ask and you shall receive"—need we fear any lack?

There are many, many more things that could be said here of prayer of liberation. We could see how prayer liberates in the face of every created power by placing it in the context of true power—God's. We could indicate how true prayer increases our attentiveness, so that we are more constantly and fully in touch with reality; how prayer increases our creativity, so that the real problems of life are perceived, new alternatives are seen, and ultimately God's answers are found; how prayer increases awareness of responsibility, so that we do not need to be coerced to do our share, but rather humble ourselves for failures and seek forgiveness through genuine conversion; and how prayer even increases relaxation, so that we can let go of more and more of our defense mechanisms and freely relate with our fellow humans.

Prayer liberates. But it does far more than that. It revolutionizes. Ultimately in prayer we come to understand the quintessence of Christian belief and practice, the Good News.

May 9, 1981

1983

Christmas in New York

George W. Hunt, SJ

This past Christmas was the first in my life when I was alone at suppertime. After sharing in the pre-Christmas spirit so spiritedly, I was grateful for a respite. It was curiosity, that congenial companion of loneliness, that induced me to walk outside of *America* and see what the other America was doing at 6 P.M.

New York is ever a city of shocks. That most of these are less than kind is a truth dating back to Peter Stuyvesant; more sentimental versions of the same thing became inspirations for the likes of O. Henry and Damon Runyon, who pumped up the ordinary to soften the shock. This night, an unnaturally warm one, I don't know what I expected, but I did anticipate a sleepy, near empty city.

So, shock number one. Any demographer would expect to see Jews, Irish, Italians, blacks—not just the city I once knew, but the city everyone sees. Not this night. I walked down Sixth Avenue, once grittily ugly, now revived after the three decades' detritus of the old El into the Avenue of the Americas. No native New Yorker can call it that with a straight face, but tonight it was the avenue of the entire world. Families of Pakistanis, Indians, Orientals of who knows what country, were coming from who knows where, giddy and happy despite the gentle drizzle, with a purposeful tiredness that was touching. I guessed most of them were Muslims, Hindus or Buddhists—tonight the city was theirs.

When I got to Rockefeller Center, I met remnants of the Sixth Avenue crowd, but here the majority was Hispanic. The skating rink had been transmuted into a village center where families gathered in clusters. Most were young, and nearly every man and woman held a baby and was very gently cautioning toddlers in tow. They were whispering to those in their arms and, while pulling at the toddlers, repeating in alternate Spanish and English, "Look! Look!" pointing toward the tree.

There were hundreds of these families, and they seemed oblivious of the crowds. Instead, it seemed all were for a few minutes privy to a collision of mutual kindnesses in a city where the tree they pointed at was actually a dead, uprooted tree. All of them knew this, of course, but like all things partly pagan and partly Christian, their very looking at it transformed it by intention and so infused it with life.

I sought out something more comfortable and went to St. Patrick's Cathedral. To my surprise, it too was packed with pre- and post-tree gapers, but here their behavior was enhanced. On entering I was pushed toward an obviously long-married couple who evidently were continuing a heated argument begun on the street outside. Suddenly the husband turned and said in a grave whisper, "Not here!" It worked. Ah, sanctuary.

Historians tend to trace the rhythms of Christian faith through the groundbreaking ideas of great theologians and the thawings and/or gellings consequent upon church councils. However, popular devotions—to whom people pray, what they say when they do, and the way they go about preparing for it—are usually more revealing. St. Patrick's holds many side chapels, all equipped with kneelers, and the saints honored there have long represented a judicious selection to satisfy the pious expectations of New York's very varied ethnic population. Tonight all of the side altars were ignored, save two. St. Francis of Assisi's narrow alcove drew a crowd of two and three lines deep, with some waiting patiently for a kneeler and others content to stand in silence. None of them looked distinctively Italian to me.

No surprise here: St. Francis remains the church's most cosmopolitan saint. But if the association of Christmas with St. Francis seemed right, I was a bit jarred to discover that the other crowded side altar was the one that displays the replicated imprint on Veronica's veil, showing the stark effect of Christ's Passion. Immediately I thought, oh well, the macabre attracts a crowd, until I noticed that the many people praying were looking down and not gazing greedily at the imprint.

My liturgical calendar was disrupted all the more when I moved on to the area behind the main altar. This area is less well-lit, and I happened upon what seemed like a hangout for reverent teenagers.

In a rear right aisle stands Partridge's rather heavy-handed version of Michelangelo's *Pietà*. Relaxed knots of these teenagers, polite and quiet, were grouped near the statue according to gender, waiting for a spot on the narrow kneeler. When their turns came, they prayed the way boys and girls always have: The boys were quick and intense; the bargain made, they moved on. The girls prayed with an enviable composure that comes from practice; also, their lists were longer and no abbreviations were allowed.

I couldn't tell whether the groups knew each other, but after noting some discerning scouting and awkwardness, I thought not. When I walked farther back to the Lady Chapel, I saw other teenagers, these a couple of years older, who clearly did know each other. About seven couples were seated in separate rows, holding hands in silence and facing forward toward the simply lit statue of Mary. I detected no restlessness or embarrassment; they seemed to like the place, as simple as that. No doubt their neighbors and all those apparently in the know suspected they were up to no good tonight. New York is a city of shocks.

Within a few short steps I felt that I had left the Christmas season entirely, until I moved around and behind the main altar and came upon the Christmas crib. The crib was situated in a rear aisle against a far wall, and those surrounding it stood so pressed together that, in an orderly division, the crowds would have been eight to ten lines deep. For a brief moment the crowd split as if by magic, while a cathedral attendant stepped into the crib to gather up the hundreds of bills tossed into the manger.

The attendant seemed glumly self-conscious as he went about his business, reaching under and around the Infant, while the crowd cooed quietly in support. A father next to me had hoisted his three-year-old son to his shoulders so that the boy could see. He turned his face upward and asked, "You like this?" and the boy answered—very loudly—"I hate it!"

Another man standing directly behind them, obviously the boy's uncle, reached out and pinched the boy's cheek, grinned broadly and said in a heavy accent to him, "You like it someday, someday, eh?" The boy at first didn't seem so sure, but then he smiled brightly and pointed toward the crib. I followed the direction of his finger and went home; when I got there, I laughed out loud.

January 15, 1983

1992

Praying

William J. O'Malley, SJ

Praying is a bit like sex. If we engage in it, we're rather nervous talking about it, and parents wouldn't dream of telling their children what goes on when they do it. In the case of prayer, that's sad, really, since according to Jesus we should be praying "always," and our job as parents and catechists is to bring children and God together.

But of course prayer is also not at all like sex, since few of us find need for alibis about not engaging in sex; "I really can't find the time; I know it's important, but there are so many other things that are . . . well, you know: *laborare est orare* ('work is prayer')."

Not only does our reluctance to open up a few minutes a day to God deprive our own lives of a realization of the genuine dimensions of those lives, but it also leaves our young laboring as fruitlessly as Sisyphus in our theology classes, which—without a personal relationship with their Subject—become as gratuitous and ultimately forgettable as factoring quadratics. After 12 years of Catholic education, most of our students know a great deal *about* God. But not too many of them seem to know *God*.

In class, we get so lost in explaining the signs that point to God—sacraments, scripture, rules, history, church—that we forget to make youngsters look in the direction all the signs are pointing. The God-signs become God-substitutes. It is easier to teach rules and history and doctrines than it is to teach praying—just as it is easier to teach fractions and Latin grammar than to teach a love of order and a sensitivity to nuanced language. We don't come to know persons analytically—they must be approached directly, me to you. Till then, we're doing background research on an interview that never takes place.

Obstacles

The first obstacle to encouraging the young (and not so young) to make praying part of their lives is making prayer seem worth the trouble, and the major part of this essay will devote itself to showing how *not* praying is actually self-impoverishing. That motivation strikes a chord in young people who, by the very nature of their present stage of development, are *self-absorbed*. But there are other obstacles as well: fear of silence and solitude, finding the time, the impracticability of praying and impracticality's corollary: short-circuiting the calculating intelligence.

Silence and Solitude. Probably never in history has there been a generation so addicted to noise. Put a city teenager in an Iowa cornfield and you're risking mental meltdown. Some kids tell me, if there's no one else home, they turn on the TV, the stereo *and* the radio! What did people do when they were walking to school before they invented the Walkman? But the reason is deeper than we might think offhandedly. My suspicion is that their *self*-chosen noise is a wall against all the *other* noise: not just screeching subway wheels and blaster boxes and sirens but against "When are you going to . . . ?" and "How come Melissa Stephenson can . . . ?" and "You guys didn't give 110 percent out there today." Like the little boy in the Swedish film *My Life as a Dog*: drumming his ears with his palms, shouting, "I'm not *lis*-tening to what you're *say*-ing!" Ultimately, that musical fortress is merely one more manifestation of a pervasive fear of yielding, of being vulnerable or becoming a loser. That fear shows in the refusal to admit they are wrong, even when they tell you later they knew they were. It shows in the refusal to commit oneself—to study, to a team, to a college, to a permanent spouse, to public service, to a vocation—because something better might come along. Thus anything teachers and parents can do to establish the context of trust also helps smooth down an obstacle to praying, because prayer is, after all, yielding.

Finding Time. Finding time to pray depends, of course, on the importance one attaches to praying. But those of us who will beg off, however
shamefacedly, "Of course praying is important but . . ." hardly ever find a
day when we can't find 15 minutes to shower, shave or put on makeup and
dress our outer selves to face the public (nobody'll see the inner shambles).
All of us have some kind of "fat" during the day—riding to work or school,
mind-numbing sitcoms, the phone, the guitar, the stereo. Nothing wrong
with them, only with their tyranny.

Impracticality. The only time praying is practical is when one is in need
of a handout or some answers. "But God doesn't give me what I ask or solve
my problems." Personally, I've pretty much given up on prayers of petition,
since I said Mass every day for three years that my mother could die (she'd
been suffering so long), and she didn't. Nothing wrong with petitions; the
best One of us prayed in Gethsemane for release from the torment ahead
of Him. Like Our Lady at Cana, He was simply telling a Friend there was
a need. When we pour out our sorrow to a friend at a wake, we aren't
expecting the friend to bring back the dead. We draw strength to go on
from a friend who supports us by letting us know we're not alone. God
doesn't play the game for us, just lets us know—if we allow it—that the
game is played in a larger context than we're ordinarily aware of. And I
sometimes wonder if, when we pray for answers, we spend so much time
prattling along that God must say, "Look, I'll *try* to suggest a few things if
you'll only shut up and *listen!*"

The Analytical Intelligence. Akin to uprooting that need to dominate
God is the difficulty of short-circuiting the discursive intelligence, which is
in full gear most of our day. Even students who don't slog away at the books
still spend a great deal of time trying to outwit the rules. We add up bud-
get figures, diagnose illnesses, follow recipes, try to figure out kids, keep to
schedules—all day long, *clickety-clickety-click*. We've got to pull ourselves off
to the side of the road and find out where we're going—and why. We have to
open the spirit within (something the analytical intelligence can't even comprehend) and allow the Spirit of God to invade us. But that's difficult, again,

because it means yielding center stage in our concerns to the One who has *been* center stage since before we even joined the cast.

It is critical that parents and teachers in early grade school create within the young a felt sense of the numinous all around them in nature, art, people *before* the self-absorption and defensiveness and fear of yielding arise in adolescence. What's more, that is the time to begin teaching children methods of centering prayer—before the pseudo-sophistication sets in.

Push back the desks (or take them to a church) and tell them beforehand all that you're going to do before you do it. When you finish setting everything up, you are going to leave, and any one of them may leave, too, *as long as* they are extra careful not to disturb those who want to stay. Loosen the ties; take off your shoes if you want. Now sit on the floor with your backs against something, close your eyes and just relax. For 15 minutes or so, the world can get along without you. Rotate your head and let all the tension drain down into your shoulders. Feel gravity pulling all the uptightness and the control out of your shoulders, down your back, through your seat and your legs and into the floor. Peace . . . peace.

Now take a deep breath—a really deep breath; hold it for five counts; out for five counts; in for five counts; out for five counts. Think of all the air in this room; we use it, then pass it on, never knowing whom it has kept alive before us; we share that life-giving force. In. Out. Now go beyond this room to the envelope of air that surrounds the whole earth; you're a part of that—leaving us, crossing the Atlantic and Asia and the Pacific and back to us. In. Out. Now, as you breathe in that air, say inside the innermost room of yourself: "God, my good Friend," and as you breathe out, "somehow You're alive in me." Say that again, several times, and quietly withdraw.

It won't work for all of them, at least the first time, but it will work for some. The important thing is to elicit their receptivity to the *process*. Before beginning, be sure to tell them not to ask themselves, "What's this supposed to be doing to me?" or "Is everybody looking at me?" or "Am I doing this right?" Just yield; let go and let God. And, personally, I'm dead against some kind of prayer journal, measuring progress or treasuring "lights." That's too much like weight-lifting in front of a mirror. The focus is in the wrong place.

What's in It for Me: Humanizing

We are not just teachers; we are also salespeople. Young people as well as adults have a perfectly reasonable question: "What's in it for me?" We can teach and test theology; as to the value of belief and religion, powers of persuasion must come into play.

There are many worthwhile effects from taking time to meditate that have no religious connection at all. Since grace builds on nature, perhaps we can lure them into genuine praying by showing its personal advantages to them first. Here are only five: simplification, perspective, freedom, feeding the soul, and wisdom.

Simplification. No emergent adult would deny that life is too confusing. We live in the most complex time in history: Hurry, bustle, keep it moving, have it on my desk by yesterday. Every free moment, our senses are assaulted by billboards and ads and commercials shouting at us to buy this, buy that—or else! A hydra of conflicting expectations: parents, peers, teachers, teammates, girls, boys, muggers. Report cards, college boards, traffic cops, tryouts. Who's playing quarterback and who's the prom queen? "Drop out! . . . Get involved! . . . Smoke grass! . . . Go to Mass! . . . Demand your rights! . . . Do what you're told!" It's like being locked in an asylum for insane carnival pitchmen.

"Leave me *alone*!"

Okay. Here's your chance.

Each of us, at the very depths, has a human need to become a hermit at least 15 minutes a day. Not a hermit cocooned in the Walkman. A hermit. Without an eye of peace in the hurricane of our days, we're going to be swallowed up by the crapstorm. Whenever mothers come to confession, I always assign this penance: "A half-hour before the kids come home, kick off the shoes, relax, and find out what's really important." No mother ever objected.

Only for a few moments, detach yourself from everything that fluctuates and, at rest, let all the tension drain out: all the confusion, deadlines, questions. Merely be there: emptied, at peace, receptive. As Chesterton said, poets and contemplatives don't go mad; the "solvers" do.

Life is an infinite sea, but solvers try to cross the infinite sea, thus making it finite. All they find is frustration. The poet and contemplative float easily on the infinite sea and enjoy the view.

Perspective. After seeing enough pictures of starving children in Kurdistan, Ethiopia, or Cambodia, at least the sensitive soul feels a twinge of guilt when complaining that Mom has forced tuna casserole and broccoli on us again. Similarly, pulling out of the hurly-burly for a while shows us what is really important in our lives, in others' expectations, in all those shouting voices.

One day my friend Ed Bartley was grading *Macbeth* tests at his desk when his little daughter came up and said, "Daddy! Come quick! The birds!" But Ed was a man who got papers back the next day. With hardly a look, he said, "Not now, honey. Daddy's busy." He went on, unaware for a few moments that she was standing next to his desk, a fat tear running down her cheek. In that moment, he really saw her. She was more important than *Macbeth* and "promises to keep." Wisely, he let her lead him to the apartment window, and for ten minutes they looked at the birds on the roof. They weren't accomplishing anything, but something was happening. And three years later, Ed died.

William Carlos Williams says the same wise thing:

> so much depends
> upon
>
> a red wheel
> barrow
>
> glazed with rain
> water
>
> beside the white
> chickens

Freedom. Most of the young have a ludicrous idea that somewhere "out there" totally unencumbered freedom is possible. But even Genghis Khan was *subject* to the law of gravity. He had to submit, humbly as a child, before storms and earthquakes. Whether he wanted to or not, he had to eat and sleep, endure toothaches, grow weary. There was a limit to what he could drink before passing out. If he had conquered all the world, he was still powerless as a peasant before death.

But most of the limitations on our freedom are *self-imposed*: enslavement to others' judgments, gigantification of our shortcomings, and at the root—fear. If we could just lay hold of our inner selves—beyond the power of others to warp that self-possession—we might find "the serenity to accept the things that can't be changed, the courage to change the things that can be changed, and the wisdom to know the difference."

True freedom comes from what St. Ignatius Loyola called "detachment" or "indifference." Neither term implies that a person must become insensitive. The real meaning is "impartiality," that one seeks the freedom to do the truth, no matter what choosing the best option might cost. One chooses without possessiveness, without self-serving ambition, without impulsiveness, without greed. One counts the cost to the self later—if at all.

No one achieves real freedom until he or she can find what freedom truly means. And it doesn't mean living random lives.

Feeding the Soul. We are all smothered by reminders to build up our bodies—nutrition, workouts, rejecting drugs—and the young hear them with Buddhist attention. They are also smothered with reminders to build up their minds—reading, learning to think by learning to write, getting those verbal and math scores up—which the young hear with somewhat less attention. But there seem far fewer reminders that what differentiates us from animals is not our bodies or our brains, which they share, but our souls—which they do not.

It is not difficult to show young people that the human soul does in fact exist and that starving the soul is self-impoverishing, because the soul is the self: who-I-am. When they look at me, they don't see *me*; they see only my body. They can make educated guesses from what I say and do as to what kind of self I am, but they don't see that self. The guards in Nazi extermination camps had bodies and brains, but the reason we can call them "bestial" is that they had lost their souls. When I honestly fall in love, it's not the yearnings of my flesh or the calculations of the brain that say, "Yep! This is the one!" It's my soul. When I stand in awe of a snow-capped peak at dawn or Michelangelo's *David* or a baby's fist around my finger, it's not my body or mind that say, "Gasp!" It's my soul. My intellect is intrigued; my soul is stirred. It's where all that's nebulous in me resides: honor, awe, loyalty, remorse, patriotism, faith, hope and love. Oh, the soul is there, all right.

Wisdom. Kids understand the difference between knowledge and wisdom, between someone who's a "brain" and someone to whom to bring their pain. Someone wise does know which things cannot be changed and which can, and he or she is at peace with that. The wise person accepts things as they are, his or her position in the universe: far better than a rock or carrot or pig; far less than God. Science is not God, nor is Progress, nor is Money, nor, most certainly, am I.

Wisdom does not come from suffering. If it did, animals in experimental laboratories would be wiser than all of us. Wisdom comes from suffering reflected on, accepted, assimilated. But if one is so busy doing and experiencing that he or she has no time for quiet reflection, then life becomes, not a connected whole, but a pile of beads without a string. We have to take time to withdraw from the transitory in order to discover the permanent.

What's in It for Me: Divinizing

Becoming aware that one has been divinized by Jesus Christ, invited into the Trinity family, is not the same as the self-aggrandizing divinization of Roman emperors. Rather, it is a felt realization of the numinous presence of God, not only all around us, but *within* us. God is there all the time, waiting, but, like God's forgiveness, God's will to share the divine aliveness with us can't activate until we invite it. It is the heart-stopping understanding that, despite our shortcomings, despite our seeming insignificance to most of those around us, the God who dwells in unapproachable light dwells within me.

On the one hand, relating personally to a God vaster than the universe takes a little doing. On the other, the Ancient of Days on a throne both risks becoming an idol and flies in the face of what we know about reality, that God inhabits a dimension beyond the limits of time and space: God has no beard, no throne, no right hand, no genitals. Yet I still have to deal with God, person-to-Person. Personally I find a less unsatisfying answer in physics—or rather in *meta* physics, in "Einstein-plus."

Suppose there were a reality faster than light; it would be everywhere at once, so super-energized that it would be at rest. And scientists now believe when they crack open the innermost kernel of the atom, it will be nonextended energy. Every object we see—though it appears rock-hard—is actually just another form of energy: $e = mc^2$. Couple that science with all we know from religion: encounters with God so often described as fiery bushes and pillars and tongues of flame. And realize that, when Moses asked Yahweh His name, the answer was: I am who am. God is the pool of energizing existence out of which everything draws its "is," "the dearest freshness deep down things." It may not help everyone, but when I pray, I pray to a Person made of light.

This is an adaptation of a Sufi meditation on light and God. Relax and get rid of all the in-charge-ness, then focus on a candle flame. Let your imagination draw a circle around it and expand the flame until it fills the whole circle. The light is like the invisible-but-present atoms that bond air, flame and candle. Then slowly imagine the light swelling beyond the circle to fill the room. Then beyond the building, beyond the whole country, beyond the globe. And then beyond. Into the immeasurable source of all light.

"The world is charged with the grandeur of God." So are you. Bow to the divine in you.

Choice or Chance?

Prayer is essential for ourselves and our children, not only as humans but as Christians. As humans we need time to regain inner stability, time to re-collect the self—not the vague and surface "I" of everyday life but the real "I." And the solitude that prayer demands lets us face our selves without all the posturing and pretense that help us bluff our way through the day. As Christians, too, we need prayer. Without real contact with the person about whom the theology texts speak and whom the Mass celebrates, no wonder the texts are no more meaningful than the insights of a dead rabbi and the liturgy no more involving than a long lunch for a Guest of Honor who never shows up.

There is no "only" way or time or place to pray. Like Goldilocks, we have to try a lot of them to find which "feels" best. Some find it best after work, after the dishes are done, after the late news and before bed. Some like to sit quietly; others prefer walking; still others pretzel themselves into a lotus. But the most important element is to have a focus to come back to when you're distracted. And you will be distracted. The body gurgles; limbs cramp; noses itch; you suddenly remember, "I didn't call Sue!" The focus brings you back to your center.

Anything will do: a crucifix, a candle, a rock. But some of the most "professional" pray-ers in the world use a mantra, a phrase repeated over and over as a focus.

People say they don't say the rosary anymore "because I never think of what the words mean." That's real left-brain, analytical, insight-mongering talk! The whole *purpose* of the prayers, repeated until the words have no meaning, is to *short-circuit* that calculating intelligence! None of our conversations are worth recording, but there is always a more important conversation going on underneath: "I enjoy being with you."

The Jesus Prayer is a mantra, too. On the long easy intake of breath: "Jesus, Son of David," and on exhale: "have mercy on me, a sinner." You could do it with any line you love: "And I, except You enthrall me, never shall be free, nor ever chaste, except You ravish me." Just being with. Acknowledging who's who.

Others pray as Ignatius taught: applying all the senses to a gospel scene so "You Are There," savoring the brittle matzoh and the tang of the wind, breathing the sweat, kneeling and taking the disciples' feet into your hands and washing them, feeling the texture of the skin. Then looking up and seeing that those you work with have taken the disciples' places.

But the critical difference between praying and merely clearing the mind is the "connection": from the beginning of the praying and consistently through it, being explicitly aware that Someone else is there—silent, perhaps, but there, the God whose faithfulness, and forgiveness and fondness for us are forever.

That sure looks to me worth finding time for.

June 13, 1992

1992

Attempting the Impossible

Robert Inchausti

A dozen years ago, at St. Vincent's Preparatory School for boys in central California, we began every class period with a simple prayer. I would say, "Let us remember," and the students would reply, "that we are in the Holy Presence of God."

We did not call it prayer, though; we called it "attempting the impossible." It was a good description of what we did. Just trying to get the students to be quiet for the few minutes it took to recite the prayer was nearly impossible, never mind the exalted ambition of connecting with God.

Some of the students approached the prayers with hands neatly brought together, fingers pointing toward heaven, faces scrunched up in abject concentration. Others took prayer-time as a wonderful opportunity to be irreverent—making noises, pretending to be asleep or staring around the room at the "fools" who were taking this hocus pocus seriously.

I really did not know how to respond to their varied reactions. Aside from the more boisterous disrupters, I let each student respond to silent prayer in his own way, for I myself had yet to fathom the full significance of this practice beyond its status as an "official" school ritual. But as the year progressed, I found more and more value in "attempting the impossible."

At first I wasn't very good at it. I would try to remember the presence of God, but I was more truly trying to imagine it—trying even just to conceive of it. I knew that this was wrong, so during the prayers I tried to stop thinking altogether, to stop the chatter of my mind for a few seconds as one does in meditation.

I wasn't able to do this either, so I ended up just watching my thoughts course through my mind, trying not to get caught up in any of them. If I found myself inside some idea or emotion, I would simply return my attention to my breath. After doing this, I noticed the same set of concerns popping up every day: Will I be able to fill up this hour? Will I get some time to relax today? What will I do if Marty acts up? Will I remember everything I am supposed to say? What if Mr. Strapp visits my room? Is my lesson plan any good? What do I have to do next?

These same worries arose so often that I soon had them numbered, and so during prayer I could simply let them go. "Oh, there's personal preoccupation number four. No need to bother about that again." As a result, at times I was able to bring to my prayers a purity of motive that I had never before achieved, and this brought me some profound moments of rest during those three-minute reflections.

But then beneath those surface concerns, I found another layer of stress. During prayer time, I would suddenly remember some stupid remark I had made to Mr. Strapp a week ago, or a look of disdain on a student's face that I had seen last month but had never registered. Or I'd suddenly remember something I was supposed to have done several days ago. During one meditation I suddenly recalled an argument I had in high school with my English teacher. It was as if my mind refused to let me attend to the reality before me, as if silence and peace were impossible to obtain.

Brother Blake, my 67-year-old mentor-teacher, assured me that thoughts and images such as these bubble up in our minds all the time. We just never slow down enough to perceive them. Their logic makes up our moods. When we first try to focus upon God in prayer, we reveal to ourselves the preoccupations of our own preconscious minds. I wasn't to try to move beyond this stage, he suggested. I was to enjoy it, learn from it, catalog my worries as the first step in liberating myself from them.

This was a wonderful time in my prayer life. Every class period began with opening a package sent special delivery from my deep self. "Oh! I'm still thinking about that? My conversation with Linda affected me more than I thought." "Oh, look at this fear I never knew I possessed."

Occasionally I would grow so bored with all my thoughts and feelings, plans and projects, obligations and responsibilities, that I would find my mind becoming clear and the chatter would cease. Time and space would disappear. This would usually happen a day or two after an especially difficult meditation when letting go of some particular thought had felt tantamount to dying. The students would sometimes even have to call me back to consciousness. "Mr. Inchausti, the prayer is over. Mr. Inchausti? Are you still here? Earth to teacher, Earth to teacher."

When I would emerge from one of these prayers and look at my students, their presence often struck me as miraculous, and I would listen to them with renewed interest and attention in hopes of discovering *who* they were and *how* they got here.

It took me a good three months before my quest for purity of motive got God's attention, but then suddenly—out of nowhere—there it was. There was a presence within me—listening. And with God's attention, I suddenly got bigger. I felt less trivial. The classroom became an authentic battleground. Life, the school, my quest for vocation, seemed to matter more.

The students, I found, often evaluated their days by whether or not their teachers were in "good" moods. At first, I took this as the typical psychological defense of blaming others for one's own problems, but after a few weeks of silent prayer I could see their point. Events in themselves do not dictate our response to them. A teacher in a "good" mood simply handled stress better than one in a "bad" mood. Why not simply resolve never to be in a bad mood, since it is merely the result of invidious interpretations anyway?

So I tried not to get caught up in my own self-drama or thought stream. I tried to stay true to the memory of the presence of God and see each class as if for the first time. I don't think I could have ever remembered to do that if it weren't for that opening prayer ritual.

As the semester progressed, I began to see more and more of my life as prayer—that is, as attempting the impossible. I experienced my teaching and my praying in almost the same way: as a quest for perfect, undistracted attention to the task at hand. And each task was seen as an end in itself, a door to bliss—infinitely interesting and complex.

Silent prayer was an activity that was admittedly useless, and so you could not fail at it. It didn't produce anything. It didn't satisfy any requirement. It didn't require elaborate lesson plans, and it couldn't be graded. It simply stopped everything for a minute, punching a hole in my busy, failed day, and in any myth of educational progress. It was done for itself and nothing more. It was a great center of calm in my stormy day, and I began to look forward to it.

Once, I promised my class that as long as they stayed silent, there would be no lessons, no assignments, no work. "If you want to," I said, "we will spend the entire period in silent prayer. But if anyone talks, it's over."

Of course, the students tried to remain silent, but they could never do it. Someone always spoke before three minutes were up. It astonished me, but they were simply incapable of being silent for more than three minutes—even when they wanted to be. They found self-control exhausting, and they were quite happy to get back to the routine of class work, after such ventures into the "impossible."

I was beginning to see that prayer was one of the most important but least understood elements in the school's curriculum. It was nothing but silence before the mysteries of life, yet that silence opened up to infinite intuitions. When the obsessions through which one apprehends the world are allowed to dissolve, everything is revealed in a new light.

Of all the discoveries I made that first year, the power of prayer was one of the most important to me, for it helped me to get out of my mind and attend to the world in its pure, sensuous reality. It provided me with a method that bore in on phenomena instead of carrying me away into abstract speculations. I learned to rest in the presence of things *as they were* instead of constantly fleeing from them by "figuring them out." I learned, in other words, how to let down my defenses just long enough to see through my own grandiose misperceptions. I was beginning to break out of my 19 years of schooling to a renewed faith in my own native intelligence and its spiritual core. I was at last beginning to see my students rather than merely *think* about them, and prayer was my way back to this kind of independent knowledge.

I looked back into my past to find the reason why it had taken me so long to learn this simple truth. And I had to admit that my ambitions and desires had robbed me of the simple, revolutionary truths of perception. I had sold my soul for success in school, popularity, approval. But through it all there had remained a part of me unconvinced by the world. And this was the pain evoked by prayer, by doing nothing, by attempting the impossible, and I thanked God it was still there.

It also dawned on me that teaching itself was *attempting the impossible* and so it too was a form of prayer—provided one did not attach oneself to the fruits of one's labors, but quietly and continually tilled the soil of teenage awareness, expecting nothing, really desiring nothing and therefore dreading nothing. Just seeing everything and providing a space for spirit to express itself. Prayer had taught me that to be a teacher one didn't need to act, nor was it enough merely to wait. One caused things to happen by opening up a space in one's heart to register the subtle movements of the students' souls toward real change. And one could do this only if one remained unimpressed by the old forms of power—progress, ability, ambition, results—and rested in the creative, unique, never-again-to-be-obtained moment of simple awareness of that which is.

My students loved to read the *Book of World Records*. They could sit for hours amazing each other with excerpts from the text. I tried to figure out why they were so enraptured by the longest basketball game or the tallest human being. Then it dawned on me that what my students were really look-ing for were concrete examples of human achievements.

What they found, however, was trivial. But this didn't bother them because at least these were "real" accomplishments. I knew, of course, that most "real" accomplishments cannot be seen, let alone measured, and occur in places of the mind of which my students were only now just beginning to become aware. Most accomplishments are hard to see because you need imagination and competence to comprehend them. Novels and scientific breakthroughs require imagination to be seen. Most people never do perceive the accomplishments of Einstein or even Tolstoy. But world records provide concrete, measurable, specific achievements that can be grasped by even the most literal mind. My students' interest in them testified to their longings for excellence and to the paucity of avenues through which they could find it.

I didn't try to change this. I just noticed it.

December 12, 1992

1994

The Journey Within

Rev. John B. Healey

Many thoughtful observers of the moral condition of the world today are convinced that, if the human race is to survive, we must regain a sense of the transcendent in our lives. That is to say, we must somehow learn to open our minds and hearts to the love and power of the one who made us, and so regain our sense of identity and of the meaning of human experience.

During his visit to Denver last summer, Pope John Paul II summed up this conviction in one striking statement that made headlines. He said: "America needs much prayer, lest it lose its soul."

This bold sentence of the Holy Father echoed the prophetic word of the eminent German theologian Karl Rahner (1904–84), SJ, who wrote that "the Christian of the future will be a mystic or he or she will not exist at all. . . . By mysticism we mean a genuine experience of God emerging from the very heart of our existence."

Prayer. Who of us does not believe in prayer? And yet, in the context of the pope's analysis of today's spiritual problems, we know that Pope John Paul II meant that we must pray in a way that most of us have never prayed before. We know that he meant that we must not only "say prayers" individually and together, valuable as this is, but that we must learn to pray from the depths of our being, in a way that will change our minds and hearts, pray with deep faith, conviction, fidelity and perseverance. We know that he meant we must pray in a way that will bring our innermost being to an experience of the transcendent God and gain for us a new perspective on ourselves and the meaning of human life. In other words, John Paul II was issuing a call to contemplative prayer, to what Father Rahner called "mysticism."

The pope and the theologian were, however, speaking of what has already begun to happen. There have been clear signs in recent years that the Holy Spirit is calling many, if not all, of us to contemplative prayer. Everywhere there is increasing evidence of a hunger for silent prayer.

The 1960s were the watershed for the resurgence of spirituality in our time. In that decade, many young people turned to meditation, especially to Eastern techniques of meditation, and the Second Vatican Council declared that we are all called by God to holiness. Since then there has been a proliferation of books on spirituality and renewed interest in classic mystics like St. Teresa of Ávila and St. John of the Cross. The writings of Thomas Merton have been unfailingly popular now for decades. Retreats and workshops on spirituality are in demand and well attended.

Perhaps a brief account of the spiritual journal of this writer, a veteran priest, will serve to exemplify the change in the way of praying that the Holy Spirit is effecting today and for which Pope John Paul II pleaded in Denver.

I am 82 years of age, and have been an ordained priest for 57 of those years. One would ordinarily expect that a priest who has been active in the ministry of the church for so long a time would, by the very nature of that experience, be truly knowledgeable and practiced in the ways of Christian prayer. Not so with me. Even though for as long as I can remember I have said countless prayers, alone and with others, it is only now, in the twilight of my days, that I am finally learning how to pray and, by God's grace, becoming a prayerful person. Only within the last few years have I begun to enter into the mystery of prayer and, again by the grace of God, to lead others along with me.

How is it possible that I, a priest who has been serving God and His people to the best of my ability for more than half a century, can say that I am only now beginning to pray? Was I a hypocrite all those years? No. Did

I attend regularly to liturgical and private prayer? Yes. Did a gracious God accept the prayers I said? I truly believe so. Then what was lacking? What was lacking was my heart. The longest journey I have made in my life has taken me half a century—from my head to my heart. And that journey will continue to the end of my life and beyond.

I consider myself a miracle of God's grace. By that I do not mean that I now see myself as holier than anyone else. Far from it. What I mean is that, in spite of my long-standing emotional immaturity, and the negligence and self-centeredness in praying that resulted from my human weakness over five decades, I have now in the waning years of my life been blessed with the gift of contemplative prayer and have somehow been able to lead others into the practice of deep personal prayer.

Prayer in my life has been mostly a head trip. This is not surprising. Each person's devotional practice depends on many factors, especially upon his or her understanding of faith and religion, as well as upon emotional development and temperament. Given my experiences, it was inevitable that my prayer would be preponderantly intellectual, almost entirely in concepts, articulated in appropriate and approved verbal expression.

From childhood my intellectual gifts served to hide and compensate for my lack of proportionate emotional development. That is a disparity that I had to deal with all the years of my life, but an account of its ongoing resolution is not pertinent here.

My intellectual approach to faith and to prayer found a most agreeable climate in Rome during my six years of study there in the 1930s in preparation for ordination. Those years were the very peak of the anti-Modernist era in the Catholic Church, when individualism and the slightest hint of subjectivism in faith and devotion were suspect.

In our studies in Rome, heavy emphasis was placed on dogmatic theology, somewhat less on moral theology, while our spiritual development for the most part was left to our own individual initiative and effort. We did learn something about the Ignatian, Carmelite and Sulpician approaches to prayer. Official church teaching, however, was our supreme concern. When ordained, I was top-heavy with doctrine. I knew much about God, but I did not know God.

During the 25 years of my priestly ministry before Vatican II, this intellectual emphasis in religious matters was pervasive among Catholics. Our model of the church was hierarchical. In our religious practice we were mostly concerned with "right" (i.e., authoritative) answers to religious questions and with approved practices in our devotional life. An individual Catholic's questions about faith and preferences in devotional practice were of little account compared to magisterial teaching and the unfailing efficacy of the sacraments.

Mystical prayer and experience, especially for ordinary believers, were frowned upon, even ridiculed. Among priests, "there's one in every parish" was a commonplace way of referring to someone who had a strong or exceptional personal relationship to God. The usual response to such cases was to remark that the church recognized the possibility of a direct relationship to God, but this experience was better disregarded. Mysticism was dangerous. Solid doctrine, frequent reception of the sacraments and approved devotional practice were all we needed to "save our souls."

In 1973, a priest now for 36 years, I became so discouraged and depressed that I wished (and even tried) to hospitalize myself for psychiatric care. God planned otherwise. That same year, for no particular reason, I attended a weekend Cursillo with a few other priests. It was my first conscious experience of the power of the body of Christ. In chapel one morning I was moved to utter aloud a prayer, in my own words, no less, for a priest a few feet away. My audacity and freedom surprised and delighted me. My brother priest smiled in appreciation.

Later that year I reluctantly attended a charismatic retreat with 70 other priests from around the world. While there I experienced a sudden and overwhelming spiritual renewal. Some call it being "baptized in the Holy Spirit." Whatever it was, it motivated and enabled me for the next 10 years or so to preach and teach at home and abroad to charismatic groups. Those were powerful, joyous days of constantly praising and thanking God. In the midst of these enthusiastic gatherings I experienced the presence and power of the Holy Spirit in the body of Christ.

Even so, I had not as yet entered into the mystery of prayer. All the while I was being unknowingly prepared for it. Charismatic prayer is usually freeing, articulate, festive, affirmative and emotional. Many need this type of prayer. I did. Still, it can remain peripheral in one's life; its enthusiastic experience can remain superficial, emotional, concerned more with being healed than with carrying one's cross.

Sometimes, even after years of joyous charismatic involvement, one may lose the taste for this kind of prayer without realizing that one is being called to a deeper, silent, wordless, often dry and difficult type of prayer—that is to say, contemplation. I know now that this, in fact, has been happening to many charismatics as it happened to me.

About 10 years ago, the writings of Thomas Merton began to provoke my interest in contemplation. I spent more and more time in silent, wordless prayer. Two intense retreats under the direction of Abbot Thomas Keating, a Trappist, made me realize that at last I had found the way to pray that my heart had always longed for, though I knew it not. Having been a teacher all my life, I felt that I must try to bring others to the same realization. I set about doing so.

Five years ago I took up residence with other priests in retirement in Queens, a borough of New York City. Not knowing what to expect, I initiated two weekly "centering" meetings, one at our residence, the Immaculate Conception Center in Douglaston, N.Y., the other in a local parish, Our Lady of the Snows in Floral Park. The response was overwhelming. In the last five years, hundreds of men and women have attended these sessions, some for all of them, others for various periods of time.

To this day 60 or 70 people gather weekly to sit in absolute silence for 20 minutes, eyes closed, hands on their laps, body relaxed. The lights are dimmed. They remain practically motionless, alone with God in the midst of the body of Christ, waiting for someone who is already present. When a signal is given, they begin a slow, meditative walk in single file around the church to prepare for a second 20-minute session. They listen to a short instruction on prayer and the spiritual life and with a mutual blessing conclude the meeting. This format never changes.

Almost without exception participants attest to a radical change for the better in their lives because of their ongoing practice of contemplation through this method called "centering." In fact, it seems that no one who "centers" for any length of time is left unaffected.

To put it most simply, "centering" is to come into the presence of God within us and allow the Holy Spirit to do the praying. It is to "get out of the way," so to speak, with our own thoughts, images and feelings in order to focus (center) upon and maintain an awareness of the presence of God within us in the darkness of faith. In this method one uses a holy word or two (e.g., "Jesus" or "my God") as a sort of mantra to replace unwanted thoughts and to renew one's intention of maintaining awareness of God's presence.

Hardly a day goes by that I do not meet or hear of someone who is being drawn to contemplation. Where can these seekers go to satisfy this God-given desire? Where can they learn about it and enter into its practice with others? I am convinced that, if it is to happen on any appreciable scale, the teaching and practice of contemplative prayer must take place in the local parish. Few parishioners have the means and opportunity to attend retreats and workshops on prayer. The parish is the center of their spiritual lives; it is there they celebrate the Eucharist and their children attend the parish school. And it is there they must learn to pray. Priests and religious coordinators must take the lead.

In conclusion, I humbly make this plea to my fellow priests: My brothers, everywhere, every day, our people are calling to us out of their misery and need, as the disciples called to Jesus, "Lord, teach us to pray." Their faith and hope are being extinguished in the face of grinding poverty, unemployment, violence, addictions, loneliness and loss of direction in life. Many with empty hearts are trying to escape life's absurdity and meaninglessness in the vain pursuit of pleasure, possessions, power and prestige.

Knowingly or unknowingly, they yearn for meaning, for direction, for real life, for the God who made them and died for them. They do not know where to turn. They hunger for the spiritual food that we were called to give them. Feeding the lambs and sheep of Christ is our priestly privilege and obligation. Who will feed them if we, their shepherds, do not?

Pope John Paul II had it right in Denver. Unless they and we pray, really pray, we are on our way to "losing our souls." In Father Rahner's words we "will not exist at all'" as Christians unless we become persons of deep, personal, intuitive prayer, unless we become "mystics."

Do not be afraid, my brother priests. Reach out to them. Teach them to pray. Pray with them. Lead them. Do not claim ignorance or inability. Learn as you go. The Spirit will teach you and so will your people. Their spiritual gifts are numerous and powerful. We are a communion of saints, the people of God, the body of Christ. How can we fail when the Holy Spirit is calling us and guiding us? Come, Holy Spirit!

February 19, 1994

1994

Rummaging for God: Praying Backward through Your Day

Dennis Hamm, SJ

About 20 years ago, at breakfast and during the few hours that followed, I had a small revelation. This happened while I was living in a small community of five Jesuits, all graduate students in New Haven, Conn. I was alone in the kitchen, with my cereal and *The New York Times*, when another Jesuit came in and said: "I had the weirdest dream just before I woke up. It was a liturgical dream. The lector had just read the first reading and proceeded to announce, 'The responsorial refrain today is, *If at first you don't succeed, try, try again.*' Whereupon the entire congregation soberly repeated, '*If at first you don't succeed, try, try again.*'" We both thought this enormously funny. At first, I wasn't sure just why this was so humorous. After all, almost everyone would assent to the courageous truth of the maxim "If at first . . ." It has to be a cross-cultural truism ("Keep on truckin"!). Why, then, would these words sound so incongruous in a liturgy?

A little later in the day, I stumbled onto a clue. Another, similar phrase popped into my mind: "If today you hear his voice, harden not your hearts" (Ps. 95). It struck me that that sentence has exactly the same rhythm and the same syntax as: "If at first you don't succeed, try, try again." Both begin with an "if" clause and end in an imperative. Both have seven beats. Maybe that was one of the unconscious sources of the humor.

The try-try-again statement *sounds* like the harden-not-your-hearts refrain, yet what a contrast! The latter is clearly biblical, a paraphrase of a verse from a psalm, one frequently used as a responsorial refrain at the

Eucharist. The former, you know instinctively, is probably not in the Bible, not even in Proverbs. It is true enough, as far as it goes, but it does not go far enough. There is nothing of faith in it, no sense of God. The sentiment of the line from Psalm 95, however, expresses a conviction central to Hebrew and Christian faith, that we live a life in dialogue with God. The contrast between those two seven-beat lines has, ever since, been for me a paradigm illustrating that truth.

Yet how do we hear the voice of God? Our Christian tradition has at least four answers to that question. First, along with the faithful of most religions, we perceive the divine in what God has made, creation itself (that insight sits at the heart of Christian moral thinking). Second, we hear God's voice in the Scriptures, which we even call "the word of God." Third, we hear God in the authoritative teaching of the church, the living tradition of our believing community. Finally, we hear God by attending to our experience, and interpreting it in the light of all those other ways of hearing the divine voice—the structures of creation, the Bible, the living tradition of the community.

The phrase, "If *today* you hear his voice," implies that the divine voice must somehow be accessible in our daily experience, for we are creatures who live one day at a time. If God wants to communicate with us, it has to happen in the course of a 24-hour day, for we live in no other time.

And how do we go about this kind of listening? Long tradition has provided a helpful tool, which we call the examination of consciousness today. "Rummaging for God" is an expression that suggests going through a drawer full of stuff, feeling around, looking for something that you are sure must be in there somewhere. I think that image catches some of the feel of what is classically known in church language as the prayer of "examen."

The examen, or examination, of conscience is an ancient practice in the church. In fact, even before Christianity, the Pythagoreans and the Stoics promoted a version of the practice. It is what most of us Catholics were taught to do to prepare for confession. In that form, the examen was a matter of examining one's life in terms of the Ten Commandments to see how daily behavior stacked up against those divine criteria. St. Ignatius includes it as one of the exercises in his manual, *The Spiritual Exercises.*

It is still a salutary thing to do but wears thin as a lifelong, daily practice. It is hard to motivate yourself to keep searching your experience for how you sinned. In recent decades, spiritual writers have worked with the implication that *conscience* in Romance languages like French (*conscience*) and Spanish (*conciencia*) means more than our English word "conscience," in the sense of moral awareness and judgment; it also means "consciousness."

Now, prayer that deals with the full contents of your *consciousness* lets you cast your net much more broadly than prayer that limits itself to the contents of conscience, or moral awareness. A number of people—most famously, George Aschenbrenner, SJ, in an article in *Review for Religious* (1971)—have developed this idea in profoundly practical ways. Recently, the Institute of Jesuit Sources in St. Louis, Mo., published a fascinating reflection by Joseph Tetlow, SJ, called "The Most Postmodern Prayer: American Jesuit Identity and the Examen of Conscience, 1920–1990."

What I am proposing here is a way of doing the examen that works for me. It puts a special emphasis on feelings, for reasons that I hope will become apparent. First, I describe the format. Second, I invite you to spend a few minutes actually doing it. Third, I describe some of the consequences that I have discovered to flow from this kind of prayer.

A Method: Five Steps

1. **Pray for light.** Since we are not simply daydreaming or reminiscing but rather looking for some sense of how the Spirit of God is leading us, it only makes sense to pray for some illumination. The goal is not simply memory but graced understanding. That's a gift from God devoutly to be begged. "Lord, help me understand this blooming, buzzing confusion."

2. **Review the day in thanksgiving.** Note how different this is from looking immediately for your sins. Nobody likes to poke around in the memory bank to uncover smallness, weakness, lack of generosity.

But everybody likes to fondle beautiful gifts, and that is precisely what the past 24 hours contain—gifts of existence, work, relationships, food, challenges. Gratitude is the foundation of our whole relationship with God. So use whatever cues help you to walk through the day from the moment of awakening—even the dreams you recall upon awakening. Walk through the past 24 hours, from hour to hour, from place to place, task to task, person to person, thanking the Lord for every gift you encounter.

3. **Review the feelings that surface in the replay of the day.** Our feelings, positive and negative, the painful and the pleasing, are clear signals of where the action was during the day. Simply pay attention to any and all of those feelings as they surface, the whole range: delight, boredom, fear, anticipation, resentment, anger, peace, contentment, impatience, desire, hope, regret, shame, uncertainty, compassion, disgust, gratitude, pride, rage, doubt, confidence, admiration, shyness—whatever was there. Some of us may be hesitant to focus on feelings in this over-psychologized age, but I believe that these feelings are the liveliest index to what is happening in our lives. This leads us to the fourth moment:

4. **Choose one of those feelings (positive or negative) and pray from it.** That is, choose the remembered feeling that most caught your attention. The feeling is a sign that something important was going on. Now simply express spontaneously the prayer that surfaces as you attend to the source of the feeling—praise, petition, contrition, cry for help or healing, whatever.

5. **Look toward tomorrow.** Using your appointment calendar if that helps, face your immediate future. What feelings surface as you look at the tasks, meetings and appointments that face you? Fear? Delighted anticipation? Self-doubt? Temptation to procrastinate? Zestful planning? Regret? Weakness? Whatever it is, turn it into prayer—for help, for healing, whatever comes spontaneously. To round off the examen, say the Lord's Prayer. A mnemonic for recalling the five points: LT3F (light, thanks, feelings, focus, future).

Do It

Take a few minutes to pray through the past 24 hours, and toward the next 24 hours, with that five-point format.

Here are some of the consequences flowing from this kind of prayer:

1. There is always something to pray about. For a person who does this kind of prayer at least once a day, there is never the question, What should I talk to God about? Until you die, you always have a past 24 hours, and you always have some feelings about what's next.

2. The gratitude moment is worthwhile in itself. "Dedicate yourselves to gratitude," Paul tells the Colossians. Even if we drift off into slumber after reviewing the gifts of the day, we have praised the Lord.

3. We learn to face the Lord where we are, as we are. There is no other way to be present to God, of course, but we often fool ourselves into thinking that we have to "put on our best face" before we address our God.

4. We learn to respect our feelings. Feelings count. They are morally neutral until we make some choice about acting upon or dealing with them. But if we don't attend to them, we miss what they have to tell us about the quality of our lives.

5. Praying from feelings, we are liberated from them. An unattended emotion can dominate and manipulate us. Attending to and praying from and about the persons and situations that give rise to the emotions helps us to cease being unwitting slaves of our emotions.

6. We actually find something to bring to confession. That is, we stumble across our sins without making them the primary focus.

7. We can experience an inner healing. People have found that praying about (as opposed to fretting about or denying) feelings leads to a healing of mental life. We probably get a head start on our dreamwork when we do this.

8. This kind of prayer helps us get over our Deism. Deism is belief in a sort of "clock-maker" God, a God who does indeed exist but does not have much, if anything, to do with his people's ongoing life. The God

we have come to know through our Jewish and Christian experience is more present than we usually think.

9. Praying this way is an antidote to the spiritual disease of Pelagianism. Pelagianism was the heresy that approached life with God as a do-it-yourself project ("If at first you don't succeed . . ."), whereas a true theology of grace and freedom sees life as response to God's love ("If today you hear God's voice . . .").

A final thought. How can anyone dare to say that paying attention to felt experience is a listening to the voice of God? On the face of it, it does sound like a dangerous presumption. But, notice, I am not equating memory with the voice of God. I am saying that, if we are to listen for the God who creates and sustains us, we need to take seriously and prayerfully the meeting between the creatures we are and all else that God holds lovingly in existence. That "interface" is the felt experience of my day. It deserves prayerful attention. It is a big part of how we know and respond to God.

May 14, 1994

1995

Praying in a Time of Depression

Jane Redmont

> I lift up my eyes to the hills—
> From where will my help come?
> My help comes from the Lord
> Who made heaven and earth.
> —Psalm 121

Nearly two years ago, Jim Castelli interviewed me, along with other Americans from varied religious backgrounds, for his book *How I Pray*. "I'm an eclectic pray-er," I told him. "I pray in a lot of different ways, some quiet and some noisy, some solitary and some communal." Jim asked whether I had a daily practice or routine. I did—at the time. Eclectic as I was throughout the day, I was faithful to an early morning sequence, moving from hatha yoga to meditation to contemplative prayer. Much of my time was spent sitting still.

Six months later, everything changed.

At the time of the interview, I was working at what I now call "the killer job." Pressed by economic necessity, I had taken on the directorship of a nonprofit organization upon completing nearly six years' work on a book. Already tired when I began, I was exhausted by the end of the job's first year. Toward the end of my second year, I resigned. I was weary of having program time devoured by administration and fund-raising, increasingly edgy with my staff, unhappy with the person I was becoming, at ideological odds with the most powerful members of my board of directors and rapidly losing confidence in my professional abilities—something I had never experienced in my life.

The early warning signal had come at the end of April 1993. Driving on a road north of Boston late at night, I became incomprehensibly dizzy, my heart beating fast and waves overcoming me—waves of what? I was not sure. I was close to fainting. My first thought was that I was having a stroke, and that I would die there on the road, in the dark, with the motor running and the car lurching out of control. I pulled the car over by the side of the highway, twice. Finally I got home, singing a chant from the Easter Vigil to steady myself.

Labor Day weekend in Vermont, 1993: I had just finished my last week as executive director, though I was due back in the office as a consultant during the fall to help the organization manage the transition. My parents, an old friend and I were resting after lunch. Around us the countryside was quiet. I became dizzy, unbearably lightheaded, felt my heart rate shoot up. I began to tremble and sweat. I called to my friend, who took my hand, then took my pulse. My heart was beating at nearly twice its normal pace. It took me two hours to calm down.

A few days later, back in Boston, the symptoms returned. Day after day, week upon week, they came and went, at all hours of day and night—3 A.M., 5 A.M., 10:30 P.M. I never knew when they were going to hit. Even at church the attacks came upon me. Externally they showed very little; inside I felt physiologically off balance and emotionally out of control.

I went to the hospital emergency room twice during the worst of the attacks, was hooked up to heart monitors, watched my heart rate go up and down, then down to normal, then up and down again. On the second of these visits I shook so violently that the technician could barely perform an electrocardiogram. "Try to keep still, dear," she said. I thought I was going to die.

Then began the parade to medical specialists. Tests for thyroid abnormalities—negative. The wearing of a Holter monitor to measure every heartbeat for 24 hours—negative. The echocardiogram, during which I watched my own heart thanks to the marvels of ultrasound technology, and listened, thud-whoosh-thud, for signs of malfunction—negative, all negative.

After I had gone for a variety of holistic treatments including homeopathic remedies and two kinds of body work, the physical symptoms began to abate. But still the fear gripped me, not a worry about something specific but an anxiety with no bottom—not something I had, but a reality that had me. Sometimes it seemed as if the electrical wiring inside my brain were short-circuiting. No amount of deep breathing, yoga and fresh air seemed to help.

One of my friends suggested I might be depressed. Not knowing there was such a thing as an agitated depression, I had at first no idea that this could be the case. Anxiety, yes, but depression? Depression, I thought, was moping, slowing down, not getting up in the morning. I was ruminating, speeding and getting up too early. One day, driving into Boston by the Charles River, I imagined myself—saw myself—jumping off a bridge. I phoned my former psychotherapist and asked to see him, fast.

I began therapy again, willingly and with a sense of urgency. Very reluctantly, a few weeks later, I started taking antidepressant medication and, soon after, an anti-anxiety drug. Even then I was in such a state of terror and agitation—and still haunted by thoughts of leaps from bridges and seventh floor windows—that I decided to check myself into the hospital.

What happened to my prayer?

Meditation was the first thing to go. I still practiced yoga, and breathing exercises gave me some mild relief from anxiety attacks. But contemplation became impossible. Still, God was present, and I knew it. I did not face the fear alone. Yet the way I prayed underwent a profound change. It continues to change to this day.

Rediscovering the Psalms

One night in September the panic attack came at bedtime, a terrible shaking and fear, causing me to tremble so hard that my steady evening companion, a large black and white cat named Alyosha, jumped off the bed from fright. I breathed as deeply as I could, calmed down enough to open the Bible I keep at bedside and began reading psalms out loud. I read aloud to steady myself, to keep the demons at bay, to make the words more real and hold them in my mouth. At last I was able to cry. The psalms gave words to my heart, and even to my body. "O Lord, heal me," says Psalm 6, "for my bones are shaking with terror. My soul also is struck with terror, while you, O Lord—how long?" They may not have called them "anxiety disorders" 30 centuries ago, but the symptoms sounded suspiciously familiar.

The first change, then, was a renewed reliance on the Bible, especially the Hebrew Bible, and above all the psalms. Praying the psalms was not so much a prayer of petition as a prayer of naming, a statement of the situation. It gave me words—ancient words written by people who had the wisdom of experience, prayed aloud by generations of my ancestors in faith, both Jewish and Christian.

In those weeks before my hospitalization, I hung onto the psalms for dear life. As I wrestled with the aftermath of what I experienced as a harmful, even evil work situation, it helped that the psalms were blunt in their language about good and evil, faithfulness and struggle, enmity and vindication. I knew I had dealt with both individual and institutional evil, but always the polite, well-bred good girl, I had sought not to think ill of anyone nor to turn my anger into anything but talk. Depression is anger turned inward, they say, especially in women. The psalms gave me back my anger, took me beyond gentility into the wrath of God for the unjust. "Smite my enemies, Lord." I would read aloud with tears rolling down my cheeks, and it felt healing. "O Lord, how many are my foes! Many are rising against me. . . . But you, O God, are a shield around me. . . . Deliver me, O my God!" (Psalm 3). I rediscovered the low-number psalms, at the beginning of the book, and was amazed at the way they spoke of my own life.

One psalm came into my life and stayed with me for months. Long after my stay in the hospital, I was still reading it each night before turning off the light. "The One who watches Israel," says Psalm 121, "will neither slumber nor sleep. The Lord is your keeper. . . . The Lord will keep you from all evil. . . . God will keep your life . . . from this time on and forever." I listened to the promise, night after night.

A Meditation on Wings and Shields

Before meditation left me entirely, one session—a guided one—gave me a revelation that proved to be a treasure. I went to visit a meditation teacher I had met through one of Boston's interreligious dialogue groups. Her school is based in India with branches around the world. I sat with Sharona, a tiny, radiant woman, sipped tea with her, told her about the great fear and heard of her unexplained headaches and dizziness—one more in the series of people who have spilled out their own stories of depression and anxiety after hearing mine. "Come to the meditation room," she said, so we went and sat cross-legged on cushions in the quiet apartment, and slowly she began, in a soft voice, a guided meditation. My friend's guiding image was God as light, and God as light was neither what I needed nor anything I was capable of perceiving at the time. I remained painfully distracted. But presently she began to speak of God wanting us to be like children, like small babies enfolded in God's arms.

At that moment in the meditation I saw, felt, imagined arms around me, then wings—long, vast, protective wings. Then the image emerged of a shield. I need protection, I thought, as the visions rushed in. Opening my eyes at the end of the meditation, I realized I was reacting to, or being reached by, images—*realities*—from the most ancient of biblical traditions. They were not images with which I had spent a great deal of time praying in the past, but they were part of me somehow, planted in me by my Jewish ancestors, by the prayer of the church, by God and God's Spirit—perhaps by all of these.

Only those realities could speak to the depths of my fear, and to the personal and social evils I had experienced with such intensity. No New Age light for me, no nurturing Great Mother, no caring Father. Give me the Watchful One, I thought, the Guardian of Israel, the shield, the rock, the fortress, the eagle's wings. In that time and that desire, God had no gender for me; God was personal but not a person. Neither warrior nor eagle, God was shield, was wings. In that time of trauma, when I felt fragile and raw, only God as heavy metal would do; and this was the God who, from the depths, came to enfold me.

Cries of Desperation

On a quick trip to New York for a consulting job, a week or two into the antidepressant drug treatment and feeling no relief, I fell into a seven-hour anxiety attack with recurring suicidal ideations. On the morning after my arrival I found I could not focus my attention, yet focus was crucial in the job I was contracted to do for 24 hours, as recorder and process observer at a conference of urban activists that was beginning later that day. I felt as if I were about to jump out of my skin—or throw myself under a truck. An hour away from the beginning of the conference, walking uptown on a noisy Manhattan street in the afternoon, I prayed. I prayed to every saint I could think of in that moment, prayed to St. Dymphna, the patron saint of people with nervous disorders, to St. Ignatius, to Mary of Magdala, to Mary the mother of Jesus, and finally to Jesus himself—perhaps out loud. I am not sure. I said with all my strength, "Jesus, I don't usually ask you for much, but I am asking you now, in the name of all those people whom you healed, in the name of the man born blind and the bent-over woman and the woman who bled for years, in the name of the man with the demons and the little girl whom you raised up, HELP ME."

Within an hour, I was calm again.

The Prayer of Others

Back at the religious house where I was staying, where the conference was about to begin, I phoned my best friend from church. "You've got to pray me through this," I said. "There's nothing else left." "I will," she said, "and my daughter too; I trust the prayers of this child even more than mine." The prayers of a child and her mother carried me. Miraculously, I was able to stay focused for the length of the conference.

This is only the most dramatic example of the way I was carried by the prayers of others. Most of the time these prayers carried me in the strong and ordinary ways they always have—through the liturgy to which I returned, Sunday after Sunday, through the daily or weekly prayers of friends of many religious paths whom I had asked to remember me in the course of their devotions or meditation. A few times an ecumenical married couple—she

Evangelical, he Catholic—prayed over me as Evangelical Christians do, and I trusted their presence and their words, and God who gave them words and had given me the courage to step out of my self-sufficiency and ask them for help.

The prayer of others also helped me to weep. One of the worst dimensions of the depression was that I was unable to cry. It was a dry depression, a depression with no tears. There were only two exceptions: my night readings of the psalms and church. The crowded Sunday liturgy was one of the few places and times I was able to cry, releasing layers of sorrow, grief, loss and fear. Why church? I wondered at the time. Perhaps because I identify crying with being safe, or being held, and because in my local community of faith I do feel held, cradled in a way by this gathering of friends in Christ. And because I am touched at a level so deep I cannot refrain from crying. Somewhere in the killer job my voice had been silenced, and in church, especially in singing, I found it again, in both the music and the words.

Receiving God's Love

I made little effort to pray during my psychiatric hospitalization. Nor do I remember praying with any coherence or clarity during the five preceding days, when I was in such a state of terror following my return from New York that I had friends stay with me around the clock, 24 hours a day, as I wrestled with the chaos inside, with looming fears of harming myself and with my emerging decision to check myself into the hospital.

But the spiritual lesson of those two weeks was perhaps the central one of this period in my life. In those five days of being loved by my friends who watched over me and waited with me, in the hospital where our main work was to heal by walking through the pain, I heard, "Let me love you. Let yourself be loved." How hard that was for me. How much easier it became through this illness.

My friend Rosalind, the Evangelical half of the couple who had come to pray over me, was one of the several loved ones who came to visit me in the hospital. When friends came, we talked, often joked, hugged, sometimes walked together. The day Rosalind came, I was weary and not my talkative self. She found me lying on my bed, asked what I wanted, then sat in silence by my side, rubbing my back. Half asleep, I gave thanks for the receiving.

It all came together: the knowledge that I was safe, that I was "good enough" and did not need to "try harder," that I would be all right and that God—more deeply than I had known or let myself believe—loved me; that it was all there, there for me, "without money, without price," in the words of Second Isaiah.

At night I read Psalm 121. The insomnia of the past two months came to visit again the first night, then left for good. I slept deeply. Mostly, it was time in a safe place simply to be human and attend to my feelings, not to perform, produce, put the needs of others first or be Ms. Cheery Supercompetent, the great coper.

With letters and visits came flowers and a collection of devotional objects. One friend, a Brooklyn-born, Harvard-educated physician, arrived bearing a rosary and a laminated card of St. Dymphna. I—the intellectual, the Catholic meditator—loved the cards and the beads. The Catholic *tchotchkes* to which I had little attraction two decades ago as a convert in my early twenties were perfect for the circumstances. They were concrete and comforting. Like the Guardian of Israel, Mary and the saints watched calmly, images speaking when I had no words left to pray.

Meeting Evil Face-to-Face

Leaving the hospital was hard. Today the insurance companies determine what length of time it takes for one's psyche to heal, or at least to be removed from mortal danger. Both medical and psychiatric patients are sent home, as the saying now goes, "quicker and sicker." A garden-variety severe depression rarely warrants an inpatient stay of more than one or two weeks. Most of us are discharged too soon. Even those who are ready to leave find the first weeks difficult.

I was discharged after 12 days, still shaky but trusting that I would heal, step by small step. Six days out of the psychiatric unit, on a Sunday evening, the pull toward death came to visit—not from my will, for my will wanted to live, but from somewhere between the biochemical and the metaphysical, a wave of death, a compulsion born of a combination of malfunctioning neu-rotransmitters and the powers of evil and sin, somewhere demonic, some-where I knew was not from God or from anything good, a wave of death that would not go away.

I busied myself, paying bills, making phone calls, sorting papers, fighting the demons with tiny acts of the will, barely praying, scattered and tense, all the while thinking I knew exactly where there was a razor blade, in the tool chest, in the guest room closet, on the upper shelf.

Most of all I felt alone. I knew I could not struggle in solitude. The threat was too great, I began phoning again, this time to call for help. "It's war-fare," one of my friends from church said categorically, "spiritual warfare." She invoked angels, archangels, the vanguard of the Catholic pantheon, pro-tecting and armed for battle. I phoned the ecumenical couple with the high-tech careers, who had promised that they were available for prayer anytime, day or night. I asked if they could pray on the phone with me, for me. In simple words they spoke to God. I remember their saying that I needed safety and protection, that evil was real and present, that they trusted God; God would be with me. Please, God, they said, be with her, and your angels too.

Remembering what I had learned in the hospital, I made a plan for going to bed, step by step: Take a hot bath, drink warm milk, swallow the evening medicine. If sleep does not come, I decided, I will watch and pray, but I will not let this get me—and if worst comes to worst I will go to the emer-gency room and beg for the psychiatrist on call, since I am, after all, in a state of emergency. After the bath I crawled between the flannel sheets, under the down comforter, taking with me a stuffed bear, a box of tissues and a broken string of rosary beads. I awoke after sleeping for eight solid hours. Alyosha, the cat, was asleep on the comforter, sloped against my feet. The rosary was still in my hand. "The One who watches Israel will neither slum-ber nor sleep," says Psalm 121, "will keep your life."

Writing as Meditation, Healing and Prayer

That evening I sat at the computer and wrote a long poem about the experi-ence of the preceding night. By the time I was halfway through, I knew that

I was on the mend, that the antidepressant medicine had "kicked in," or that God had navigated me through the waters, or both. I felt alive and well. I was no longer silent. My voice was out in the world again.

The next writing to emerge was a reflection on social and political realities and their psychological consequences. In early 1994, delving into the past, I wrote about my family's experience with the McCarthy era, an essay that had sat inside me for at least 15 years and suddenly spilled out, provoked by Admiral Bobby Ray Inman's remarks on how criticism of his nomination for Secretary of Defense was tantamount to McCarthyism. I reviewed the attributes of the real McCarthyism and spoke of the effect this national hysteria had on one small family, the one into which I was born. I wrote about my father's refusal, at the age of 31, to testify against an innocent man, of his immediate loss of employment and blacklisting for a decade, about his working as many jobs as was necessary to support his young family. I wrote about the unspoken anxiety that sat, like a still murky pond, underneath my parents' efforts to move beyond the trauma to give my brother and me the happiest and most stable childhood they could provide. No wonder, I thought as I read my own words, no wonder I developed anxiety attacks three decades later. My father cried when he read the essay. For our whole family it was healing, simply because it had been spoken onto paper, a personal sequel to a memoir my father had published a year earlier. The story I told is still in search of a publisher, but it is alive now and cannot go back into the pool of silent dread where it sat for years.

Already a practitioner of social analysis after years of theological education and social activism, I found myself even more politicized by this illness. I began to notice realities at which I had only glanced before: the burden of carrying all at once mental illness, poverty and parenthood, as several of my brother and sister patients did; the tyranny of the insurance system and the illnesses aggravated by lack of health insurance; the way in which the workplace can destroy mental health; the way oppression breeds depression. Paradoxically, this time of unprecedented introspection turned into a look at causes of emotional distress that go beyond the biochemical and the intrapsychic, even beyond the family system, to the larger structures and events that shape our lives.

By summer, I was writing theology again—a commentary on Pope John Paul II's apostolic letter on the ordination of women (*America*, 7/30/94). The letter had been published in the late spring, when I was spending each Sunday liturgy in the company of my goddaughter, filtering ecclesial, theological and ministerial realities through her eight-year-old experience and grateful for her affectionate company. Having had the experience of falling to pieces, I experienced the reunion with my writing self as exquisite mending. It was both sign and cause of my renewed health.

Getting Help

Sometime in the middle of 1994, I realized my prayer had no anchor. I was better. I was working, writing, healing—and yet feeling as if I were wandering in the wilderness. No longer in crisis, not yet in steady peace. I decided it was time to go back into spiritual direction. The informal insight of peers was no longer sufficient. I needed someone older and wiser—and someone new.

Asking for help: again and again, it has come down to this. Help from therapists, from family, from God, from the local bank, from colleagues and friends. Help with the fear, help with the rent, help with untangling the emotional knot, help with employment, help with prayer.

"It doesn't work the way it used to," I complained to my new spiritual director. "I'm out of emergency mode, but I can't pray as I did before."

"Begin with your experience," he offered; "begin exactly where you are."

Praying with Body, Breath and Voice

I wanted to be gentle with myself. At the same time, I felt I ought to bring back a rhythm of prayer, the kind of discipline and fidelity which I imagined to be "right" and a sign of spiritual health.

"Bring back" was not, as it turned out, the operative word. I could not go back to the place I had sat before, metaphorically or otherwise.

My spiritual director encouraged me to pray with what "worked" in the present, not with what "used to work." I found that the prayer best suited to me was that which involved my body most. I was still waking up with yoga, the one practice I had not abandoned even in the hospital. Better still was the prayer involving both body and breath: singing. When all else failed this past year—and "all else" failed so often that I finally ceased trying to recapture it—I played recordings of sung psalms, chants or Gospel songs on the tape decks in my kitchen and car. I sang with them, letting the words and music carry me, entering into them with my voice, often repeating the same song two or three times. Some of the most powerful moments of communion with God came in those all-absorbing moments, not so much times of trance as periods of intense presence. Months later, I am still asking music for help: When in doubt, sing.

In the late spring, one of my friends, an Episcopal priest, 60 years old, becomes ill. It seems she has only weeks to live, perhaps days. She survives the crisis. I begin visiting her, bringing vegetables from Vermont in the late summer and giving her a massage during every visit, every week or two. Often I pray while I work on her body with scented oil. The image that comes to my mind is fire—a concentrated fire from God, almost like a laser beam, touching her bones, her muscles, her tendons. Often the massage itself is a prayer. In both words and silence, and in hands that seek to heal and flesh that receives, in the interaction, there is God. I am never tired when I leave, probably because she is, I am convinced, a truly holy woman, so full of prayer that her being passes it on like a communicable disease.

Anger and Healing, Hand in Hand

Another friend, an old school buddy, has been living with AIDS for two years. He is ambulatory and *compos mentis*—admirably and gracefully so, living a full life—but for how long? I watch every change, dare not phone too often, hold my breath against the day when his strength will wane and his sharp mind will waver. For him and for my older sister in ministry I grieve already, but mostly I am angry—that such precious, good beings will go before their time.

I like my anger. It makes me well, rather than wearing me down. But I have no idea what to do with all the anger, despite the fact that I rather enjoy it. I cannot turn it inward—it almost killed me once, it could kill me again—and so I let it rise to the surface and live with it. It moves into my conversations, my writing, my prayer. I think of how long I have been expressing anger politely, so as to make it palatable to those who need to know it. I am weary of being polite.

Where shall I put all this fury?

Fall 1994: The economic bottom has dropped out of my life. I have never quite recovered my earning power, though I am feeling well enough to work full-time. I have spent all my savings, and both my own and others' money, on getting well—acupuncture, psychotherapy, medication, some covered by my insurance, much not. In the spring and summer, I have had to stop ther-apy—a bad idea, but I have no alternative. I apply for free care at one of Harvard's teaching hospitals. It is a little like applying for welfare, though the process is less impersonal; I become a file with information that sits on a desk and waits and waits. Finally, I am declared eligible and start—once again—the slow process of building trust with a new therapist. I begin work at a part-time job that barely covers my rent; I accumulate freelance assign-ments and small consulting jobs. I write more theology, this time in the form of applications to doctoral programs.

The edge of winter finds me in a rage—at the health care system, at the insurance companies, at the killer job, at the Republican Party, at the Demo-cratic Party, at bureaucracies in general, at the Cambridge Department of Traffic and Parking, at the economy. And at God? My spiritual director asks me, as I in the past have asked so many of my own directees, whether I am angry at God. No, no, I answer. It's not God's fault that all this is happening.

Then, finally, one day in early winter, I crack. I am driving home by the river. My phone has been shut off, only briefly, because I have just paid the phone company the money I owed the auto mechanic, and now I have to pay the auto mechanic with the money I owe the landlord, which I do not have. The oil tank at home reads half an inch from "empty." I am sleep-deprived from all the work I am juggling. I begin to cry in the car and find myself screaming—at God, I think—"Enough! Enough! Enough!" All I can say is "Enough!" and cry. The next day, I feel much better for having yelled at God, and four phone calls come in offering me work, some of it decently paid. Following this I am angry, of course, that even with God, I have to raise my voice. Then it occurs to me that I am in a rotten lousy mood, and I begin to laugh: I am definitely not depressed. But in a rotten mood, oh yes, with a vengeance, dear God.

Ordinary Time

For a while, I am so absorbed with daily survival that my prayer, usually made in motion—as I walk, in the bus, on the subway, in the car—becomes reduced to two simple expressions: "Thank You" and "Help!"

I struggle, hard, with the realities of evil and forgiveness. Resentment and anger at the killer job sit inside my belly like a lump. "Some demons," Jesus said, "can only be cast out by prayer." I believe it, and I know this is one of them, but I do not know how to cast it out, nor do I know yet how Jesus will help me do it.

I am still singing in times of doubt.

I have begun, once again, to pray for others, sometimes because they ask me, sometimes because the Spirit moves me that way, placing the petitions before me and sitting me down to ponder them. Sitting me down. One day in early Lent, in this year 1995, I decide to try stillness again; I cannot pray for others on the run. I also want to sit and be with the Holy One, without words, only presence. Or perhaps it is the Holy One who wants me there, sitting and present. I make a small altar with a table my parents have recently given back to me, the small, low white table at which I sat with my dolls, books and tea parties as a child. Prayer has become wordless again. But this time I listen to music, watch candle flame and icons and lean against the memory table, eyes open.

August 26, 1995

1996

Jesuits Praying in Prison

George M. Anderson, SJ

From the time of Ignatius Loyola, founder of the Society of Jesus, many Jesuits—including Ignatius himself—have been incarcerated for their faith. Ignatius' own brief confinement came about through the Inquisition, which subsequently absolved him of any wrongdoing. But for the most part, their imprisonment was the result of conflicts with secular regimes that saw them as a threat because of the Society's ties with the Vatican. During the persecution of Catholics under Queen Elizabeth I, for example, Edmund Campion (1540–81), Robert Southwell (1561–95) and many others saw the inside of prisons. Not a few were executed or died as a result of brutal treatment. In this century, under the Nazis and later under Communist governments, scores of Jesuit priests and brothers were incarcerated for long periods.

A surprising number, however, not only survived imprisonment, but later described their ordeals in writing. What emerges again and again in their accounts is the role of prayer as a crucial factor in sustaining them. Walter Ciszek (1904–84), an American who spent 15 years in Soviet prisons and labor camps, speaks of the role of prayer in his autobiographical book, *He Leadeth Me* (1973). Prayer, he observes, led him to an understanding of his own suffering that enabled him to endure and even grow through it to a deeper awareness of his relationship with God: "I learned it only by the constant practice of prayer, by trying to live always in the presence of God. . . . If I wanted to preserve my interior peace and joy, I had to have constant recourse to prayer." In his earlier book, *With God in Russia* (1966), Ciszek underscores the fact that his prayer was based on an unshakable trust in God:

"In Lubianka [Prison], I grew firm in my conviction that whatever happened in my life was nothing else than a reflection of God's will for me."

In the accounts of lesser known Jesuits there is the same focus on prayer as a predominant source of strength. An Austrian, John Lenz (b. 1902), writing of his experience in Dachau, asserted that "it was prayer that saved us, not only in our physical but also in our spiritual need." He goes on in his auto-biographical *Christ in Dachau* (1957, in German) to make the same connection as Ciszek between prayer, suffering and the will of God. Through the school of suffering alone, he insists, was it possible to learn "the sort of prayer which pierces the soul like a sword . . . a blind submission to the divine will."

After his arrest by the Czech secret police in 1950, Ján Korec (b. 1924)—now Cardinal of Nitra—spent a total of eight years in prison. The charge against him was the one most commonly used by Communist authorities of the period: counter-revolutionary activities. For him, too, prayer and the deep sense it gave him of the presence of God was both a form of apostolic activity and a source of joy in a time of darkness. In his 1992 autobiography, *La Notte dei Barbari* (*The Night of the Barbarians*), he writes: "I felt that our Lord was with me, and thus in praying I spoke to him. I prayed with all my heart during the years in prison, because prayer was my only joy, as well as the only apostolate I could exercise during that long period of my life."

In an effort to withstand the intense pressure of the grueling interrogations, Korec made a small circle on the wall of his cell with the burnt end of a match stick. Then, gazing at the circle, he prayed: "In you, O Lord, I am strong. . . . You have given me health and strength to exist." He explains that this type of visual aid to prayer was suggested by a character in the writings of Franz Kafka; for Korec, however, focusing on the circle took on a specifically Christian connotation.

For some, conditions involving torture and the prospect of imminent execution led to a form of prayer that was highly simplified but equally intense. Franz Jálics (b. 1927), a Hungarian-born Jesuit working in a barrio of Buenos Aires during the military dictatorship of the mid-1970s, was arrested with a fellow Jesuit in 1976. Although they had received permission from the Catholic hierarchy and from their own religious superiors to live and work among the poor as a form of witness, a member of the extreme right denounced them as terrorists. Abducted by soldiers, with their heads covered for days by suffocating rubber hoods, they joined the ranks of the "disappeared."

Realizing that they might be facing death any day, Jálics prayed by constantly repeating the word *Jesus*. "We stayed with this simple prayer," he notes in the book he later wrote on the Spiritual Exercises of St. Ignatius. It was a prayer that helped them both to survive the uncertainty of not knowing from one day to the next whether they would be executed; but it also served as a means of allowing them to pray for their persecutors, particularly the man whose false testimony led to their arrest.

Four centuries earlier, the English Jesuit John Gerard (1564–1637) was tortured on the rack in the Tower of London in an effort to force him to reveal the secret location of the superior of the English mission, Henry Gamet. "You will be a cripple all your life if you live, and you are going to be tortured every day until you confess," the warder of the Tower warned him. But during a series of torture sessions, Gerard—like Jálics—found that the repetition of Jesus' name, and Mary's, gave him the strength to bear the agony of the rack. "I prayed in a low voice as well as I could, calling on the names of Jesus and Mary." When the torture resumed in successive days, he continued to put himself "in the presence of the Lord Jesus and his blessed mother." Eventually he managed to escape to the continent. There, at the order of his superiors and for the edification of novices, he wrote in Latin the long account of his underground ministry to English Catholics and his resultant imprisonment that has come down to us as *The Autobiography of a Hunted Priest*.

Seeking assistance through Mary by reciting the rosary has been another frequently employed form of prayer. During his almost 30 years of incarceration in China after his arrest in 1955, George B. Wong (b. 1918) describes how he turned to this devotion: "Not having any religious books with me, I had to rely on my daily rosaries. . . . My rosary beads consisted of 10 knots made from a torn rag like a five-inch string," he says in an article published in *The* (London) *Tablet* in December 1994, adding that possession of any longer string or cord would have been prohibited in order to prevent possible suicide attempts. Wong recited two complete rosaries in the morning and two more in the afternoon, interspersing them with meditations of his own devising. All personal reading material, including the Bible, was denied him, as it often was to imprisoned Jesuits and others of any period. A well-trained memory filled with Scripture passages therefore became an important resource.

Use of the rosary in China's prisons called for secrecy, however, because prayer was forbidden and guards watched to see that prisoners—forced to sit in silence on the floor of their cells in fixed positions all day—did not so much as move their lips. But prisoners like Wong found ways to circumvent the prohibition, as did Dominic Tang (b. 1908), the Jesuit archbishop of Canton who died in Connecticut in June 1995.

Archbishop Tang spent seven years in solitary confinement, where he was closely watched: "The warders would peep through a small hole to . . . see whether I was keeping the rules," he states in *How Inscrutable His Ways!* (1984). Nevertheless, although forced to rely on his fingers because he had no rosary, he managed to recite the prayers silently as he held his hands beneath a copy of *The People's Daily*, which was required reading for those who were being "re-educated." Since he was a Jesuit, it is not surprising to find that in addition to prayers like *Veni Creator Spiritus* ("every day there were many events which needed the light of the Holy Spirit"), his favorite prayer in prison was Ignatius' *Suscipe Domine*—"Take, O Lord, and receive all my liberty, my memory, my understanding and entire will, all that I have and possess. . . . Grant me only thy love and thy grace." After his release, Archbishop Tang spoke to a group of Jesuits in Rome about his experience; at the end of the meeting, the superior general, Pedro Arrupe, asked him to lead them in reciting this prayer together.

John Houle (b. 1914) was an American Jesuit imprisoned in another of China's prisons at roughly the same time. Locked in a 12- by 15-foot cell with 15 others, he had to struggle constantly against the surrounding distractions in order to find the inner calm that enabled him to make the early morning meditation with which he began each day: "Sitting on the floor, shoulder to shoulder with silent, suffering men, every movement, every whispered word, every noise in the corridor is a distraction." Nevertheless, as he goes on to observe in the May/June 1958 issue of *The Catholic Mind*, "in this and other hours of meditation I have really learned to love prayer and have felt gratitude to the depths of my being for little lights, little unexpected sources of strength." The theme of gratitude is an ever recurring one in the writings of incarcerated Jesuits.

In contrast to silent prayer, vocal prayer has also played an important role in their lives. Jacques Sommet (b. 1912), who, like John Lenz, was imprisoned at Dachau during World War II, speaks of it in his 1987 book, *L'Honneur de la Liberté* (*The Honor of Liberty*). He was drawn to vocal prayer by its physical aspect: "Vocal prayer has a physical dimension, tied as it is to . . . the call for God's grace. . . . It is a reliance on this grace through a route that is to some degree biological." The psalms were especially meaningful because he discovered in their cry "a sort of connaturality between [them and] our situation" in the deadly surroundings of the concentration camp.

Another for whom the psalms were a source of strength was William Bichsel (1928[–2015]), an Oregon Province Jesuit incarcerated after an act of civil disobedience at the naval base at Puget Sound in Washington State. During his confinement in the county jail in Seattle, amid tensions caused by crowding and a volatile racial and ethnic mix—he was with 15 others in a cell equipped with a single toilet—he turned to two psalm verses in particular. One was from Psalm 121: "I lift up my eyes to the hills. From whence comes my help? My help comes from the Lord, who made heaven and earth." The other was from Psalm 40: "I waited patiently for the Lord. He inclined his ear to me and heard my cry."

A number of Jesuits have found it helpful during their time of incarceration to make the Spiritual Exercises of St. Ignatius, relying on memory to recall the various meditations. Pierre Olivaint (1816–71), for instance, was one of five Jesuits arrested in 1871 when a revolutionary group seized control of Paris after the municipal government fled to Versailles as the Germans approached the city during the Franco-Prussian war. From prison, Olivaint was able to send out letters to his community. In one dated April 7 he writes: "I am taking advantage of my forced leisure to make my annual retreat." On the 13th day of it, he speaks of being so fully engaged in its dynamic that there is not a moment of boredom. Indeed, as the retreat proceeded, he was moved to extend it far beyond the usual four weeks, commenting in early May that he was by then on the 39th day. At one point, he allows himself "to rest a little," making only three hour-length meditations on the 31st day instead of the usual five. Toward the end of the same month, he and those with him, along with other priests and religious held in the same location, were put to death in a scene of mob violence.

The *Spiritual Exercises* were a help to John Gerard, too, after torture sessions in the Tower that left him barely able to move his limbs. "Now, as in the first days of my imprisonment, I made the *Spiritual Exercises*. Each day I spent four or sometimes five hours in meditation; and so on for a whole month." What aspect of the *Exercises* did he—or Olivaint and others, for that matter—find most meaningful? Gerard does not tell us, but it may well have been the third of the four weeks, devoted as it is to Jesus' passion and death, a theme suited to the situation of those subjected to torture and the prospect of execution. As an ongoing source of meditation during his years of prison in China, Archbishop Tang notes that he "liked best to meditate on the passion of Jesus."

During his incarceration in China from 1952 to 1954, the Hungarian Jesuit John Havas (1908–94) was another who had sought strength in an extended retreat experience. Locked in a pitch dark 9- by 5-foot cell as extra punishment, he decided to make a 40-day retreat to correspond with Jesus' 40 days in the wilderness. The darkness of the cell, however, prevented him from distinguishing one day from the next. He therefore made a scratch on the wall to mark what he judged to be the passage of each 24-hour period. When the punishment was mitigated and he was allowed to have light in his cell, he counted the scratches and found that his retreat had lasted not 40 days, but 55, so deep had been his spiritual involvement.

Whether in a retreat mode or not, daily prayer served an additional purpose: It was a way of establishing a supportive structure amid fear, loneliness and often chaos. In *With God in Russia* Walter Ciszek says, in fact, that while in solitary confinement in the Lubianka prison in Moscow, "I began to organize my days as if I were in a Jesuit house back home, and I made up a daily schedule for myself." He describes this schedule in considerable detail; after breakfast, reciting the Mass prayers from memory; the Angelus morning, noon and night as the Kremlin clock chimed the hour; a noon examination of conscience and another before bed when, at the same time, he prepared points for prayer the following morning.

A companion of Pierre Olivaint, Léon Ducoudray (1827–71), who was also able to send out letters in 1871 from his prison in Paris, gives a similarly detailed description of what he calls his little daily regimen: 5 A.M. rise, wash and clean cell; 6 A.M., prayer, the liturgical hours of matins and lauds; 8:45, rosary; 9, breakfast and the Office of the Blessed Virgin Mary; 10, spiritual sharing in the Mass being celebrated by his Jesuit community; 11:45, examination of conscience; noon, second rosary, and so on through the day until the Litany of the Saints at bedtime. Such a tightly arranged and self-imposed schedule was for him, as for Ciszek, a way of integrating himself back into the supportive prayer life of his Jesuit community.

As helps to remain psychologically balanced, prayer-based structures like these gave Ducoudray, Ciszek and others an advantage over their non-praying fellow prisoners. Among the latter was the cellmate of the Uruguayan Jesuit Luis Pérez Aguirre (b. 1941), who was imprisoned and tortured by the military in Montevideo in the 1980s. On one occasion the cellmate remarked that Pérez Aguirre was lucky, because he knew how to pray.

All that he himself could do during torture sessions was to count up to a thousand and back.

When, in his letter detailing the structure of his day, Ducoudray speaks of sharing spiritually in the Mass being celebrated at 10 A.M. by his brothers in their community, he is almost certainly referring to the so-called dry Mass, as is Ciszek when he speaks of reciting the Mass prayers in his cell in the Lubianka prison. The dry Mass was another form of prayer that sustained inner strength under the most difficult of conditions. Thus, John Gerard tells us that he daily "rehearsed the actions of Mass, as students do when they are preparing for ordination. I went through them," he adds, "with great devotion and longing to communicate, which I felt most keenly at those moments when in a real Mass the priest consummates the sacrifice and consumes the *oblala*."

Centuries later in China, in 1953, John Houle also found comfort in the dry Mass with, again, memory serving as a crucial aid: "Through our Lord's gracious gift, I know the Mass word for word in English and Latin, the proper of the feast of the Sacred Heart, and one of the Masses of our Blessed Mother. . . . This is the really happy hour of the day," he concludes, "[because] I am in heart before God's altar, clothed in his grace and love."

Helpful though the dry Mass was as a form of prayer, the inability to celebrate a true Mass remained a grievous source of suffering. John W. Clifford (1917–84), another American, spent three years in a Shanghai prison in the early 1950s. He speaks of this painful lack in *In the Presence of My Enemies* (1963): "I had not said Mass or received holy Communion for 888 days. . . . No one but a priest can fully realize the significance of that deprivation."

Unlike others less fortunate, however, Clifford eventually did find the means to celebrate with supplies smuggled in from the United States. Family members in California sent him a package through the Red Cross. In it were two small bottles labeled *Pabulum Vitae*—Latin for "food of life." One contained wine; the other hosts concealed between nickel-sized slices of sugar candy. When inverted, the stopper of the wine container became a miniature chalice.

The significance of the labels was lost upon the prison authorities, who allowed Clifford to keep the two bottles. Each evening, he waited until midnight before celebrating his secret Eucharist. Once assured that his cellmate was no longer awake, he lay on the floor and began. His small supply of wine and hosts lasted 41 days.

Are such stratagems a thing of the past? By no means. In our own time . . . Vietnamese Jesuit Joseph Nguyen-Công Doan (b. 1941), who spent nine years in prisons and labor camps in Vietnam starting in 1980, was finally able to celebrate Mass when a fellow priest-prisoner shared some of his own smuggled supplies. "That night, when the other prisoners were asleep," he said in an interview, "lying on the floor [of my cell] I celebrated Mass with tears of joy." Later, when he had been sent to a labor camp, a pharmacist friend was able to send wine to him in bottles labeled vitamins—a method similar to the one used by Clifford's relatives. But whereas Clifford's supply ran out, Doan's did not, and he continued to celebrate each night for the remainder of his nine years: "My altar was my blanket folded as a pillow, with my daily clothes as priestly garments," he said in an interview, "but I felt myself at the heart of humanity and of the whole of creation."

But for some, even prayer could not prevent their being shattered psychologically, if not physically, by their experience of incarceration. Although a work of fiction, Shusaku Endo's novel *Silence* tells the story of two Jesuit missionaries in Japan during a time of persecution. Arrested and imprisoned, both eventually apostatized. Who can say that such crumbling under intense pressure was not frequent over the centuries? Nevertheless, whether through a dry Mass or a real Mass, or simply by the constant repetition of the name of Jesus, the sustaining power of prayer, in whatever form, is evident in the words of the Jesuits described in these pages. Many others, men and women, lay and religious, Catholic or not, have also found prayer to be the source of their survival under inhuman conditions. The brief overview of the Jesuit experience presented here is simply meant to offer one aspect of that wider picture.

October 12, 1996

1997

Give Comfort to My People: Praying in the Spirit

Richard J. Hauser, SJ

I remember when I learned to pray. I was teaching as a Jesuit scholastic at a mission in South Dakota. Our life was very difficult. Our regular daily order included rising at 5:00 A.M. and retiring after the students were asleep around midnight. We were expected to do an hour of meditation before 6:30 Mass in the mission church. Eventually sheer physical exhaustion drove me to begin sleeping late, getting up only in time for Mass. Daily meditation had always been presented to me as essential for living the Jesuit life, so I experienced continual guilt for skipping it.

Every evening, however, after the students had quieted down in the dorms, I'd walk down the highway under the stars, often for over an hour. I recall being discouraged and lonely and pouring out my heart to God. I also recall returning from these walks peaceful, feeling close to Christ and wondering how I could survive without these walks. My conscience continued to bother me for omitting daily meditation, but one night I had a startling realization: I was not skipping daily meditation, I was doing it at night! I was walking down that highway each night to be with the Lord—not to fulfill a religious obligation. I had discovered a rhythm of being totally open to and comforted by God. I had learned to pray.

My nightly mission walks had uncovered my own almost desperate need for a fuller coming of the Lord into my life. I was praying, actually, in the spirit of Advent, which has become my favorite liturgical season. Advent, from the Latin *adventus*, "coming," commemorates the threefold coming of the Lord to the human family: the historical coming of Jesus in Bethlehem 2,000 years ago, the final coming of the Son of Man at the end of the world, the daily coming of Christ to the hearts of believers. The third, the daily coming, is the most central to the season—and the most neglected. We energetically celebrate the historical coming of Immanuel (God-with-us), and we all but ignore the implications of that coming, his abiding with us.

In this liturgical season the church invites us to pierce through the levels of our habitual consciousness and discover those areas where Christ does not yet abide. Having exposed our emptiness, we are invited to pray the Advent prayer, *Maranatha*, "Come, Lord Jesus!" The spiritual discipline *par excellence* for Advent is thus the prayer of longing, longing for the fuller coming and comfort of the Messiah to the human family, a longing classically expressed by the Hebrew prophets of old, "Rouse up your might and come!" We acknowledge with the prophets the depth of human restlessness, realizing it can be quelled only by a fuller openness to the Lord, which occurs only through a fuller opening to God's Spirit. So my Advent observance now centers on attentiveness to the voice of the Spirit.

Regularly in Advent I receive requests to give talks on prayer in preparation for Christmas. Usually I'm told that the group would like some practical methods for improving the quality of their prayer. I am uncomfortable with the assumptions behind these requests. My own experience tells me that praying well involves more than the conscientious use of methods—I'd been doing that for years before my breakthrough at the mission. My experience tells me that prayer happens best when we find a time and place that enable us to be in touch with God's Spirit—and with our own deepest selves. At that moment God's Spirit joins our spirit, and we truly pray from our hearts. In this context Paul's remarks about God's Spirit aiding our prayer make great sense: "The Spirit too comes to help us in our weakness. For when we cannot choose words in order to pray properly, the Spirit himself expresses our plea in a way that could never be put into words, and God who knows everything in our hearts knows perfectly well what he means, and that the pleas of the saints expressed by the Spirit are according to the mind of God" (Rom. 8:26–27).

The Second Vatican Council called us to a renewed appreciation of the role of the Holy Spirit within the church and within spirituality. Chapter One of the "Dogmatic Constitution on the Church" expresses this eloquently:

> The Spirit dwells in the church and in the hearts of the faithful as in a temple (cf. 1 Cor. 3:16; 6:19). In them he prays and bears witness to the fact that they are adopted sons (cf. Gal. 4:6; Rom. 8:15–16, 26). The Spirit guides the church into the fullness of truth (cf Jn. 16:13) and gives her a unity of fellowship and service. He furnishes and directs her with various gifts, both hierarchical and charismatic, and adorns her with the fruits of his grace (cf. Eph. 4:11–12; 1 Cor. 12:4; Gal. 5:22).
>
> In order that we may be unceasingly renewed in him [Jesus] (cf. Eph. 4:23), he has shared with us his Spirit who, existing as one and the same being in the head and in the members, vivifies, unifies, and moves the whole body.

Pope John Paul II's encyclical *Lord and Giver of Life* (1986) reflects Vatican II's emphasis on the centrality of the Spirit in Christian life. The Pope succinctly summarizes the connection between the redemption of Jesus and our sanctification by the Holy Spirit: "The redemption accomplished by the Son in the dimensions of the earthly history of humanity—accomplished in the 'departure' through the cross and resurrection—is at the same time, in its entire salvific power, transmitted to the Holy Spirit: the one who 'will take what is mine'" (No. 22).

The Pope reminds us that we adequately understand the Christian vocation only when we understand the role of the Holy Spirit: The entire effect of the redemption is brought about by the Holy Spirit. Post-Vatican II Christians are challenged to renew their understanding of the work of the Holy Spirit—an understanding all but lost before the council—and then to rethink their approach to every spiritual discipline, including personal prayer.

The Spirit and the Self

Treatment of the role of the Spirit within ourselves must begin with the Last Supper discourse in John's Gospel. Jesus is comforting his disciples, having told them of his imminent departure: "But now I am going to the one who sent me, and not one of you asks me, 'Where are you going?' But because I told you this, grief has filled your hearts. But I tell you the truth, it is better for you that I go. For if I do not go, the Advocate will not come to you. But if I go, I will send him to you" (Jn. 16:5–7).

Jesus explains why it is better for his followers that he goes: The Spirit he sends will take his place, guiding and strengthening them in their mission. Indeed this union with himself through the Spirit is the condition for apostolic effectiveness. The Gospel could not be more clear: "Remain in me, as I remain in you. Just as a branch cannot bear fruit on its own unless it remains on the vine, so neither can you unless you remain in me. I am the vine, you are the branches. Whoever remains in me and I in him will bear much fruit, because without me you can do nothing" (Jn. 15:4–5).

Jesus' prediction is fulfilled at Pentecost, when the Spirit descends on the community. The Acts of the Apostles gives witness to the working of the Spirit in the apostolic church. Note the difference in the disciples before and after the coming of the Spirit.

Among New Testament writings, the letters of Paul are also a most eloquent witness to this power of the Spirit—a power he received only after his conversion to Christ at Damascus. For Paul, belief in Jesus, with the subsequent infusion of the life of the Spirit, is a new principle of life, a new creation. This principle of life infuses the Christian community forming one body, the Body of Christ, with every member united and animated by the same Spirit: "The body is one and has many members, but all the members, many though they are, are one body, and so it is with Christ. It was in one Spirit that all of us, whether Jew or Greek, slave or free, were baptized into one body. All of us have been given to drink of the one Spirit" (1 Cor. 12:12–14).

What can we Christians expect from this presence of the Spirit? The answer presupposes three modes of activity flowing from the three dimensions of our being—physical, psychological and spiritual. One may imagine three concentric circles. The center is the spirit, the middle is the mind, the outer is the body. Every human activity engages all three levels. Our physical and psychological activities are obvious to all, but what are our spiritual activities? The spiritual level is the level of our freedom, our freedom to *respond* to the Spirit or not to respond. The Holy Spirit joins our human spirit, *initiating* within us the desire for goodness—without the Spirit's presence we would not even have the desire. Responding to the Spirit then transforms the other levels of our being, the physical and the psychological. The Spirit is the principle for all Christian life. Traditionally this indwelling of the Spirit has been called sanctifying grace. Personal prayer—like every spiritual activity—is a response to the Spirit.

Unfortunately the Vatican II theological renewal concerning the Holy Spirit still remains contrary to popular beliefs. Many of us live with a different model of the self. I call it the Western model, because it is the model I recognize as dominating the approach to God in myself and in my brothers and sisters in the Western Hemisphere. In this model God is solely transcendent—in heaven—and so not dwelling within the self through the Spirit. Since God is in heaven, God cannot be the initiator of good actions. Though the Western model duly acknowledges that we are made to know, love and serve God in this life and so be happy in the next, it gives God no role in these actions until after they are performed. Then it grants that God rewards us with grace in this life and heaven in the next. But in the Western model *we are the initiators* of our own good deeds—including personal prayer—so we never truly understand the inner dynamics of prayer. In this model sanctifying grace is often erroneously understood as the treasury of merit stored in heaven, earned by good works.

The Spirit and Personal Prayer

All this has practical implications for how we pray. We are called to live and to pray within the scriptural model of the self—not the Western model. For me prayer is simply the movement of the heart toward God under the influence of the Holy Spirit. It is a movement of the heart: no heart movement, no prayer. It cannot be identified either with words we say or thoughts we think. Indeed, prayer need not be accompanied by words or by thoughts. In Christian tradition the deepest prayer transcends both. And the movement can occur only when we are under the influence of the Holy Spirit. We have seen that the Spirit abides with us as a permanent indwelling gift of God. Though the Spirit, or sanctifying grace, is always present, we are not always in touch with that presence. But in prayer we set time aside to allow God's Spirit to join our spirit and to raise our hearts to God.

And in prayer the movement of the heart under the influence of the Spirit is ultimately toward God—toward the Father and toward Jesus. Just as Christian theology sees the Spirit as the bond of union between the Father and the Son in the Trinity, so the Spirit is our bond of union with the Father and Jesus. Note that we do not really pray to Mary and the saints; more accurately we go to them to pray *with* them to the Father and Jesus. In the communion of saints the Spirit unites us with Mary and the saints. And we on earth are united with them as they now are in heaven. In heaven they exist in continual movement of love and praise to the Father and Jesus; as such they can be privileged intercessors for us. With them we move toward communion with the Father and Jesus, since the deepest yearnings of our hearts are also toward the Father and Jesus. It's impossible to imagine Mary not wanting to unite us more deeply to her son and to our Father.

And Christians must pray, for in prayer we experience our deepest identity. Often we erroneously assume that we pray simply to seek specific favors from God. Deeper reflection reveals, however, that what we are really seeking is a confirmation of God's love for us. Though we may be led to prayer to seek specific favors, as we continue praying we eventually realize our deepest need is for God's presence and support; the Spirit has transformed our initial desires. The process is not unlike Jesus' transformation in the Garden of Gethsemane. Initially he begins by seeking to have the chalice of suffering removed, but he concludes by yielding to God's presence and energized to do God's will. I believe I experienced this same type of surrender during my nightly walks at the mission. I wait expectantly for a similar renewal each Advent.

The "trick" to praying well is discovering the conditions that best facilitate the movement of the Spirit. The time, place and setting for prayer are important. We choose the best available time, place and setting. For me at the mission, this was late at night walking down a highway, and definitely not early in the morning when I was half-asleep. I am presenting the following conditions and methods as the ones that regularly best facilitate my own daily response to the Spirit in personal prayer. Each person's conditions and methods will be distinctive, related to personality and schedule.

First, the *time*. As it happens, I now do manage to pray early. After rising, showering and shaving, I light a candle before my prayer wall. I spend 60 to 90 minutes in the following spiritual disciplines. After getting coffee, I begin by writing in my journal; then, putting the coffee aside, I move to the morning office; finally, I go to personal prayer for the last 20 to 30 minutes. I never rush, spending as much time journaling as needed. The journaling clears my head and allows me to process what has built up in my psyche, matter that could emerge as distractions in personal prayer. Often journaling provides the topic for the subsequent prayer.

Next, the *place*. I pray in my own room—which doubles as a bedroom—in a chair next to a large window with an eastward exposure overlooking a secluded garden; the chair faces my prayer wall. It is upholstered and comfortable but supports me firmly in an upright position. Alongside the chair on a side table I place all the materials I need: my journal, a Bible, the daily office, a lectionary, meditation books related to the liturgical season. I love this room. It is away from my offices; the window, open in warm weather, gives direct access to the sights and sounds of the garden and to the warmth and light of the rising sun. My prayer wall is hung with favorite icons, prints and crucifixes gathered over the years, which I rearrange for different liturgical seasons and feasts. I also have music tapes that I occasionally use as background. The physical setting—the time, place, furniture arrangement—is key. The regular rhythm of entering this environment at this time each day not only prepares the conditions for facilitating the Spirit but often occasions immediate communion with the Lord. Given the desire for communion with God, praying can be simple. Just find the right time and place and go there regularly.

Use of prayer methods may also help or hinder the movement of the Spirit. Most of us pray using the method of *lectio* prayer. In this prayer we choose an aspect of God's word to focus our attention, and then we wait, listen and respond to the word of God—under the influence of the Spirit. This method is based on the conviction that God is present and can speak to us through the word. But the "word of God" has multifold meanings. God is present in the *scriptural word*; traditionally most have found the scriptural word has been the most helpful starting point. God is also present in the *created word*; some find focusing on God's presence in creation—the beauty of nature—a more effective beginning. God is also present in the *existential word*; many find focusing on God's presence in events and people of their lives the most effective beginning. But any aspect of creation or embodiment of creation—images, poetry, music—is a word of God and possible starting point for prayer, since God is present in all aspects of reality, sustaining them in existence and using them to bring us into communion: "Creation proclaims the glory of God."

The Christian tradition affirms a wonderful truth: By focusing on the word of God we can be led by the Spirit to the highest levels of communion with God. This tradition, enshrined in Benedictine spirituality, describes internal transformation as moving from thinking (*meditatio*) about God's presence in the word, to praying (*oratio*) to God about our reactions to this presence, to simply resting (*contemplatio*) in God's presence without either thinking about God or even consciously praying to God. Guigo II, a 12th-century Carthusian abbot, gives in his *Ladder of Monks* (*Scala Claustralium*) the classic expression of the internal dynamic of this prayer:

> You can see . . . how these degrees are joined to each other. One precedes the other, not only in the order of time but of causality. Reading (*lectio*) comes first, and is, as it were, the foundation; it provides the subject matter we must use for meditation. Meditation (*meditatio*) considers more carefully what is to be sought after; it digs, as it were, for treasure which it finds and reveals, but since it is not in meditation's power to seize upon the treasure, it directs us to prayer. Prayer (*oratio*) lifts itself up to God with all its strength, and begs for the treasure it longs for, which is the sweetness of contemplation. Contemplation (*contemplatio*) when it comes rewards the labors of the other three; it inebriates the thirsting soul with the dew of heavenly sweetness. Reading is an exercise of the

outward senses; meditation is concerned with the inward understanding; prayer is concerned with desire; contemplation outstrips every faculty.

The goal of the process is contemplation, which "outstrips every faculty" and rests in communion with God. Our activity recedes; God's increases: God holds us to God's self with little or no effort on our part.

For me, two other methods of prayer complement *lectio* prayer. Centering prayer is based on the truth of God's presence in the *center* of our being, beyond the level of thoughts and desires. It presumes the scriptural model of the self. I find it most helpful when the Spirit brings me to the contemplation mode of *lectio* prayer. After I have reached a level of interior quiet I experience no need to verbalize thoughts and desires to God and am drawn by the spirit simply to rest in the Lord. To symbolize my intention I choose a favorite appellation for God, such as, "Father," "Abba, Father," "Jesus," "Lord," repeating my prayer word only when distractions arise. The rest of the time I simply sit in faith before the Lord. The method, taken from the 14th-century English classic *The Cloud of Unknowing*, is more useful for those who have been praying regularly. In this method the Spirit holds us in communion with God without the mediation of thoughts and desires.

The assumptions and dynamics of mantra prayer are similar to those of centering prayer. In mantra prayer we also respond to God directly, unmediated by reflections on God's word. Having reached a level of interior quiet, we sustain our prayer not by a prayer word but by a mantra. Most mantras have four phrases; we slowly repeat the mantra, coordinating its four phrases (indicated below by asterisks) with our inhaling and exhaling (most, though not all, authors suggest coordination with breathing). The desert fathers preferred: "O God * come to my assistance * O Lord * make haste to help me." The most famous mantra in the Christian tradition, however, is the Jesus Prayer of the fifth-century Greek Fathers: "Lord Jesus Christ * Son of God * have mercy on me * a sinner." I frequently recast scriptural passages into mantra form. Among my favorites: "The Lord * is my shepherd * there is nothing * I shall want"; "You are my servant * whom I have chosen * my beloved * with whom I am pleased"; "I am the vine * you are the branches * without me * you can do nothing." Mantra prayer enters the Christian tradition formally in the fifth century in the *Conferences* of John Cassian.

When thoughts arise in centering or mantra prayer, the practical advice for handling them is simple: Resist no thought, react to no thought, retain no thought. Simply return to the prayer word or mantra. Thoughts even have a positive quality to them, because as we let them pass we are evacuating from our psyches obstacles to the contemplative communion with God. They are actually part of the purification process. Handled well, they move us toward interior silence, "which outstrips every faculty."

The Best Method of Prayer?

There is no best way to pray. Whatever works is best for us. Since the goal of all prayer methods is communion with God, and since only the Spirit can bring about this communion, our role is to discover the conditions that facilitate the movement of the Spirit. Communion remains a gift. I once believed— erroneously—that it was my conscientious use of a particular method that guaranteed good results in prayer. Through trial and error we discover how best to be open to God. Robert Frost's poem "Not All There" catches the challenge for praying well:

> I turned to speak to God,
> About the world's despair;
> But to make bad matters worse,
> I found God wasn't there.
> God turned to speak to me
> (Don't anybody laugh);
> God found I wasn 't there—
> At least not over half.

The following are some additional reflections on what helps me "be there" in prayer. I am not presenting them as ways everyone should pray.

The starting point for prayer is usually my life, the existential word of God as I am experiencing it. I have had little luck—and in the past wasted much time—forcing myself to reflect on meditations written by others, unrelated to my daily life. I believe God continually manifests God's self in all creation and history—and in my life—through the Spirit. I choose some aspect of God's word from my previous day, a person or event. I bring the matter to mind and begin focusing my attention upon it. I put distractions aside as they occur and attempt to keep my mind gently on God's word. I *wait* in God's presence, *listen* to God's speaking through the word in my heart and *respond* in any way the Spirit moves. The Spirit directs our attention to the word (*lectio*); the Spirit transforms our minds, prompting suitable thoughts about the word (*meditatio*): the Spirit transforms our wills, prompting suitable desires and affections about the word (*oratio*); the Spirit leads us to rest in God's presence beyond thoughts and desires (*contemplatio*). I believe that *listening to God* is a better metaphor for the prayer process than the traditional expression, *speaking to God*. We speak only in response to the Spirit and only after we have listened.

But frequently, after lighting my candle, settling into my prayer chair, sipping my coffee and journaling, I find myself already held to God by God with no further effort needed on my part, so I stop journaling. I am already centered; no method is needed. I have developed a facility for being drawn by the Spirit into communion by the regularity of being present to God each morning at this time and in this place. The setting has not only prepared me for praying but has actually itself occasioned it. Perhaps my journal recordings have brought to mind some blessing, some word of God, from the previous day. The blessing becomes the occasion, the sacrament, for awakening consciousness of God and for resting gratefully in the presence of God. The Spirit moves me from gratitude to communion and contemplation. All I know is that I have no desire either to reflect upon or pray over the blessing. Or perhaps the recordings have recalled a need. The need then becomes the occasion for awakening consciousness of dependence on God and resting in silent acknowledgment of my helplessness without God: "Be still and know that I am God." At this point I often use mantra prayer and then centering prayer to sustain my attention.

Occasionally my attention is caught unexpectedly by some aspect of the garden outside my window. I see the sun rising through the trees; I hear a song of a bird or rustle of leaves; I smell the fragrance of the garden and feel the wind on my face. I then have no desire to continue reflecting or pray-ing. I find myself held by God to God; I am centered. Nature has become the sacrament occasioning communion with God and contemplation. Again mantra prayer or centering prayer may help me sustain attention.

Frequently also my attention is caught by one of the icons or prints on my prayer wall. My favorite images include these: the Vatican Museum's fourth-century sculpture of the Good Shepherd, the Vladimir *Madonna*, Fra Angelico's *Annunciation*. I also rotate favorite works of art relating to the cur-rent liturgical season; I believe the Spirit offers graces to help savor the season. Each season finds me anticipating and responding anew to my favorite art works: for Christmas, Giorgione's *Adoration of the Shepherds*; for Lent, Perug-ino's *Crucifixion*; for Easter, Fra Angelico's *Noli Me Tangere*. During Advent, Edward Hicks's *Peaceable Kingdom* seems best to evoke my yearning for a fuller coming of the Lord to the human family—and to my life. I find myself held by God to God through these images, often with no desire to think about them; I am centered. The images have become sacramentals occasion-ing communion with God and contemplation. Again I may move from this *lectio* prayer on the word of God to mantra prayer to centering prayer.

The Coming of Immanuel

We may arrive at Advent preoccupied and discouraged by the events of our year. But the prophet Isaiah's words hearten us: "Comfort, give comfort to my people, says your God. Speak tenderly to Jerusalem." We dare to hope again for a better life and a better world through a fuller opening to God's presence. And in prayer we dare to pray for an actual experience of this pres-ence. Despite our preoccupations we can always pray, for we have been given the Spirit to help us in our weakness. I think Paul had his own tumultuous life in mind—and perhaps also Jesus' experience in Gethsemane—when he wrote to the community in Rome, a community experiencing persecution and even death for their faith in Christ: "The Spirit too comes to help us in our weakness. For when we cannot choose words in order to pray properly, the Spirit himself expresses our plea in a way that could never be put into words, and God who knows everything in our hearts knows perfectly well what he means, and that the pleas of the saints expressed by the Spirit are according to the mind of God" (Rom. 8:26–27).

In Advent we seek to experience again the truth of Augustine's famous dictum, "Our hearts are restless until they rest in Thee." And sometimes in the stillness of our prayer we are touched in the center of our being and taken out of time and beyond the ability of words to explain. God holds us to God's self. It is the experience of T. S. Eliot's "still point of the turning world" in *Burnt Norton*:

> Neither movement from nor towards,
> Neither ascent nor decline. Except for the point, the still point.
> There would be no dance, and there is only the dance.
> I can only say, *there* we have been: but I cannot say where.
> And I cannot say, how long, for that is to place it in time.

Immanuel has come!

November 29, 1997

2001

Why Do You Pray?

William A. Barry, SJ

Often people ask, "Why do you pray?" In all honesty, at one time I prayed because I was a Jesuit. In other words, my answer was, "I'm supposed to pray." Prayer was an obligation and, to be frank, a burden. At times I have prayed in order to placate God—to get God off my back, as it were. Many times I have prayed in order to obtain something, a favor, for example. Such an answer to the question makes prayer utilitarian. No doubt, my motivation for prayer still has vestiges of these answers. However, in my better moments my answer to the question is, "I pray because I believe in God." Let me explain. In the process I hope that I will also say something helpful about how to pray.

Why did God create this universe? Let's play with the image of the garden in the second and third chapters of the Book of Genesis. The image becomes clear after the sin of the first man and woman. We read:

> They heard the sound of the Lord God walking in the garden at the time of the evening breeze, and the man and his wife hid themselves from the presence of the Lord God among the trees of the garden. But the Lord God called to the man, and said to him, "Where are you?" He said, "I heard the sound of you in the garden, and I was afraid, because I was naked; and I hid myself." (Gen. 3:8–10)

If we sit with this image for a while, we realize that the earth is visualized as a garden where God and human beings engage in daily work and get together in the evening to pass the time of day, perhaps to talk over the day. The man and woman are unafraid before God; their transparency is symbolized by the fact that they are naked and show no shame. This image speaks to my heart, and I hope that it will speak to yours. It tells us something about God's dream for our world.

God wants a world where we work in harmony with God's intention in creation, a world where God is active and we are active, where, indeed, we cooperate with God in developing the planet. God wants us to be partners in this creation and to be intimate in our relationship with him. Sin throws a spanner into the works. Human beings act contrary to God's intention and become ashamed and afraid of God. The relationship of intimacy is broken.

But God does not give up on his desire. Of course, there are consequences to human sin. The next few chapters of Genesis describe them. Cain kills Abel; human beings die at an earlier and earlier age; incest and other abominations follow; finally, in Chapter 11, human beings lose the ability to communicate with one another at the tower of Babel. Yet God does not give up.

Chapter 12 of the Book of Genesis begins the story of God's efforts to bring us back into right relationship. God calls Abraham, from whom will come the chosen people, a people chosen not just for themselves but to be light for the world. You can read the following chapters of the Abraham cycle as a story of growing intimacy between God and Abraham and his wife, Sarah. In other words, the reversal of the catastrophe of human sin comes about by the recovery of an intimate relationship with God, a relationship in which human beings once again are asked to become partners with God. God chooses Abraham, and through him the Israelites, to be the carriers of God's dream for the reversal of the effects of sin. The culmination of this choice of Israel, of course, is the appearance of Jesus of Nazareth. We who are followers of Jesus are to be the light of the world by living his way of partnership and intimacy with our Father.

So the God in whom we believe wants a relationship of intimacy and partnership with each of us and all of us together. He wants us to be one family. If this is true, then God's creative desire, which brings the whole universe and each one of us into existence, touches us in the depths of our hearts. We are made for union with God, and our hearts must want that union at a very deep level. Augustine wrote, "You have made us for yourself, and our hearts are restless until they rest in you." Julian of Norwich echoes the same idea: "For by nature our will wants God, and the good will of God wants us. We shall never cease wanting and longing until we possess him in fullness and joy. Then we shall have no further wants." Why do I pray? I pray because I believe in this God. Not only that, I pray because my heart aches for God even though I also am often afraid of closeness with God. I have met many people who express this longing for God.

All of this brings us to the question of how to satisfy this longing for God. The simplest answer is to engage in prayer. Here is where the hope that I might have something useful to say about how to pray comes into play. If God wants a relationship of intimacy and partnership with each of us (and all of us as a people), and if we have a reciprocal desire for such a relationship, then prayer is similar to what happens in any relationship of intimacy. Intimacy between two persons develops through mutual self-revelation. So in prayer I try to let God know who I am and ask that God reveal himself to me. It's that simple. As with Abraham, it is a matter of growing mutual transparency. As we grow in trust in God, we reverse the results of the sin of Adam and Eve. We are not ashamed to be naked before God, that is, to be open with all our thoughts, feelings and desires.

Of course, even in human relationships what seems simple can become complex and difficult because of our fears and insecurities. So in our relationship with God: fears and insecurities can get in the way. We may feel that we are not worthy of God's attention and love. It is true, of course, that we are not worthy of God's love, but God loves us anyway, freely and, it seems, with reckless abandon. So our fears are, in fact, groundless. But we have to grow out of these fears, and the only way to do so is to engage in the relationship with God and find out for ourselves that God is hopelessly in love with us.

In principle, then, prayer is a simple thing. I tell God what is going on in my heart and wait for God's response. The psalms are examples of this kind of prayer. In them the psalmists tell God everything that is going on in their hearts, even things that we shudder to say. Psalm 42 tells God how much the psalmist longs for God. Psalm 104 praises God for the beauties of creation. Psalm 23 speaks of trust in God even in a dark hour. Psalm 51 begs

God to pardon sins. Psalm 13 pleads angrily with God: "How long, O Lord? Will you forget me forever?" The beautiful Psalm 137 ends with this chilling prayer against the Babylonians: "Happy shall they be who take your little ones and dash them against the rock." These psalmists let it all hang out in prayer. The psalms also record God's communication to the psalmist and to the people. For example, in Psalm 40: "I waited patiently for the Lord; he inclined to me and heard my cry. He drew me out of the desolate pit." In other words, the psalmist experienced God's presence as a lifting of spirit in a hard time. And in Psalm 50: "Hear, O my people, and I will speak, O Israel, I will testify against you. I am God, your God. Not for your sacrifices do I rebuke you." Prayer is a simple thing, but it requires a growing trust that God really wants to know everything about us, even those things that seem unsavory, and that God wants to reveal himself to us.

What happens when we pray in this way? Just as two friends change because of their deepening intimacy, so too we are changed by a deepening intimacy with God. But the change comes about through the relationship itself, not through sheer willpower. As we relate to God in this way, we become more like God. This happens in human relationships, does it not? We become like our best friends in our likes and dislikes, in our hopes and desires. So too we become like God through the kind of prayer indicated. We become like what we love.

The best way to become like God is to grow in our knowledge and love of Jesus of Nazareth, God in human flesh. When making the full Spiritual Exercises of Ignatius of Loyola, I come to a point where I desire to know Jesus more intimately in order to love him more and to follow him more closely. But I can know another person only if that person reveals himself or herself to me. So this desire to know Jesus more intimately is a desire for Jesus to reveal himself. If I have this desire, I must then take the time with the Gospels to let them stimulate my imagination so that Jesus can reveal himself, that is, reveal his dreams and hopes, his loves and hates, his hopes for me. As I engage in this kind of prayer, I will be surprised by what I discover about Jesus and thus about God, and about myself. In the process, I will come to love Jesus and become more like him.

Why do I pray? Because I believe in God who loves us with an everlasting love and wants us as partners and friends. I pray, in other words, because God has made me for it.

June 4–11, 2001

2001

Desiring Prayer

Jerry Ryan

During the first few years I spent in the choir of St. Mary's Orthodox Church, I wrestled mightily with the intricacies of Byzantine chant. When I had a couple of other basses surrounding me I could follow along all right, but when I had to hold up the part on my own it was usually a disaster.

One Pentecost Sunday, facing a very complex hymnology, I began to panic when none of the other basses appeared. I was sure I was going to screw everything up. In my corner of the choir there is a big icon of St. Nicholas on my right, a much smaller one of St. John the Evangelist lower down and a large icon of St. Vladimir behind me. In the Eastern tradition an icon is a quasi-sacramental presence of what it represents—so I looked at the three icons surrounding me, chose St. Nicholas and pleaded for help. A soft but clear voice came to me: "You picked the wrong one, pal. I can't sing for beans."

This was as close as I have ever come to a supernatural experience—and it is also pretty typical of the kind of relationship I have with God and his kingdom (in all fairness to St. Nicholas, another bass showed up during the second antiphon).

There are a few people I know who live in constant contact with the supernatural. They discover the hand of God in everything. All sorts of mysterious and wonderful things happen to them. They believe and they see, and I have no reason to doubt their authenticity. Such is not my lot, however. I usually have no clue as to what is going on and have given up trying to make sense out of it. I figure the best I can do is to roll with the punches more or less gracefully. There are many mansions in the house of the Father. I have the quiet conviction that God wants me to walk with him in twilight and poverty, in doubt and weakness, in communion with all those who find it difficult to believe and hope and pray, with those who are scandalized by his silence. My place is there with the poor, the ordinary guy—not to preach or set an example but as a co-sufferer and partner in their obscurity.

The other day I received a pamphlet offering all sorts of books, cassettes and videos on meditation and contemplation, drawing upon different traditions—Christian, Jewish, Sufi, Hindu, Celtic (druidic) and others. All these time-tested techniques and theories certainly have their value for persons with the leisure and setting to put them into practice. I am not one of them. After a day of often hard and usually boring physical work I am pretty much wiped out, and any attempt to establish the silence recommended by the how-to books would be interrupted by snoring. I would like very much to get away to a monastery or a solitary place for a prolonged retreat, but that too is a luxury I cannot afford. So I have to do the best I can with what I have, trying to weave prayer into the texture of my daily life.

Psychologically my relationship with God varies. There are better days, when we seem to get along well. Occasionally I get mad at him. I get bored with God often. Sometimes I wonder if I have any relationship with him at all and whether this whole business is not one big illusion. This worm of disbelief lurks in the back of my mind. I know it is there, and I cannot ignore it no matter how hard I try.

The apparent inefficacy of our prayers does not help either—not just my personal prayer but the prayers of the church and the prayers of Jesus himself while on earth. For two millennia we have been supplicating God for the coming of his kingdom and for our daily bread, for peace and unity; but we experience kingdoms of evil and famine, wars and divisions. He who promised that we could move mountains with the faith of a mustard seed remains silent in spite of the importunities and insistence of his children. It is almost as if they were given vipers instead of bread. There is no way of sugarcoating this. Karl Barth once wrote that disbelief should not be taken seriously. This is good advice. I try to follow it, though it is not easy.

In this context I have doubts about the reality of my so-called prayer life. It is one thing to have ideas about God and play intellectual games with them or have poetical intuitions concerning the mysteries of faith. It is quite another thing to be truly in relationship with the living God of Abraham, Isaac and Jacob. I am afraid that much of my "contemplation" is simply a monologue with myself. For one thing, there is far too much noise. I find myself scheming, organizing my life, watching myself live, imagining what could happen, what might happen. Other people populate my mind too, some beneficially, others less so. Is there, beneath all this, a zone of silence and simplicity open to the Immortal One? I honestly don't know.

Near the end of his life, Charles de Foucauld wrote how everything had become difficult and painful for him, even to tell Jesus he loved him. He no longer "felt" anything—but that, finally, was unimportant. "When one wants to love God, one loves him and when one wants to love God above all things, one loves him above all things." I think the same can be said about prayer. Whatever might be our psychological predispositions at a given time, the desire to pray is in itself a prayer. There are so many factors, both inside and outside ourselves, that impede concentration and make sustained attention difficult. For instance, we are not always mindful of the theological virtues. The masters of the mystical life often stressed the importance of being ready to leave behind all our ideas of God, all our "sentiments," in order to enter into the life of God in his thrice-holy mystery. And there is the whole weight of genetic sin, of inherited hang-ups and complexes: social sin, the hypocrisies and lies in which we live, breathe and have being; our personal sins, our cowardice, the habits we cannot shake, the vulnerabilities that just won't go away; the mystery of evil which finds its complicities in us.

In the midst of all this, it is difficult to find points of reference. For my part, I have discovered nothing better than Foucauld's simple truth, phrased a bit differently: "When one desires to pray, one prays. When one desires that prayer be the center of one's life, it is." In this I find a certain peace amid all the apparent difficulties and failures.

But how serious and authentic is this will to pray? Here I feel the need to translate it into something concrete and objective. My solution is not very original, nor what would be expected of a guy usually considered a wild-eyed radical. I have been reciting the Divine Office daily, come hell or high water, for the last 12 years in Latin, according to the Tridentine rubrics as reformed by Pius X. (That just happens to be the only breviary I have.) It is not just my prayer; it is the prayer of the church into which I enter. There is the old notion that the prayer of the church compensates for our personal distractions. This gives a setting to my day and is a constant reminder to renew my desire to pray. I do not pretend to hold this up as a method for anyone else—but it works for me.

Helpful, too, has been my rediscovery of—and subsequent immersion in—the spirituality of the Eastern churches. On the one hand, the mysticism of the East has enabled me to see my own traditions in a new light and to discover things there I would not have imagined. And, on the flip side of the coin, my Western heritage allows me to appreciate better the riches of Orthodoxy. I thus have the best of both worlds. Being able to "breathe with both lungs" (as Pope John Paul II put it) has made a wonderful difference. It is a grace I wholeheartedly desire for the universal church.

When all is said and done, my prayer life is not for me to know or discern. St. Paul, in 1 Cor. 4:3–5, is very succinct: "It matters little to me whether you or any human court pass judgment on me. I do not even pass judgment on myself. Mind you, I have nothing on my conscience, but that does not mean that I am declaring myself innocent. The Lord is the one to judge me, so stop passing judgment before the time of his return. He will bring to light what is hidden in darkness and manifest the intentions of hearts. At that time everyone will receive his praise from God."

I am not afraid of this judgment of Christ on the day of his revelation, for his judgment will be just and true, and I thirst for truth and justice. Surely I shall discover that his holiness is far greater than anything I could have imagined and that my nonconformity to his image is far more pathetic and tragic than I ever suspected. But I shall also discover the magnificence of his mercy, which surpasses all understanding and which I can only begin to measure by the illuminated realization of my misery. Jesus knows of what clay he has fashioned me—and has promised that anyone who comes to him will not be cast out.

December 24–31, 2001

2001

Does God Communicate with Me?

William A. Barry, SJ

"You say that God wants to engage in a relationship of mutuality with each of us, and you indicate that God communicates with us. But I don't hear God speaking to me." I can imagine someone responding in this way to my article "Why Do You Pray?" (*America*, 6/4/01). I would like to answer the question of the title as best I can.

In the earlier article I argued that God creates the world in order to invite each one of us into a relationship of intimacy, friendship or mutuality. If this is true, then God is always making overtures to each of us, is always communicating with each of us. So the answer to the question of the title is yes, and the real question should be, How do I pay attention to God's communication? God, the creator of the universe, is not the god of the deists, one who created the world and then left it to carry on by itself, much as a clockmaker makes a watch. As Ignatius of Loyola wrote in the *Spiritual Exercises*, God is always at work in this universe, calling us to intimacy and friendship with God and with one another. So the question is, How does God communicate with me—or with anyone?

When we are attracted to anyone or anything, we are attracted by the existing beauty of that person or thing. But we do not exist until God desires us into existence. In so desiring us, God makes us desirable to God and to others and makes us desirous of God. God's action of desiring us into existence is not a once-for-all act in the past; it is ongoing, ever present. At every moment of our existence we are being created by God's desire for us.

Do we experience this creative desire of God? I believe so. Every so often we are almost overcome by a desire for "we know not what" and, at the same time, are filled with a sense of well-being. At these moments we are experiencing God's creative desire for us and our own corresponding desire for God. God is the object of this desire for "we know not what," for the all, for what we cannot even name. In Anne Tyler's novel *Dinner at the Homesick Restaurant*, we find a description of such an experience. An old woman, Pearl Tull, asks her son to read from her childhood diary. It seems that before she dies, Pearl wants to remember an experience she had written about long ago:

> Early this morning I went out behind the house to weed. Was kneeling in the dirt by the stable with my pinafore a mess and perspiration rolling down my back, wiped my face on my sleeve, reached for the trowel, and all at once thought, Why I believe that at just this moment I am absolutely happy. The Bedloe girl's piano scales were floating out her window . . . and a bottle fly was buzzing in the grass, and I saw that I was kneeling on such a beautiful green little planet. I don't care what else might come about, I have had this moment. It belongs to me.

Over and over again I have found that people respond positively when I ask whether they have had experiences like this. These are experiences of God's communication to us.

Once when I was discussing such experiences with a class of graduate students, an Australian nun spoke up. She had had such experiences, but she had also had experiences that were different. She had worked in the inner city of one of Australia's large cities. Often in the evening, after an exhausting day, she would take time for prayer and would be overcome by sobs of deep sorrow. In the quiet that followed I asked her whether she would want to have more such experiences. She said, "Yes, but not only those." In the class there was a deep silence. I believed then, and still believe now, that she had experienced God's sorrow at what we have done to this "beautiful green little planet." I have come to believe that when we spontaneously experience great sorrow and compassion for another human being, we are experiencing God's own compassion.

The prophet Hosea fell helplessly in love with a prostitute and continued to love her in spite of her continued infidelity. As he pondered his own passion, he realized that he was experiencing some of God's own pathos over faithless Israel. When we really love and forgive someone who has done us wrong, I believe, we are experiencing God's love and forgiveness. David Fleming, SJ, maintains that when we pray in the First Week of St. Ignatius' Spiritual Exercises for shame and confusion because of our sins and the sinful condition of our world, we are asking to experience Jesus' shame and confusion as a human being for what human beings have done to other human beings, to the planet and to God. In other words, we are asking to experience God's shame and confusion over us sinners. The prophet Micah puts these poignant words of complaint in God's mouth: "O my people, what have I done to you? In what have I wearied you? Answer me" (6:3). The creator of the universe begs his people for an answer, almost as if puzzled and ashamed at what they have done. This sounds like the shame and confusion for which Ignatius asks the retreatant to pray. Perhaps when we experience such shame and confusion at our own sins and at the horrors perpetrated by our fellow human beings, we are experiencing God's communication to us.

I have met people who show tremendous compassion for others. One is a pastoral care worker in a hospital, who is often moved to tears of compassion for suffering patients. Her heart is nearly broken by the suffering of these strangers who become her family. Another is a man whose wife is suffering from a brain disease that has changed her personality. He told me how he loved her so much and how his heart was broken that she no longer knew how much he loved her. When I hear of experiences like these, tears well up in my eyes; I feel an awe and warmth that convinces me that I am in the presence of God, a God who loves others through the hearts of these people. When we experience compassion for others who are suffering, we are experiencing God's compassion. God is communicating to us and through us to the other.

Recently I acted generously without premeditation. In fact, as I described it later, it was an act of spontaneous generosity for which I could not take credit. I had been planning to use a gift certificate for some books for myself, when, at lunch, I asked an elderly Jesuit if he could use some classical CDs. I do not know where this idea came from, but when he said he would like some of Beethoven's symphonies, I just went out and used the gift certificate for them. While I was doing this, I never thought of myself as generous; in fact, I did not think of myself at all. This is not my usual way of acting, as you can tell by the fact that I was surprised by it. In this situation, I believe I experienced God's generosity poured out in me. It reminded me of an experience recorded by Frederick Buechner in his memoir, *The Sacred Journey*. He had just signed the contract for his first novel. As he left the publisher's office, he ran into a college classmate who was working as a messenger boy. Instead of feeling some pride that he had succeeded while this classmate had not, he felt sadness, even shame, and realized, as he writes, "that, in the long run, there can be no real joy for anybody until there is joy finally for us all." He says that he can take no credit for this insight or this feeling. "What I felt was something better and truer than I was, or than I am, and it happened, as perhaps all such things do, as a gift." When we are surprised by feelings, desires and insights that are "something better and truer" than we are, I maintain, we are experiencing God's presence drawing us into union with God and with all others.

What I am suggesting is that we pay attention to our experience as the privileged place where God communicates to us. Our God is actively involved in this world and with each of us. God has a purpose in creating the universe and each of us; that purpose never rests nor grows weary. If this is true, then we are the objects of God's communication at every moment of our existence. God is always knocking at our door, as it were. We are just not aware enough at the time. But we can grow in awareness if we wish. When we begin to pay more attention, we will discover, I believe, that God's communication often shows itself in those times when we forget ourselves and are concerned with the other, whether that other is something in nature or another human being.

While Jesus was explaining the Scriptures to the disciples on the road to Emmaus, their hearts were burning, but they did not pay attention to this fact until after the breaking of bread. Even though they did not notice the burning of their hearts, they were caught up in the words of this "stranger" and thus were experiencing God's communication. When they recalled the experience, they recognized what had been happening on the road. We need to take time to look back over our day to see where our hearts were burning. We may well find that we have been touched often by God during a day. Yes, God does communicate to each one of us.

December 3, 2001

2002

How Do I Know It's God?

William A. Barry, SJ

I can hear someone who reads my article "Does God Communicate With Me?" (*America*, 12/3/01) asking, perhaps with some pique, "You tell me to pay attention to my experience as the privileged place where God communicates with me. But how do I know it is God who is communicating with me? Couldn't it just be wish fulfillment or even just good digestion that makes me feel treasured by God?"

Readers of *America*, like me, live in a culture that is immersed in psychological explanations for every kind of experience, indeed a culture that distrusts religious claims. How can we know whether we are experiencing God and not just ourselves and our own projections? In our age this is a burning question, but it was also a burning one at the time of Ignatius of Loyola (1491–1556). In his *Spiritual Exercises* he develops rules, called "Rules for the Discernment of Spirits," for answering such a question. It is astounding that a set of rules formulated by a man who lived over 400 years ago could still have relevance, yet many people are finding them a help to answer the question of the above title.

Ignatius himself began to learn how to tell God's influence from other influences during his long convalescence from a battle wound in 1521. He engaged in long daydreams about doing great deeds as a knight to win the favor of a great lady—a lady so great that, it seems, he had no realistic hope of winning her—and he enjoyed the daydreams immensely. But in the absence of the romantic novels he would have preferred, he began to read the life of Christ and a book about the lives of saints. Reflecting on this reading led him to equally unrealistic daydreams; he imagined himself doing even greater deeds than these saints had done for the love of Christ. Again, he enjoyed these daydreams immensely. There was a difference, however, but for a long time he did not notice it. After the daydreams about knightly deeds, he felt sad and listless; whereas after those of imitating the saints he felt joyful and alive. One day, he said, the light dawned, and he realized that God was communicating to him through one set of daydreams, the ones that inspired continuing joy, whereas the "bad spirit" was behind the other daydreams, the ones that left him sad.

Note well: Ignatius was not praying when he made this first discernment of God's communication; he was daydreaming. Moreover, both sets of daydreams had a quality of narcissistic, unrealistic ambition to them. Yet he came to believe that God used one set of such daydreams to draw him toward a new way of life. Because of experiences like these, Ignatius came to believe that God is always communicating to us, that every experience has a touch of God in it. It is almost a motto of Ignatian spirituality that God can be found in all things. The only question is whether we will be aware of God's presence or not.

So how did Ignatius figure out that God was communicating with him in this case? He finally paid attention to his emotional states during and after the two sets of daydreams. During both he felt elated and excited, but after the daydreams about doing great knightly deeds, he felt sad and listless, while after the daydreams about following Christ, he still felt elated. The first lesson in discerning how God communicates, then, is to pay attention to our experience and to the emotional states aroused by these experiences. The second lesson, strange to say, is that Ignatius discovered God's presence through feeling happy and excited. It is strange to say because we may not often associate feeling happy and excited with God's presence. For the rest of this article I want to paraphrase the first two rules for the discernment of spirits formulated by Ignatius in the *Spiritual Exercises*.

The first rule of thumb is that one should look at one's ordinary orientation with regard to God and to one's life as a Christian. Do I try to lead a good Christian life insofar as possible? Or am I someone who cuts corners with regard to my Christian life? As an example of the latter, think of a land-lord who gouges his tenants and provides few services to make their living even halfway decent. Suppose that he were to try to engage in a relationship with God. What do you think would happen in his prayer periods? Proba-bly he would begin to feel pangs of conscience as he realizes how good God has been to him and as he considers his treatment of his tenants. He might also feel some relief from these pangs of conscience with thoughts like these: "These tenants are a lazy lot anyway; at least I'm giving them a roof over their heads." Ignatius would say that the pangs of conscience come from God and that the rationalizations that give relief come from the evil spirit or from his own unwillingness to change his lifestyle.

What about the person who is trying to live a decent Christian life even if not perfectly—say a working mother and wife who tries her best to do an honest day's work and take care of her family obligations? One such per-son felt great joy and peace in God's presence and looked forward to prayer. Soon, however, she experienced anxiety, feeling that she was being too proud to expect God to speak to her and that taking time for prayer like this was a luxury she could ill afford. She said to herself, "This is too highfalutin for the likes of me." God now seemed distant. Ignatius would say the positive experiences come from God, or the good spirit who wants to draw her into friendship, whereas the troubling thoughts come from the bad spirit or from her fears of closeness to God.

So the first rule of thumb urges us to establish the general orientation of our lives. If I am not in tune with God in my life, I can expect that God will try to get me to change my life; I will feel pangs of conscience or concerns about certain aspects of my life. These pangs of conscience, however, will not lead to anxious, scrupulous examinations of all my motivation; they will gen-tly point out where I have gone wrong. The bad spirit or my own desire not to face a change will try to whisper blandishments in my ear to convince me that all is O.K.

Here is an example from my own life. For some time I had had concerns about the amount of alcohol I was drinking and how it was affecting my health. I rationalized them away because I was functioning quite well in daily life. But I was often sleepy in the evening after dinner, when I wanted to pray. One day, because of the intervention of a friend, I realized that the concerns about my drinking were from God. I was given the grace to stop drinking and have been much happier for it. God's communication came in the form of niggling concerns that wanted to lead me to a happier and healthier life.

On the other hand, if we are trying to live in tune with God's intention, says Ignatius, God will console us, help us to move forward, encourage us in our efforts to live a good life. But the bad spirit or our own fears of closeness to God will try to make us leery of developing a closer relationship with God, as happened with the woman just mentioned. Ignatius, for example, had the thought at one point after his conversion, *How will you be able to put up with this [his ascetical life and prayers] for the 70 years you have ahead of you?* Ignatius quite rightly answered that no one could guarantee that he would live for even one more day.

The second rule of thumb follows from the first. God wants us to be happy and fulfilled. But the only way we can be happy and fulfilled is to be in tune with God's desire for the world and for us. For those who are trying to lead a life in tune with God's intention, consolation is the order of the day for the most part. This does not mean that life will be without pain and suffering; it means that God wants to be a consoling presence to us even in the inevitable pains and sufferings life has in store.

If this is true, then the terrible mental agony and torture scrupulous people go through is not from God. After all, scrupulous people are trying to live in tune with God. Ignatius himself, during the early days after his conversion in 1521, was plagued by scruples, fearing that he had not confessed all his sins. Things got so bad that he contemplated suicide. Yet at this point in his life he was trying with great fervor, indeed excessive fervor, to live a life in accordance with God's dream. He finally came to the conclusion that these scrupulous thoughts could not be from God. In other words, he finally realized that God wanted his peace and happiness, not torture of mind and soul.

We can discern, in our experience, what is from God [and] what is not from God. But to do so, we have to pay attention to what we experience as the privileged place of God's communication. If we answer positively the question of the earlier article, "Does God communicate with me?" then we are committed to faith in God as the mystery who is always trying to draw each of us, and all of us together, into friendship. Now we need to put that faith into practice by taking seriously our experience. One way to do this is to engage in the exercise Ignatius calls the daily examination of conscience, as outlined by Dennis Hamm, SJ, in "Rummaging for God: Praying Backward through Your Day" (*America*, 5/14/94). We can, indeed, know God's voice.

May 20, 2002

2003

Friendship Is a Prayer

Greg Kandra

Should I feel guilty? The question nagged at me—a good Catholic question, pecking at my conscience as I sat under a shaggy tree on the grounds of a great monastery and listened to the bell as it tolled. It was time to pray. I should have been heading to the church. Others on retreat would be inside, under the barn-like arches of the Abbey of Gethsemani, in Kentucky, chanting with the monks.

Instead I was outside with my friend Jeff shooting the breeze, being decidedly noncontemplative. I should have been spending the day being silent, meditative, prayerful. Instead I was yapping like a cocker spaniel. The bell was calling. I wasn't answering. I couldn't help but feel a twinge of guilt.

We had come to this remote place on a hot July weekend to share a little time, take a break and catch up. Jeff and I attended Mass and a few of the liturgical offices. But mostly we just hung out. I scanned the skies for birds. He smoked. We wandered the woods. He scribbled in his notebook. We griped about the church and her scandals and marveled at the folly of man. We worried together, and laughed together, and solved the world's problems over gallons of black coffee, across a wooden table in the dining room, or on two chairs in the retreat house porch.

The bell tolled. Ask not for whom. It tolled for me.

What kept me from going to the church? I have always been captivated by the offices of the monks—the chanting, the bowing, the hushed calm of men collected to pray. The psalms are part of that powerful experience, of course; those 150 prose-poems contain everything we need to know about life: it is

177

glorious, it is horrible, it is maddening. And it goes on. The psalms are the human experience writ large. Out of the mouths of monks, they gain new resonance.

So why wasn't I joining them? What was I doing outside, swatting at flies?

I wondered about that, and shrugged it off. Days later, at the end of our visit, as my plane climbed over Louisville and back to New York, I wondered something else. In spite of my frequent absences from church, why did I feel so surprisingly at peace? What made me feel so—for want of a better word—graced?

I think I know. For all the riches of monastic prayer, there was another prayer that engaged me that weekend. It is a kind of everyday psalmody—found in a conversation, a laugh, a shrug, a nod. It is the prayer we all whisper at one time or another.

It is the simple liturgy of friends. For friendship is, at its best, a prayer.

It is, after all, an act of faith. It is sacred. It is an epistle, delivered from one person to another. In its best moments, friendship is a canticle that celebrates, a parable that teaches. In the close proximity of a friend, you find a cathedral where promises are kept, and a chapel where tears are shed. Friendship is a responsorial psalm: one heart speaks, another responds, and in the silences in between we hear something of God.

Jesus—no stranger to friendship, or to its swift reversal, betrayal—said that wherever two or more are gathered in his name, there he is, too.

Perhaps when we seek a friend, we are seeking God, the God who dwells in all of us, the God in whose image we have all been made. Perhaps in friendship he is there, waiting to be found, the God of laughter and companionship, the God of shared secrets and long stories and strong coffee, the God who is comfortable just kicking back. He is there to listen, because that's what friends are for. He is there to guide us on the journey, to see that we are not alone and that there is someone with us who can read the map. He is there to help us find faith in one another, at moments when that particular faith may be all that we have. He is there to let us know that someone else understands our pain, shares our joy and, thankfully, gets our jokes.

Out of that, we are encouraged and given hope. Out of that, I believe, we are given God.

There is something consoling, we know, in communal prayer. Hearts and voices join in one place, under one roof, at one moment in time, to acknowledge the Creator and ask his blessings. And in doing that, we acknowledge what we are—people bound by common faith, humility and trust.

So it is, I think, in this extraordinary prayer of friendship.

With garden chairs as a choir, and the lawn for an aisle, and the starry sky as a dome, my friend Jeff and I, on that summer weekend, prayed our own office, a private liturgy that bestowed on the two humble congregants a blessed amount of grace. The grace to be comfortable with another soul, and feel a connection. The grace to enjoy the fading of twilight, or the stirring of leaves or the simple silence that comes when there is nothing really to say—and that's just fine, too. Two or more were gathered. And God, I believe, was there.

Unfortunately, I do not think you'll find that liturgy in any book of common prayer. It's not in the Roman Missal. Other rituals can be found there, beautiful testaments steeped in history and discipline. They are the handrails that guide us through the spiritual life. Without them we are lost.

But sometimes we find another way, on our own, and still manage to stumble upon God.

So, the next time you are alone with a friend, consider it a concelebration. Kick back, open up, light up a smoke, crack a smile, heave a sigh—and listen. You may hear, gently but surely, the happy beating of your own heart, like a bell tolling, quietly announcing that prayer has begun.

March 17, 2003

2005

In Praise of Horizontal Prayer

Frank Moan, SJ

I'm 77 and retired, a priest, a celibate. You may be like me. Or you may be married still, with or without your spouse. You may be a parent, a grand-parent or, God bless you, a great-grandparent. Or you may be single, young, with the expectation of many years ahead. In any event, I hope each of you shares with me the joy of horizontal prayer.

By horizontal prayer I mean, literally, horizontal: when I'm on my back, in bed. Age has taught me that I do some of my best praying in bed. I still advocate that parents teach their children to kneel at bedside in the evening to say their prayers. But my knees will no longer let me get down there. And if I do get down, I would have to call out to someone else in the rectory to get me up. God understands. In fact, I think God can't wait till I get flat on my back in bed.

I do my best praying then. Sometimes, if I've had a very long and stressful day, I might fall asleep almost immediately. But that is rare. Generally, I have to lie there for a while before sleep comes. That's when I pray.

I converse with God about the day I've spent, how it went, where I failed God or my neighbor, what graces came my way and how well I used them. I like to talk to God about the people I encountered that day, in person, on the phone, through e-mail or snail-mail. I often tell God how I disagree with the way he is letting the world turn round. I pray for those who die each day in Iraq or Afghanistan. I pray for understanding among Muslims, Christians and Jews.

I also turn often to Mary, the Mother of Jesus. I say at least one Hail Mary to win our Lady's protection. My life in the liturgical practices of the church has taught me that the day never ends without recourse to Our Lady.

Prayer to Mary then turns my mind to the communion of saints. Over many years I have come to love and respect so many of them that I count them as intimate friends on whom I can depend to be voices for me before the Trinity. And in that number I include many people I have known over these past 77 years who have preceded me to the Pearly Gates.

At my age—those who are about my age will know what I'm talking about—I have to get up periodically to relieve my bladder. I take a nightly pill to forestall such an occurrence. But it never does. I think I take the pill just to keep my doctor happy. Anyway, I get up at least twice a night and return to bed. Now, sometimes I am lucky and soon fall back to sleep. But often it is not so easy.

So here I am again, turning to prayer. I begin to think about the next day. And the first thing I think is, *Will I have a next day? Or will God summon me before then?* It is not a pessimistic thought. Many of my relatives and friends have died before this age. The daily obituary notices recount many deaths of people my age, older and younger. So I'm wont to say that prayer I learned in childhood. It may be childish, but it is a beautiful prayer and means a great deal to me at this age: "Now I lay me down to sleep; I pray the Lord my soul to keep. If I should die before I wake, I pray the Lord my soul to take." I have known some of my fellow Jesuits who have died peacefully in their sleep or while sitting in their chair. I envy them—it's a nice way to go.

Then I turn to the coming day, if God should grant it. I recall the intention for the Mass I will celebrate. It may be for a deceased brother Jesuit, or for a relative with cancer, or for our country in this time of national crisis. I talk to God about that intention. I bring God up to date on where I am politically, charitably, socially. I must admit I do much of the talking. But sometimes God does get through. I begin to see things more clearly. I realize there were times I was hasty in judgment or insensitive in action. I see new ideas opening up before me on how I can contribute to the graces God spreads through his church, particularly through its sacramental life.

I give some thought also to the Divine Office, the breviary, I shall be reading when I get up. It will take some time over the course of the day. Nowadays I pray it with much more devotion than I did in my earlier years. I give extra attention to it because I now read it on behalf of all the priests in my diocese. I know many of them are too busy to read it, so I read it for them.

The middle of the night gives me the time to raise to God the many friends I have from over 70 years, particularly those who are now in physical distress. A 92-year-old friend prays daily that she may die. I ask, God, why don't you let her die? She would be so much happier with you than she is now with a body that refuses to respond to her willingness to love others. I pray for my friend the doctor, who, shortly after retiring, suffered a debilitating stroke. Since then he has lost a leg and, worse still, lost much of his enthusiasm for life. I pray for his wife, a nurse with physical problems of her own that prevent her from giving her husband the full attention he needs.

Dear God, you know what wonderful people these have been, how much they have done for others in very active lives. Yet now they wait. God, give them patience; give them cheer. I pray for a widow friend of 40 years' acquaintance. Not only has she lost her husband; she also buried two of her five children. Yes, she has the others to look after her. But God, she is failing. Give her courage; give her comfort. And give her children the willingness to look after her, without depriving their own children of the attention they deserve.

I could stay up all night praying for these and myriad other causes.

On a rare occasion nowadays I am awakened by the alarm to rise and go to a nearby parish to say early Mass. That breaks my momentum of prayer.

Ordinarily I can get up when I wake up. Or I can lie there for a few or many minutes. I can pray again. Today, dear God, this day is for you. You have given me another day to live, or maybe only part of the day. If you call me home today, I hope I shall be rejoicing to greet you. But if I am to live another day, may it be to your glory. Let me bring sunshine into someone else's life; let me be a support to my fellow Jesuits here in the rectory; let me learn how to converse with you, dear God, more and more. Teach me to pray.

I open my eyes. I look to see if the sun is shining on the church-school building outside my window. How I am cheered if it does. I see in my room all the souvenirs of a long life. They speak to me of so many past and present loves. They are my daily comforts. Each speaks a prayer to me; I speak a prayer to each.

Then it is time to rise. As I put my feet into my slippers, I offer a final prayer. God, I'm going about the day. I may not be as attentive to you throughout this day as I have been during this night. So please remember that I love you still. I'm here to do your will. And should you bring me to another night, I'll lie again in bed, and our conversation will go on.

February 14, 2005

2005

A Letter to Young American Catholics: On Singing a New Song

Rev. Robert P. Maloney, CM

My dear younger brothers and sisters:

I write, as an older brother, to encourage you. Last month more than a million young Catholics gathered with Pope Benedict XVI in Cologne for World Youth Day. Twenty-five thousand of them were from the United States. The Lord entrusts the future of the church to young people like them and you.

Our countryman Walt Whitman once wrote:

> Youth, large, lusty, loving—
> youth, full of grace, force, fascination. . . .
> Day full-blown and splendid—
> day of the immense sun, action, ambition, laughter

In that spirit I urge you to use the gifts of youth to be fully alive, actively responsible members of the church and alert citizens of the world community.

Many factors beyond your control will shape the future, but your response is crucial to the vitality of the church and its role in the world. Sixty-four percent of the world's population is under the age of 25. In some places, particularly in the West, religious practice has declined dramatically among young people. In Rome, where I lived until recently, it is almost fashionable for a young person to say, "I'm not a believer." Practice has fallen beneath 10 percent in Italy. In Spain, in the last five years, it has declined to 13 percent. In

France, some estimate it at 1 percent. How many young people in the United States believe and live out their beliefs? One astute writer says this: "The great problem confronting the churches today is indifference: the massive absence of God from so much of the contemporary world—with all the final emptiness, religious cynicism, or meaninglessness of that experience."

Though there are significant differences in various parts of the world, young people increasingly have the following characteristics in common:

Deepening immersion in an information culture. Most young people do not grow up in a Catholic culture, where their environment and a stable family setting support religious values. Many spend more time each week before the television than they do in school.

Plasticity. Rapid change is woven into the fabric of contemporary life. A century ago most people lived, worked and died in their home town. Today, people change jobs, homes (and sometimes spouses or religious commitments) frequently. Of course, the positive side of this plasticity is flexibility, the capacity to change, be formed and grow.

Hesitancy in making commitments. A young woman I know recently told me that she would never get married in the church. She said that she couldn't imagine saying that her marriage was forever. The word *forever* sticks in the throat of many young people. They have seen too many broken marriages, too many divided families and too many fractured religious commitments.

Yearning love. Young people long to know how to love. The desire for significant relationships occupies a huge space in their psyches. In fact, a counselor once told me that for many young people, this is the only item on their agendas. Many, too, are drawn toward transcendence. They are ultimately unsatisfied in the relationships they experience. They yearn for a love that goes beyond their everyday experience of love.

Contemporary society often attempts to sell youth the wrong dream: money, the triumphant Lone Ranger, the need to have more of everything and to have it now, perfect sex. Who, then, are the models young people seek to imitate: Jesus, the Virgin Mary, Mother Teresa, the saints and martyrs? Or are they more likely to be LeBron James, Julia Roberts, Denzel Washington and Maria Sharapova?

To use the play on words of one contemporary writer, we live in an era of "clashing symbols." The values that our faith presents often collide against those that our culture promotes, with a discordant clang.

So I urge you to sing a new song. What might that song be like?

Sing a Deeply Spiritual Song.

This seems quite obvious, but nothing is more important. To quote St. Paul (Rom. 13:14), all Christian life aims at "putting on the Lord Jesus Christ." For the Christian, Jesus is the absolute center. "I am the way, the truth and the life," he says; "no one comes to the Father except through me. . . . I am the vine. . . . I am the gate. . . . I am the shepherd. . . . I am the light. . . . I am the true bread come down from heaven. The one who feeds on my flesh and drinks my blood will live forever."

I encourage you to make a commitment today that will slowly change your life. Spend a quarter-hour each day with the Lord in silent, meditative prayer. This is not an easy commitment to keep in the midst of a busy schedule at school or at work or at home. But find a place where, in the words of St. Matthew's Gospel, you can shut the door on the noise of the world and talk to the Lord and listen to him. Read a short passage from the New Testament and ask the Lord: "Lord, what are you saying to me? What do you want me to do today?"

If you learn to live in the presence of the Lord, love him deeply and ponder his word, then you will surely sing a deeply spiritual song in life.

Let Your Song Be Not a Solo, but a Chorus.

Learn to pray with and work with others too. Pope John Paul II wrote this: "Our Christian communities must become genuine 'schools' of prayer, where the meeting with Christ is expressed not just in imploring help but also in thanksgiving, praise, adoration, contemplation, listening and ardent devotion, until the heart truly 'falls in love.' Intense prayer, yes, but it does not distract us from our commitment to history: by opening our heart to the love of God it also opens it to the love of our brothers and sisters, and makes us capable of shaping history according to God's plan" (*Novo Millennio Ineunte*, No. 33).

Our prayer together should lead to action together. Divorced from action, prayer can turn escapist. It can lose itself in fantasy and create illusions of privatized holiness. On the other hand, service divorced from prayer can become shallow. It can have a driven quality to it. It can become an addiction.

A healthy spirituality is at its best when it holds prayer and action in dynamic tension with each other.

Let It Be a Song of Service to the World.

Because of rapid transportation and communication, the world community is becoming smaller. At the same time, the gap between the rich and the poor is becoming larger. It is hard for most of us here in the United States to imagine the terrible imbalance in the distribution of this world's goods, because we rarely come face-to-face with the poorest of the poor.

Let me give you just one example. Not long ago, *Time* magazine published some remarkable statistics about Africa. The question posed was this: What percentage of the population in various African countries lives on less than $1 a day? The answer might surprise you:

Congo 91%

Ethiopia 85%

Chad 82%

Zambia 80%

Tanzania 79%

Niger 74%

Angola 73%

Somalia 72%

There are millions of people on every continent who live in dire poverty. In the spirit of today's church, make the poor a key element in your vision of the world, in your spirituality. Find practical ways of serving the poor as you study or work now and, later on, wherever you may be. Always ask yourself, What is the need of the poor person crouched in the doorway of the building nearby? What is the AIDS patient's most acute pain? What does the sick person at home or in a hospital yearn for? What are other young people calling out for in the school I attend?

Sing a Liberation Song.

Be a bearer of good news! Bring the Spirit of the Lord with you wherever you go. In the presence of a person filled with God's Spirit, people come alive. They dream new dreams and see new visions. The Spirit of the Lord inflames something in their hearts. They begin to hear the deepest voices of reality. They begin to see the possibility of a new heaven and a new earth. They become freed from the inner bonds that hold them back and eager to pour out their lives with a new generosity.

Sing this liberation song with others too. Join youth groups and form youth groups. Become a multiplying agent of God's Spirit, an ambassador. Pass on generously to others the gifts of the Spirit that you yourself have received.

When others are afraid as they look to the future, say to them, as Jesus says to you: Do not be afraid when some chaos upsets the orderly patterns of your life, because I can build a level road. Do not be afraid when darkness descends upon you, because I can make light shine in the darkness. Do not be afraid if your numbers as believers become smaller, because I can raise up a multitude from a faith-filled remnant. Do not be afraid when death approaches, because I have overcome death. I am with you. I have come to set you free.

Let Yours Be a Wake-Up Song to the World.

At one of their synod meetings, the world's bishops wrote this rousing message to young people:

> You, young people, you are "sentinels of the morning. . . ." How is the
> Lord of history asking you to build a civilization of love? You have a

keen sense of what honesty and sincerity require. You do not want to be caught up into divisive ethnic struggles nor poisoned by the gangrene of corruption. How can we be disciples of Jesus together and put into practice Christ's teaching on the Mount of the Beatitudes?

In the ancient and medieval worlds, sentinels stood guard on the city walls, looking toward the East to catch the first glimpse of the rising sun. Since there were no clocks or bell towers in those days, they beat a drum or rang a gong to wake up the city.

In a Christian worldview, the rising sun is Jesus, the risen Lord. How I urge you to rouse the world to his presence! Do not settle for indifference. Do not be lulled to sleep by a continual hunger for material possessions or an overabundant diet of them. Be aware of the presence of Jesus the risen Lord, the rising sun, and develop a profoundly Gospel-centered, service-centered spirituality in your life.

Join with other young people in living a courageously evangelical life to help create a world where:

- charity reigns among you and then radiates out to others, especially the poor;
- you support one another as friends and enjoy one another;
- you speak the truth with sincerity, humility and constancy;
- you pray faithfully and share your prayer naturally with others;
- you listen well and discern the will of God with others;
- you encourage one another to renounce immediate gratification for the sake of life's more important goals.

Over 2,500 years ago, reflecting gratefully on the mystery of God, the composer of one of the psalms cried out, "I will sing and make music for the Lord" (Ps. 27:5). I encourage you today to sing a new song. Sing a deeply spiritual song, not a solo, but a harmonious symphony, a song of service, a liberation song, a wake-up song to the world. Let your song be a rousing, beautiful hymn, a great chorus resounding to the glory of God and ringing out as good news for the world.

September 19, 2005

2006

Mysterious Tools: A New Catholic's Meditation on Prayer

Karl Bjorn Erickson

One night a few months ago, my 8-year-old son was very sick in bed. He lay there moaning and crying because of terrible pain in his ears. While my wife was on the phone attempting to get hold of a doctor, I did what I could to comfort him. We tried the usual things, but nothing worked. The choices seemed to be either to wait in an emergency room for hours late at night or try to wait it out at home. Neither option seemed like a good choice.

We could not let him go on like that, so something told me to pray over him. I took the holy water we were given at a recent church event. It felt a little strange to me, as a new Catholic, but I proceeded to make the Sign of the Cross over my son with the holy water. Then I prayed for healing. I framed my prayer along the lines that we know that children hold a special place in God's heart, and that it cannot be God's will that my son would be in pain. Something seemed different about the prayer, but I could not immediately identify what it was. Since nothing dramatic took place after I finished the prayer, I returned to our room.

Half an hour or so later that night, I noticed my son had fallen into a deep sleep. I made a passing comment to my wife that I had prayed over him earlier, but it seemed not to have accomplished anything. She pointed out what should have been obvious: he was indeed sleeping, and this fact did resemble an answered prayer. For some reason, I had not connected the prayer to his falling asleep; they seemed to be two distinct events. The next morning, my wife took him to the doctor. He was found to have a serious ear infection, but my son insisted, to the doctor's confusion, that it didn't really hurt.

Prayer often seems like a routine. When something actually happens in response to our prayer, many of us find ourselves a bit incredulous as we search for other explanations. While that's fine to a point, it may suggest why more of our prayers are not answered in precisely the ways we hoped. In thinking back over this experience, I realized that there was a different quality to my prayer. That difference seems to have been faith.

Who did not pray for snow as a youth? I remember sitting in my bed as a child and praying fervently for a heavy snowfall late one night. There was no doubt in my mind that the snow was going to come down in piles, and I remember falling asleep as I prayed with the blinds cracked open, so I could watch the falling snow. The next morning, everyone seemed very surprised at the record snowfall—everyone except me: I had faith.

Fast forward several decades, though, and it is harder for me to draw upon the child-like faith described in Mark 10:15. Why is it so difficult to imagine that God would extend his finger into our reality and perform a miracle on our behalf? The miracle, like ripples on a pond, is one of God's ways of reminding us that we worship a living and real God, one who seeks to help us in our daily walk with him. How often do we forget to thank God for answered prayers?

I recently was made aware of an ancient homily for Holy Saturday, which appears in the *Catechism of the Catholic Church*. Here is a brief excerpt from this beautiful prayer.

> Today a great silence reigns on earth, a great silence and a great stillness. A great silence because the King is asleep. The earth trembled and is still because God has fallen asleep in the flesh and he has raised up all who ever slept ever since the world began. . . . He has gone to search for Adam, our first father, as for a lost sheep. Greatly desiring to visit those who live in darkness and in the shadow of death, he has gone to free from sorrow Adam in his bonds and Eve, captive with him—He who is both their God and the son of Eve.

The prayer reminds us that God is continually searching for us and desires the best for us. While God cares for and loves us individually, this does not mean that we as individuals should put ourselves before others, or neglect the larger Christian community. In fact, as C. S. Lewis pointed out in *The Weight of Glory*, we should not say that Christ died for us because we were so important. On the contrary, it is entirely through Christ's sacrifice that we are endowed with our spiritual importance. Otherwise any potential value of the person would be eclipsed by sin. Of course, the "best" for us is not necessarily what we might imagine it to be. That is why our prayers may not always result in the kinds of answers for which we might have hoped. After all, God is not a genie, waiting to grant us three wishes. Some of us have even learned that we need to take care what we ask for—especially patience, for instance.

One should also not forget what the holy water represents. While obviously not required, it is a powerful sacramental, a physical sign of a particular sacrament as holy water reminds us of the spiritual rebirth of baptism. And in the case of my son, it seemed to play no small part.

When I think of holy water, a few observations come to mind. First, it represents the larger community of believers and the traditions of the church. If we pause and think about the cycle of a drop of water as it endlessly changes its form and location, we can catch a glimpse of this Christian community—past, present and future. Perhaps this drop of water on our outstretched finger once dropped as rain on the head of Christ himself. Second, it creates a powerful means for the dispensation of God's grace to man. As the Catholic writer J. R. R. Tolkien uses Galadriel's vial, given to Frodo, as a symbol for holy water, we are all in need of a light in the darkness.

If your prayer life is like mine, there is a lot we both can improve. One preacher in particular is a model for praying without ceasing. Billy Graham, a friend of the Catholic Church, takes prayer very seriously. Some years ago I listened to a presentation by a close friend of the Rev. Graham. The speaker recalled asking Graham what it meant to pray without ceasing, as described in 1 Thessalonians 5:17. The presenter reportedly expressed doubt as to how this could be done. He pointed out to Graham the daily distractions of things such as phone calls and meetings. A surprised Graham disagreed. Praying without ceasing was precisely what he did. He gestured toward an open Bible in his office and explained that every time he passed the Bible, he paused a moment to read a passage, reflect and pray.

Billy Graham makes the following observations in his latest book, *The Journey*: "Nothing can replace a daily time spent alone with God in prayer. But we also can be in an attitude of prayer throughout the day—sitting in a car or at our desks, working in the kitchen, even talking with someone on the phone." This also emphasizes the way prayer can ensure that our minds are calm and focused. A friend who serves nearby as a Carmelite brother recently drew my attention to this need for preparation before deep prayer in the contemplative writings of St. Teresa of Ávila.

The Catholic tradition brims with examples of devout men and women of prayer. It is through the study of these lives lived for Christ that we begin to catch a glimpse of what it means to be "created in the image of God." If we read works like G. K. Chesterton's biography of St. Francis or St. Augustine's *Confessions*, we realize that saints were just as human as we are today, but they learned to do more for God than their human capabilities alone could have accomplished. They achieved this through prayer, devotion and love.

Through prayer we move closer to childlike faith as we become the men and women God intends us to be, co-workers in the building of the kingdom. As we read in John 14:3, when we invoke the saving name of Christ in sincere prayer, we become instruments of peace in the hands of God, tools mysteriously necessary to fulfill and reveal God's will.

July 3–10, 2006

2006

A Lesson in Consolation

Drew Christiansen, SJ

In some ways I am an old-school Jesuit. In a succession of assignments and apostolic responsibilities, I have lived by St. Ignatius Loyola's perplexing maxim that he preferred a man of self-denial to one of prayer. I am scandalized, but only slightly, by some young Jesuits' need for the spiritual satisfactions of direct pastoral experience. One of the first lessons Ignatius learned during his hermit period at Manresa was to forgo what he called the consolations of prayer and to reduce his physical austerities for "the good of souls." Ignatius, one of the great Spanish mystics, loved prayer; but he encouraged detachment from its satisfactions and even advised sacrificing time from prayer for the sake of uniting oneself to God's will in bringing spiritual progress to others.

I learned that lesson in a different way early in my Jesuit life, as a novice at Calvary Hospital for the Cancerous Poor in the Bronx. The first patient I was assigned to look after was a big-boned Irishwoman known for her cheerfulness, who was suffering with a brain tumor.

Veronica was everyone's favorite patient. But for the two weeks she was in my care, she was ill and sedated. It was as if she were comatose. She sipped her water, swallowed her food, but uttered not a word. The first response I received from her came the day I introduced her to my replacement. She said, "I know you. You have taken care of me. Thank you." It was as if she arose from the dead with words to pierce my soul.

That experience of the value of an emotionally unrewarding task stayed with me afterward, sustaining me in difficult tasks and hard times. Doing

God's work serving humanity is often without immediate satisfaction. It does not require spiritual consolation to sustain it. Mother Teresa, after the vision that led her to found the Missionaries of Charity, is said to have prayed in desolation the rest of her life. She once said, "When I meet Jesus, I will say, 'I loved you in the darkness.'"

I thought about spiritual consolation and its absence recently as I read Karen Armstrong's autobiography, *The Spiral Staircase* (2004). A prolific writer on the history of religions, Armstrong spent seven years as a nun in a community whose rule was inspired by St. Ignatius, our Jesuit founder. The version of Ignatian spirituality imparted to Ms. Armstrong focused on breaking the will, but without "the mysticism of service," Joseph de Guibert's description of Ignatius' apostolic charism. Such a spirituality is bleak enough; but in addition, Armstrong reports, in the course of seven years in the convent, she did not enjoy one moment of spiritual consolation.

I do not have a particularly vivid prayer life, but I cannot imagine what it would be like to be deprived of all spiritual consolation. "I never felt caught up in something greater," Armstrong writes, "never felt personally transfigured by a presence that I encountered in the depths of my being." She could not even still herself, she reports, "to wait on God." Only 20 years later and after a life filled with disappointments, did she have her own *metanoia*, as she wrote her well-known *History of God* (1993). Then she understood "true religion" as a practice that opens the heart to others. "The habit of empathy," she wrote, "had to become part of my life, and it had to find practical expression." Her transformation had begun. She experienced what Alfred North Whitehead describes as one of the fruits of prayer, "the love of mankind as such." Her most recent book, *The Great Transformation* (2006), an interpretation of the origins of the world religions, has as a key theme the primacy of compassion and nonviolence in the growth of religious consciousness.

Over the years, I had some memorable moments of prayer: when, for example, after a personal crisis I rediscerned my Jesuit vocation, or when, as I prayed in a mountain meadow over "the lilies of the field," I felt God's providence at work. But mostly my consolations have been unspectacular, what St. Ignatius describes as "every increase of faith, hope, and love, and all interior joy that invites and attracts to what is heavenly and to salvation of one's soul by filling it with peace and quiet in its Creator and Lord."

That said, I am all the more in awe of those, like Mother Teresa, who do beautiful things for God deprived of even these everyday sorts of consolations. My respect for Ms. Armstrong's often inspiring scholarship is all the greater knowing how her insight was wrested from her own peculiar darkness. And I wonder at God, who gives light to some and not to others and accompanies us all in darkness as well as light.

July 3, 2006

2007

Friends in High Places

James Martin, SJ

The best-known prayer among American Catholics, after the Our Father and the Hail Mary, may be the one to Anthony of Padua, which goes, "Saint Anthony, Saint Anthony, please come around. Something is lost and cannot be found." How many times have you turned to the Portuguese-born Franciscan after losing your keys?

There are petitionary prayers for almost every need. Looking for a boyfriend or a husband? Try a prayer to Mary's mother: "Saint Anne, Saint Anne, find me a man." An addendum was recently suggested to me during a talk on the saints at a local parish. After I mentioned that popular intercessory prayer, one woman in the audience shouted out the correct final line.

"As fast as you can!" she said to general laughter. Another woman in the audience said, "Now I finally know why it's been taking so long in my case: I wasn't saying the last line."

Now, I know that some readers may already be rolling their eyes. The concept of intercession makes many contemporary Catholics uncomfortable. (And I haven't even mentioned the prayers to Mother Cabrini and Thérèse of Lisieux to find a parking space.) Often when I mention praying for help to a particular saint, Jesuit friends will grimace or, with polite silence, communicate their theological disapproval. Why the distaste?

First, it smacks of superstition. (What is the difference between those rhyming prayers and a magic spell?) Second, it irks those who feel that intercessory prayer encourages believers to bypass God. (Why not pray to God directly?) Third, it may seem frivolous, even absurd, to ask members of the communion of saints to search for something as minor as a lost wallet. (Admittedly, it is odd imagining St. Anne searching for husbands from her heavenly post.) Fourth, it can reduce the saints to people whose primary role is reduced to obtaining favors for us. ("Find me a man!") Overall, it is said to be inconsistent with a mature Christian theology.

But intercession has a distinguished history that reaches back to the earliest days of Christianity. In her book *Friends of God and Prophets*, Elizabeth Johnson, CSJ, delineates two main historical models of devotion to the saints: companion and patron. Many Catholics may be more comfortable with the saint as companion, the one who accompanies us along the way to God, and whose story and example helps us to lead a more Christian life.

But the patron model is also an integral part of the Christian tradition. In her book, Sister Johnson notes that intercessory prayers can be traced to requests scratched as second-century graffiti on the walls near the martyrs' graves in Roman cemeteries. "Calling upon the martyrs was a specific way of evoking the solidarity that existed between pilgrims on earth and those who had been sealed with the victory of Christ," she writes.

Today this part of Catholic heritage finds echoes not simply in expressions of personal piety but also in liturgies celebrated by the whole church. It appears most visibly during the Easter Vigil and at ordination Masses, with the chanting of the ancient Litany of the Saints. In response to the invocation of the names of the saints, the congregation sings, "Pray for us." Such prayers are expressing the same desires as those of the early Christians.

For me, it is both natural and sensible to call on the saints for help from time to time. Since we often ask for prayers from friends on earth, why would we not turn to our friends in heaven?

When it comes to serious matters, like a life-threatening illness, the intercession of the saints is easy to explain. Why wouldn't someone as generous as, say, Thérèse of Lisieux want to help us during difficult times, just as she prayed for her sisters, for missionaries in Vietnam, and for a notorious murderer, during her life? The doctor of the church specifically hoped for this role in the afterlife. "After my death I will let fall a shower of roses," she wrote. "I will spend my time in heaven doing good on earth."

Even with less significant matters, like the lost set of keys, the saints may be happy to help us, much as a big brother or sister will bend down to help a younger sibling tie a stray shoelace or zip up a winter coat.

How does all this work? Beats me. All I know is that when I get to heaven I plan to do a lot of thanking, to the Father, Son and Holy Spirit, and to the Blessed Mother, to be sure, but also to quite a few patrons and companions. And given my forgetful nature, I'll start with St. Anthony, who for over 40 years has faithfully been coming around.

May 28, 2007

2007

Surprising Teachings on Prayer

Daniel J. Harrington, SJ

Seventeenth Sunday in Ordinary Time (C)
Readings: Gen. 18:20–32; Ps. 138:1–3, 6–8; Col. 2:12–14;
Luke 11:1–13
"Lord, teach us to pray." (Luke 11:1)

Our Sunday Gospel readings this summer from Luke's journey narrative provide a framework or outline for developing a sound Christian spirituality. One essential element in any variety of Christian spirituality is prayer. Luke's Gospel is an excellent place to learn about biblical prayer. Luke tells us that at the most decisive and important moments in Jesus' ministry—his baptism, choice of the Twelve Apostles, sermon on the plain, transfiguration and especially during his passion—Jesus prayed. In fact, if you want to know what events Luke regarded as most important, look to his many references to Jesus at prayer. Luke also provides two large blocks of Jesus' surprising teachings about prayer, which is why Luke is sometimes called "the Gospel of prayer." In the first block, read today, Jesus tells us what to pray for, how to pray and why we should pray.

Jesus' first instruction on prayer is set within his own practice of prayer. Luke's notice that Jesus was at prayer indicates the importance of what follows. In response to his disciples' request, Jesus gives them and us a sample prayer. It is the short version of what we call the Our Father or the Lord's Prayer. The longer version that is more familiar to us appears in Matt. 6:9–13, in the Sermon on the Mount. With this sample prayer Jesus teaches us first of all to address God as a loving father. Next he prays for the full coming of God's kingdom and for the time when all creation will acknowledge and celebrate the holiness of God. Then he teaches us to ask the Father for sustenance in our everyday life, for forgiveness of our sins (provided we forgive others) and for protection during the trials or tests accompanying the full manifestation of God's kingdom.

Having shown us what to pray for, Jesus then teaches us to pray—with persistence and boldness. His parable of the friend at midnight reflects a common experience. Often a friend or family member (especially a child) will be so persistent in making a request that we find it easier to give in rather than continue to resist. We grow weary of hearing, "Please, please, please . . ." The surprising point of Jesus' parable is the idea that if we are persistent and bold enough in prayer, God will eventually give in to our petitions. The reading from Genesis 18 about Abraham bargaining with God illustrates this biblical attitude perfectly. And Jesus' own repeated insistence on the almost automatic efficacy of the prayer of petition ("ask and you will receive") further encourages persistence and boldness in prayer.

The best reason why we should pray is that God wants to answer our prayers. This point is made by the parable about the father who wants to give good gifts to his son. If human parents naturally want to give good gifts to their children, how much more does God want to give us good gifts. And God wants to give us the greatest gift of all, the Holy Spirit. These are indeed surprising teachings on prayer.

July 16–23, 2007

2007

Persistence in Prayer

Daniel J. Harrington, SJ

Twenty-ninth Sunday in Ordinary Time (C)
Readings: Ex. 17:8–13; Ps. 121:1–8; 2 Tim. 3:14—4:2; Lk. 18:1–8
"Jesus told his disciples a parable about the necessity for them to pray
always without becoming weary." (Lk. 18:1)

Luke's Gospel is sometimes called "the Gospel of Prayer" because in it Jesus prays at the most important moments in his life and because it contains two substantial instructions devoted to Jesus' teachings on prayer (11:1–13 and 18:1–14). In the first passage Jesus offers a sample prayer (the Lord's Prayer) and gives encouragement to be bold and persistent in prayer, since God really wants to answer our prayers. The second prayer instruction reinforces the theme of persistence in prayer (today's passage) and insists on the importance of humility in prayer (next Sunday's text).

Luke introduces the parable of the persistent widow with the comment that it illustrates the need to "pray always without becoming weary." Today's Old Testament reading from Exodus 17 exemplifies that teaching in an almost cartoonish way. As long as Moses keeps his hands raised (presumably in prayer), Israel's battle against the Amalekites goes well for them. When he puts his hands down, then Israel begins to lose. So Aaron and Hur come to Moses' assistance, keeping his hands raised until evening. By that time Amalek has been defeated, and Moses' prayer has been answered. Here persistence in prayer is taken quite literally, even comically.

Today's parable from Luke 18 features two characters: a widow and a judge. In the ancient world a widow was among the most defenseless and powerless persons; unless she had adult sons who were influential, a widow had no social standing and no political power. The other character is a judge, who in this case is an opportunist and a pragmatist, without respect for God or other people. One might imagine that nothing good could ever come from any interaction between them, but when the widow brings her case before the judge, she prevails. She prevails not because she is influential or powerful and not because the judge is honest or compassionate. Rather, she prevails only because she is persistent. She keeps after the judge and finally wears him down. Because the widow will not take no for an answer, the judge decides to give her what she wants in the hope of getting rid of her. The point of Jesus' parable is clear. If a defenseless and powerless widow can wear down a corrupt judge through her persistence alone, how much more can we expect that God, the just and merciful judge, will hear our prayers and answer them positively if we persist?

How can we pray "always"? When we hear the word *prayer*, most of us instinctively think of formal prayers like the Lord's Prayer. And we should, since formal prayers are integral to Christian spirituality. There is another way of thinking about prayer in Christian life, however. It is the effort to make our whole life into a prayer—that is, to pray always. This kind of prayer involves offering all that we are and have and do to the service of God, calling ourselves into the presence of God at various times during our day and making all our personal encounters and actions into a kind of prayer. This form of prayer means bringing all our successes and failures, joys and sorrows, and highs and lows to God in prayer. This habit of prayer, of course, needs to be complemented by formal prayers. But the combination of the two can add up to praying always.

The reading of Scripture has often been the starting point for both formal and personal prayer in the Christian tradition. Today's selection from 2 Timothy insists that "all Scripture is inspired by God." In this context "Scripture" would have meant the Old Testament, since the New Testament was still being written. Nevertheless, we can take the opportunity offered here to consider the place of Scripture in Christian prayer and spirituality. Scripture reveals to us that God the creator and Lord of all is the God of Israel and the Father of our Lord Jesus Christ. Scripture describes our history and religious heritage as the people of God; it provides us with the language and theology of prayer. Scripture serves as the repository of human wisdom and teaches us how to live wisely and justly. It also points us to Christ as the key, so that what is hidden in the Old Testament is revealed in the New Testament.

For those who are serious about prayer, today's Scripture readings provide good advice about both content and style. Scripture, both the Old Testament (especially the Psalms) and the New Testament (especially the Gospels), offers valuable starting points to prayer. The parable of the persistent widow encourages us to be bold and persistent in our prayers of petition. The challenge to pray always can open up for us a habit of prayer that encompasses our entire life.

October 15, 2007

2007

Humility in Prayer

Daniel J. Harrington, SJ

Thirtieth Sunday in Ordinary Time (C)
Readings: Sir. 35:12–14, 16–18; Ps. 34:2–3, 17–19, 23;
2 Tim. 4:6–8; Lk. 18:9–14
"Whoever exalts himself will be humbled, and the one who humbles
himself will be exalted." (Lk. 18:14)

Today we consider the second part of Jesus' second instruction about prayer in Luke 18. The parable of the Pharisee and the tax collector reminds us that God hears the prayers of some surprising persons and that we all must approach God in prayer with humility.

The Old Testament passage from Sirach 35 summarizes the recurrent biblical conviction that God gives special consideration to the prayers of the oppressed and needy and of those who seem least important in society, the orphans and widows. Psalm 34 affirms that the Lord is close to the brokenhearted and crushed in spirit and hears the cries of the poor. The parable of the Pharisee and the tax collector makes a similar point, that God hears the prayers of some very surprising persons. To appreciate this parable, we need to place the two characters in their historical and social context.

In the Gospels the Pharisees often appear as negative characters. They are the most persistent opponents of Jesus, and he often criticizes their attitudes and behavior. In English today the word *Pharisee* can refer to a hypocrite or a religious fraud, someone who pretends to be devout and observant but is not so in reality. In Jesus' time and place, however, people would have heard the word *Pharisee* differently. The Pharisees were members of a prominent Jewish religious movement. Many of them were in fact devout and observant.

They were also the progressives of their day, seeking to adapt the biblical laws to the demands of everyday life. They gathered regularly for prayer and study, and their meals together celebrated their communal identity and religious commitment. Of all the Jewish groups of Jesus' time, Jesus was perhaps closest to them; he shared an agenda with them and sometimes agreed with them (about the resurrection of the dead, for example). Those who first heard Jesus' parable would have considered the Pharisee as a positive example of learning and piety.

In Jesus' time and place, the tax collector in the parable would have been regarded as the opposite of the Pharisee. Taxes were usually let out for bid. The Roman government official or the agent for Herod Antipas might specify the amount to be collected from the inhabitants of a certain area. A tax collector would then contract to pay the specified amount to the government; what he collected above that amount was his to keep. So in Jesus' day tax collectors were suspect on two counts. They were suspected of dishonesty by overcharging the people and keeping excess profits for themselves. They were also suspected of being collaborators and instruments of the Roman occupiers.

These two men went up to the temple area to pray. Whose prayer was heard by God? The Pharisee's prayer was not heard because he exalted himself. His prayer was so focused on himself, his superiority to the tax collector and his own spiritual accomplishments that it was hardly a prayer at all. It was more self-congratulation than prayer. By contrast, the tax collector, whatever his failings may have been, knew who God is and who he was before God. He prayed sincerely, "O God, be merciful to me a sinner."

Whose prayer does God hear? If our prayer becomes an exercise in self-congratulation like that of the Pharisee, our prayer will not be heard, because it is not a prayer at all. If our prayer celebrates the justice and mercy of God, however, if it acknowledges our dependence on God, our sinfulness and our need for God's mercy, then God will hear our prayer, because it is genuine prayer made in a spirit of humility proper to us as God's creatures.

During this next week we will observe All Saints Day and All Souls Day. Today's selection from 2 Timothy 4 describes how a great saint, Paul the apostle, faced life and death. Paul compares his impending death first to pouring out a libation or drink offering, that is, as a sacrifice freely offered to God. Then he evokes the images of an athletic contest ("I have competed well") and a race ("I have finished the race") and affirms that he has kept the faith.

In the face of death, Paul remained confident and hopeful. He was convinced of the truth of the Gospel that he preached, and he believed that eternal life had already begun for him at his baptism into Jesus' death and resurrection. He could disregard his condemnation by a Roman judge, because he regarded God as the only real judge and trusted that the Lord Jesus Christ would rescue him and bring him safely to his heavenly home. In life and in death, Paul provides a model for all saints and would-be saints, for all who approach God in humility and hope.

October 22, 2007

2007

Brother Lawrence and the Chimney Bird

Stephen Martin

As I laid my cell phone on a bookshelf near the door and stepped outside into the late winter afternoon, I remember thinking, *What can happen in just 30 minutes?*

True, my wife's due date for our first child was just a few weeks away. It's also true this fact made me quiver on occasion like an over-bred hunting dog. I was a man with many worries, desperate to be updated and informed at all times, and so my cell phone went with me everywhere. On this day, though, more than anything I needed a head-clearing run through the neighborhood, so I left the phone behind—just this once.

A couple of miles later I came chugging up the hill toward my house. The stop sign that served as my finish line lay just ahead. I was approaching a state largely foreign to me—relaxation. That should have tipped me off. As if on cue, the screen door of my house burst open, and my wife appeared on the front stoop. She was yelling. For me. *Good God*, I thought, veering blindly across the road and up the driveway, *What now? Is she sick? Is the baby on its way?*

"Calm down," my wife told me as I lunged, heaving and fearful, up the steps. "It's not the baby. But we've got a problem. A bird just came down the chimney."

To understand why the drama now unfolding is worth an essay, it helps to know how this day started—with an early morning dash to the emergency room. My wife awoke that Sunday morning with pain and soreness in her calf. Not a big deal, it seemed. But a quick call to the doctor yielded disturbing news. In a pregnant woman, these symptoms could be the sign of a blood clot. We went straight to the hospital, where we spent the morning talking with doctors and agreeing to various tests and mostly just cooling our heels in a little curtained room where I read the sports section four or five times. In the end, we were told it was just muscle spasms. We headed home much relieved, but to tell the truth, I had never been too worried from the start. This was rather astonishing for me, considering my family's penchant for excessive worrying, which can be traced back to at least the Civil War and blamed for more than one nervous breakdown. How to explain this uncharacteristic calm? The credit went not to modern anti-anxiety medication but to a lowly cook from a 17th-century monastery.

It had been about a year since I'd stumbled upon *The Practice of the Presence of God*, the classic collection of letters and teachings by Brother Lawrence, who spent his life chopping vegetables in a kitchen in France and thanking God for it anyway. I read his little book in a weekend, and it quickly became a companion nearly as constant as my cell phone. It taught me two points I had failed to learn from St. Augustine, Pascal, Thomas Merton and a raft of other great spiritual figures to whom I had turned over the years—that prayer is our greatest vocation and that the surest way to God is in our current circumstances, however pedestrian they might seem.

As I raked leaves, collected the trash and slogged through dozens of other humdrum tasks that for years had seemed merely a waste of time, I could hear Brother Lawrence urging me to find new meaning in each one. "Lord of all pots and pans and things," he prayed, "make me a saint by getting meals and washing up the plates!" His teachings inspire. They are also demanding and unsettling, because they are about letting go. "We ought to give ourselves up to God," Brother Lawrence taught, "with regard both to things temporal and spiritual, and seek our satisfaction only in the fulfilling of His will, whether He lead us by suffering or by consolation."

On this particular Sunday morning visit to the E.R., God led us by inconvenience, but I did not object. It was a unique victory for me, and I couldn't resist congratulating myself. Out on my deck that afternoon, flanked by quiet woods in bright sunshine, I captured this triumph in a journal entry. As that hectic morning unfolded, I wrote, "I found myself almost naturally resorting to prayer instead of freaking out or getting anxious, and that's an improvement for me. . . . It was also a chance to practice dealing with situations as they arise and having the flexibility to stay calm." Then I took my notebook back inside the house, changed into shorts and a sweatshirt and headed out for my cell-phone-free run.

"Make it your study, before taking up any task," Brother Lawrence advises, "to look to God, be it only for a moment." I have this nugget of wisdom underlined in his book in black ink, but it was well out of my mind by the time I stalked into our living room to confront the offending bird. Small, dark and sparrow-like, it was hopping around the grate inside our fireplace, chirping unhappily behind the glass doors. As I fumed at our bad luck, my plucky wife grabbed a large towel and reached for the fireplace doors.

"What are you doing?" I roared.

"I'm going to get it out," she said.

"I don't think that's a smart move when you're pregnant," I snapped.

"Oh, please," she said. "Since I got pregnant, you won't let me do anything." That was true and hardly worth disputing.

"Just let me have the towel," I said.

As I gingerly opened the glass doors, I knew I had a better chance of delivering our baby myself than catching a furious bird in a towel, transporting it to the front door and setting it free without getting an eye pecked out. The bird wasn't up for it either. No sooner had I cracked the doors open than it jumped onto the hearth and took off.

I don't recall the exact pattern of its flight, but it covered a lot of airspace in our living and dining rooms as I stood rooted to the hardwood floor holding an empty beach towel and swearing earnestly. We should "so rule all our actions that they be little acts of communion with God," said Brother Lawrence. It was too late for that.

After a couple of desperate loops, the bird smashed into our dining room window and dropped to the floor. It lay there dazed for a moment, long enough for me to stop feeling sorry for myself. I yanked open the front door, propped the screen open and dashed back to the dining room.

The determined bird was airborne again, and I was ready for redemption, ready to defend my vulnerable, helpless, pregnant wife, who in the interim had wisely closed all the doors leading to the rest of our house and thus saved the day. The bird had perched along the wall—and was still a step ahead of me. With a burst of beating wings, it rocketed straight through the dining room at chest level, across the living room and right out the front door in a smooth ascending arc skyward, zipping beneath the upper left corner of the door frame and into the open air like a football just squeezing through the uprights. Any illusions I had about my progress with prayer and patience flew out the door with it.

In explaining to a colleague how he prayed, Brother Lawrence wrote, "Everyone is capable of such familiar conversation with God, some more, some less. He knows what we can do. Let us begin, then." It is in this beginning, of course, that reality, the reality of our wandering minds, collides with our spiritual ambitions, and our failures pile up high in the wreckage. It is hard to keep the conversation with God going. We forget about grace as we sweep floors and sit in traffic and stagger around a dark room in the middle of the night hunting for lost pacifiers; then we remember, and then we forget again.

Looking back on his journey of prayer, Brother Lawrence observes that it was replete with shortcomings, that he "fell often, and rose again presently." Faith, he reminds us, is less about moments of mystical union and mostly about getting knocked down and standing back up—like the bird in my house as it bounced off the window, hit the floor and took flight again, like my own restless faith straining to break free of the limits I impose, searching for that open door, for that sudden flash of warming sky and the promise of springtime coming.

December 24–31, 2007

2008

Shadows in Prayer: The Seven D's of the Spiritual Life

James Martin, SJ

One challenge for readers of *Mother Teresa: Come Be My Light*, the collection of Blessed Teresa of Calcutta's letters published last fall, is to distinguish among the terms *darkness, dryness, desolation, doubt, disbelief, depression* and *despair*—the "seven D's." On a popular level, some journalists, media analysts and bloggers conflated Mother Teresa's "darkness" with "disbelief." Christopher Hitchens, the atheist author of *God Is Not Great*, was not the only one who asked, after reading selections from the book, whether the "saint of the gutters" was a closet atheist. Even devout Catholics had difficulties grasping how Mother Teresa, considered a paragon of faith, could have suffered from a feeling of abandonment by God. While some Catholics saw her example as one of remarkable fidelity, others were disturbed to read such lines as, "I have no faith." One woman asked me, "How can I expect to pray at all, when even she couldn't believe?"

Such reactions show how easy it is for the media and the public to be addled sometimes by the complexities of the spiritual life and, also, how confused terminology can become, even among those familiar with prayer.

The "seven D's," however, are distinct, and Christian spiritual masters have long used specific terms to refer to distinct experiences. One may experience dryness without depression (for example, during a retreat when one suspects that the period of dryness in prayer is temporary). One may encounter darkness without disbelief (as did St. Thérèse of Lisieux, who continued to believe despite spiritual aridity near the end of her life). Experiences can overlap, too. Darkness can lead to occasional doubt, as in the case of Mother Teresa. And depression can lead, as even atheists and agnostics know, to despair.

Darkness Visible

Darkness has been an important theme in Christian spirituality since St. Gregory of Nyssa in the fourth century. Perhaps the most often quoted source on the topic is St. John of the Cross, a Spanish mystic. Ironically, he may be the most misquoted as well, as illustrated by frequent references to the "dark night of the soul." His original 16th-century poem is called simply *Noche Oscura*, "Dark Night."

"Dark night," however, is only one way of describing a particular state of feeling isolated from God. Around the same time St. John was writing, St. Ignatius Loyola wrote of "desolation" in his *Spiritual Exercises*. So even the most educated Christian can be forgiven for wondering, *Are the two saints talking about two phenomena that are the same, or similar or different?*

To add to the confusion, where one spiritual director uses "darkness," another might use "dryness" to describe the same experience. "And sometimes directors can be presumptuous, too," says Jane Ferdon, O.P., who has trained spiritual directors in California for 20 years. "People may say that they are in darkness, and we spiritual directors assume we know what they're talking about!"

Perhaps confusion stems not only from an imprecise, overlapping and shifting use of terms but also from a failure to recognize that everyone who prays will at some point encounter many of these states.

What are these states? How do they affect our relationships with God? Lent is a good time to reflect on these categories, not only as a way of taking stock of our spiritual life but also as an invitation to meditate on Jesus' own expression of isolation on the cross, "My God, my God, why have you abandoned me?"

What follows is a brief overview of the seven D's, beginning with some simple definitions, followed by comments from past and present spiritual masters.

Definitions and Descriptions

1. Darkness is a feeling of God's absence after having developed a personal relationship with God. For St. John of the Cross, there were two types of "dark nights." The "dark night of the senses" is an experience of one's own limitations and the removal of attachments to the consolation felt in prayer. It is "an inflowing of God into the soul whereby he purges it of its habitual ignorances and imperfections," wrote St. John. At a later stage, some experience the "dark night of the spirit," which is a more profound challenge to faith. But both are steps toward deeper union with God.

Janet Ruffing, R.S.M., professor of spirituality and spiritual direction at Fordham University, describes St. John's dark night as a "mystical experience of God that overwhelms our normal way of apprehending God, and leads not only to an increase in faith, hope and love, but also eventually into a place of light." She believes that while almost everyone who prays seriously will encounter the dark night of the senses, relatively few will experience the dark night of the spirit.

An experience of darkness can be a gateway to finding God in the *nada*, or nothingness, and an entry into the *via negativa*, the negative way. Ruth Burrows, a Carmelite nun, writes in her book *Essence of Prayer* that God "wants us to trust him enough to live with him unafraid, totally defenseless in his presence. We can truly say that John of the Cross's teaching has as its sole aim to bring us to this inner poverty."

A person in darkness feels isolated from God. Yet with patience (whether or not one can identify which "dark night" one is experiencing), one can let go of the need to feel God's presence constantly and gradually move through the darkness to discover greater intimacy with God.

2. Dryness is a limited period of feeling emptiness in prayer. "Dryness is more temporary than darkness," says William A. Barry, SJ, author of *God and You: Prayer as a Personal Relationship*. Anyone who prays will at times feel dryness in prayer, when nothing seems to be happening. "There is little in the way of sensible consolation," Father Barry said in an interview.

These natural parts of the spiritual life can increase our appreciation for richer moments. One never knows what kind of inner change occurs during "dry" times, and being with the living God in prayer is always transforma-tive. As a Jesuit novice, I once confessed to my spiritual director that nothing was happening during my prayer. It seemed a waste of time. "Being in the presence of God is a waste of time?" he asked.

Much as even a close friendship goes through some quiet or dull times, so our relationship with God may go through dry patches. But being with a friend in such times is necessary if the friendship is to be sustained and grow in intimacy.

3. Desolation is feeling God's absence coupled with a sense of hopeless-ness. St. Ignatius Loyola describes it as "an obtuseness of soul, turmoil within it, an impulsive motion toward low and earthly things, or a disquiet from various agitations and temptations." It is more than feeling dejected or sad. "Desolation is often confused with simply feeling bad," says Barry. "But it's more accurate to say it is a feeling of estrangement from God."

Margaret Silf, a columnist for *America* and author of *Inner Compass: An Invitation to Ignatian Spirituality*, notes that desolation has a quality of isola-tion. "Those in desolation are turned away from the light of God's presence," she told me, "and more focused on the shadows." Father Barry agrees. "In desolation it's more about the person than it is about God," he says. "Ulti-mately this leads to despair."

Desolation is distinct from St. John's dark night. In desolation, writes St. Ignatius, one is moved toward a "lack of faith" and is left "without hope and love." In the dark night the opposite is happening, as one moves toward com-plete abandonment to God. "For the one experiencing this, it may be easier to see this in retrospect," says Janet Ruffing. "But in the Ignatian worldview, the dark night is actually consolation."

The desolation Ignatius describes may seem far removed from the lives of average Christians. But it is a common, painful state experienced by many people, coupled as it is with feelings of "gnawing anxiety," as Ignatius puts it. He counsels that in these times one should, among other things, redou-ble one's efforts in prayer, remember times when God seemed more present or remind oneself that it will eventually pass. He also reminds us that all the fruits of prayer are really gifts from God, which we cannot control.

4. Doubt is an intellectual indecision about God's existence. Many believers face doubt at some point in their lives. "Most people are relieved to be able to talk about doubt in spiritual direction," says Ruffing. "But no one reaches adult faith without doubt. And frequently people encounter doubt and then move toward a faith that is more complex, paradoxical and, ultimately, more adult."

Doubt is a supremely human experience, shared by nearly every Christian since St. Thomas the Apostle. Recently, in John Patrick Shanley's Pulitzer Prize-winning play, *Doubt*, a priest (who faces his own doubts and the doubts of his parishioners about his background) points to this universality in a homily: "When you are lost, you are not alone."

5. Disbelief is an intellectual state of not accepting the existence of God. Some commentators concluded that because Mother Teresa suffered darkness, she did not believe in God. Once, in her letters, she bluntly wrote, "I have no faith." But, as Father Barry explains, "She was still praying and writing letters to God."

Sometimes disbelief is a way of discarding old images of God that no longer work for an adult believer. Margaret Silf reflects on her own experience: "I've been through times when all the old props have fallen away, and have felt that I just couldn't go on believing. So what to do? Bolster this old system, or let things be and see what happens? For me, this finally enabled me to break through to a deeper level of faith, which I would call trust." Disbelief is a serious challenge in the spiritual life. If the journey ends at that point, there will be little space for God. The key is to continue seeking, even in the midst of disbelief.

6. Depression is a profound form of sadness. In the medical and psychological community, it has a more technical definition. "It's a clinical category that is often able to be treated medically," says Barry, who is also a psychologist. "We don't want to spiritualize primarily psychological problems," says Jane Ferdon. "But today," she adds, "we can also psychologize spiritual issues. So it's very important to discern the root causes of depression."

In "The Dark Night and Depression," an essay in Keith J. Egan's book *Carmelite Prayer*, Kevin Culligan, a Carmelite priest, writes that in the dark night there is an acute awareness of one's own incompleteness. However, in this darkness one seldom "utters morbid statements of guilt, self-loathing, worthlessness, and suicidal ideation," as one does during a period of clinical depression.

So one can be in darkness but not be depressed. What about the other way around? Father Barry responds, "Rarely is the clinically depressed person able to experience consolation in prayer."

Therese Borchard, who writes a blog on depression, "Beyond Blue," for the spirituality Web site Beliefnet, has suffered from depression herself. She understands it from both a theoretical and a personal point of view and agrees with Barry. "When you're depressed you feel so angry at God," she told me. "For some people it can lead you closer to God, as you struggle to express your anger and also cling to God as a last hope. For others it can distance you and lead to turning away from God. In general, though, depression usually leads to darkness and dryness in prayer." Clinical depression needs to be treated by medical professionals as well as to be addressed in a spiritual setting.

How do spiritual directors and counselors distinguish between darkness and depression? "When I'm with depressed people, I feel swallowed up by their depression," says Janet Ruffing. "It's the opposite with people going through the dark night. Once, I accompanied one of our sisters, who was dying, through an experience like this, and in her presence I felt God's luminosity—though she couldn't touch it at all."

Sadness is different from depression. As Barry notes, "Sadness over a painful reality in your life can be a sign that you are in touch with God." Jane Ferdon says, "These are some of the people who are the most alive, since they are feeling deeply."

7. Despair is a feeling that all is, and will remain, hopeless. The Trappist monk Thomas Merton defined despair in his book *New Seeds of Contemplation* as "the ultimate development of a pride so great and so stiff-necked that it accepts the absolute misery of eternal damnation rather than accept that God is above us and that we are not capable of fulfilling our destinies by ourselves." The form of despair Merton describes implies that we know better than God does, and what we "know" is that things can never get any better. Such pride leads to a spiritual dead end: despair.

This may sound harsh. For those living in poverty, facing a life-threatening illness or confronted with some other tragedy, despair may seem a rational response. It can also stem from depression. "When you are depressed you are often without hope," says Therese Borchard, "and this can lead to despair."

Jane Ferdon thinks that sometimes despair is not a spiritual dead end, but appropriate. She remembers one woman describing her painful circumstances by saying, "I feel like I'm walking among the living dead." Ferdon always asks people if they can find God in this state. "Also, it's important to know if the despair is a reflection of something else, say, aloneness or depression, and what happens when the person brings that despair to prayer. Sometimes the person doesn't want to pray about it, and if not, why not? That may be where Thomas Merton's notion of pride comes in."

Ferdon respectfully disagrees with Merton in definitively identifying despair with pride. "It may be that pride is actually the opposite of what is happening. Despair can be an experience of letting go of our need to control everything, and it can lead to change, revitalization and even consolation." So while a despair that says, "Nothing can change" is perilous in the spiritual life, a despair that says, "I can't do it by myself" could lead to growth.

Distinctions and Deliverance

One need not be a scholar of Christian spirituality, a spiritual director or a person under spiritual direction to see that disentangling these spiritual strands can be encouraging, clarifying, consoling and freeing. Understanding that most of these experiences are common can encourage us by reducing anxiety. "These are stages in everyone's spiritual life," says Janet Ruffing. Knowing that these stages are not identical can be clarifying and help us discern the correct responses to different events in our spiritual lives. (St. Ignatius, for example, prescribes definite steps to take when one is in desolation.) Being able to bring such experiences to prayer can be consoling, since it can deepen our relationship with God, in the same way that speaking about a thorny problem with a friend can strengthen a friendship and lead to greater intimacy.

Finally, knowing that all these experiences can lead us to God can free us from fear, which can cripple our spiritual lives. For the God by whom Jesus felt abandoned on the cross is the same God who delivered Jesus from death, giving him new life. "My God, my God, why have you abandoned me?" is the beginning of Psalm 22. A few lines later, though, the psalmist sings another song. "For he did not hide his face from me, but heard me when I cried to him."

March 17, 2008

2008

The Heart of the Matter: Rediscovering a Time-Honored Devotion

Rev. David N. Knight

There was a time when devotion to the Sacred Heart needed no introduction. Not anymore. Many people today have never even heard of it. Should we try to revive it or let it die?

Before answering that question, let us recall that at least two popes have written encyclicals presenting this devotion as "no ordinary form of piety" but rather "a summary of all our religion." These are strong words. Four popes have been calling for a "new evangelization." What better time to launch a revival of the devotion to the Sacred Heart than during the Year of Paul, which began on June 29, 2008?

The devotion to the Sacred Heart as we know it today began with a vision of Christ given to St. Margaret Mary Alacoque in 1673 at Paray-le-Monial, France. In that vision the heart of Jesus was visible, on fire with love, pierced by a lance and thorns. Christ's words were, "See the heart that has loved so much and receives so little in return." Christ's desire was to focus people's attention on his love. He asked that individuals and families display a picture of his Sacred Heart in their home.

The devotion encouraged people to begin each day with a morning offering, to consecrate themselves to the Sacred Heart and dedicate themselves to making reparation through prayers and penance for the failure of people to respond to Christ's love. Devotion to the Sacred Heart encouraged frequent

Communion and adoration of Jesus in the Blessed Sacrament, especially during a holy hour before the first Friday of every month, in order to promote "a truly grateful love for Jesus."

How might each of these elements be practiced today in ways consonant with the progress Catholic spirituality has made since the 17th century?

The Image

Focusing on the image of the Sacred Heart should recall us to a deeply personal relationship with Jesus Christ as the very center of our spirituality. We need to live and experience our religion, not as a system of laws and practices, but as a spirituality of exciting, personal and even passionate interaction of love and friendship with Jesus. Christianity is a religion of love aroused by an awareness of God's love for us first. In St. Paul's words, it is the "love of Christ" that "urges us on."

Consecration

The act of consecration fundamental to Christian life is baptism. We need to deepen our understanding of the commitments inherent in the sacrament that made us Christians, until we all say with St. Paul, "I live now, not I, but Christ lives in me" (Gal. 2:20). This is the mystery of our identity as Christians. The image of the Sacred Heart reflects the promise of the Christian identity bestowed by baptism. Contemplating that image should lead us to live as the saving Christ, fired by his love. This means inviting Jesus constantly to act with us, in us and through us to "save" and lift up all of our activities and engagements—at home, at work, in our social and civic life.

Our act of consecration and morning offering are combined in the ongoing affirmation of our baptismal promises: "Lord, I give you my body. Live this day with me, live this day in me, live this day through me." We extend this by repeating the WIT prayer before everything we do: "Lord, do this *with* me; do this *in* me; do this *through* me."

Reparation

Reparation to the Sacred Heart is realized in the prayers and penances we offer to Jesus to make up for the failure of people to respond to his love. For ordinary Christians leading busy lives in the world, the most practical form reparation can take is repair work. We need to respond effectively to the landslide loss of faith among those around us, to the distressing defection of Catholics who no longer attend Mass and to the uncritical acceptance of the distorted values of our contemporary culture, including the relativism that Benedict XVI has called the "greatest threat to faith in our day." We need to recognize and resist the implicit idolatry of so many for whom religion is just a part, and not even the most important part, of their life. Our resistance should be fundamental and radical.

Baptism commits us to such a response. The minister's words as he anointed us with chrism were, "As Christ was anointed priest, prophet and king, so live always as a member of his body." This is our job description as Christians: to bear witness as prophets, to minister to everyone with love as priests by baptism, and to take responsibility for the transformation of society as stewards of Christ's kingship. This is radical reparation.

As *prophets* we can repair the damage sin has done and is doing to the world by bearing witness to the Gospel through a lifestyle that wins people to faith. If we contemplate the contrast between Christ's passionate love and the lukewarm response given to it by most believers, the image of Christ's heart will motivate us to live a lifestyle radically different from the conventional expectations of our society.

Pope Paul VI defined witnesses as those who "radiate faith in values that go beyond current values, and hope in something not seen, that one would not dare to imagine. Through this wordless witness, they stir up irresistible questions in the hearts of those who see how they live: 'Why are they like this? Why do they live in this way?'" Witnesses are those whose lifestyle raises eyebrows.

To commit oneself to a life of witness is to change one's whole standard of morality. We would never ask again just whether something is right or wrong, but whether it bears witness to the values of the Gospel. This is reparation that echoes the teaching of Paul: "If with Christ you died [in baptism] . . . why do you live as if you still belonged to the world? . . . Live your life in a manner worthy of the Gospel of Christ" (Col. 2:20).

As *priests by baptism* we say in our hearts to every person we encounter, "This is my body, given for you; my flesh for the life of the world." The contemplation of Christ's heart, wounded by the denial of love, leads us to recognize those same wounds now borne by others; it motivates us to make reparation through the healing ministry of love.

It is not just the heart of Christ that is wounded by the absence of love in the world; all of us are. People sin because they are not loved. People sin seeking love. People live mediocre lives because they feel they are only moderately loved. People do not respond to God with passion because they do not believe God loves them with passion. And they do not believe this because they do not experience the passionate love of Jesus reaching out to them in the visible members of his body.

The problem with the world is that the church does not love enough. The heart of Christ is not a vivid presence in today's world, because it is not sufficiently visible in his body on earth. The Sacred Heart needs to be seen as a living heart, full of love for living people.

When we "presented our bodies" at baptism "as a living sacrifice to God," we pledged that we would be "sacrificed" to continue the mission of Jesus, both priest and victim. As Christians, we never deal with anyone on a purely professional or impersonal level, ignoring their humanity. Paul saw ministry as the mystery of bringing Christ to birth and to full stature in every member of the human race. Our ministry of reparation must "build up the body of Christ" in love.

As *stewards of Christ's kingship* we repair what sin has done to the world. We address the social structures, policies and practices that produce environments that breed destruction and deceit.

Our baptismal anointing as sharers in Christ's kingship makes us responsible for extending the reign of his love over every area and activity of human life on earth. This commits us to leadership, to taking the initiative in promoting the changes we perceive as desirable in family, church, business, politics, social life and neighborhood. If we love Jesus Christ and understand his love for the world, we cannot remain indifferent or passive in the face of false principles and destructive policies that block the "peace and unity of his kingdom."

Jesus said that in devotion to his heart, people will find "all the sanctifying and saving graces needed to draw them back from the abyss of destruction." John Dear, SJ, has identified this abyss in "The Politics of the Sacred Heart" (National Catholic Reporter Conversation Café, 6/19/07):

> Today we stand at the brink of unprecedented global destruction, global warming and global violence. This violence pushes us personally and internationally ever closer to the abyss of destruction, but the grace of the Sacred Heart—with all its burning social, economic and political implications—has the power to convert us into people of Gospel nonviolence, pull us back from the brink, and create a new world of peace with justice. . . . If we were to adopt the image of the Sacred Heart as our image of a nonviolent, peacemaking God, and live not just individually but communally, nationally and globally according to that nonviolent, radiant love, the world would be disarmed.

If we love Jesus Christ and share his love for the world, we will "make reparation" for the sins of the world by working against anything that delays what Paul described as God's "plan for the fullness of time," which is to "gather up all things in Christ, things in heaven and things on earth" so that Christ might be "all in all."

Adoration

Adoration has always been part of devotion to the Sacred Heart, especially before the Blessed Sacrament. But adoration, in its pure form, is just wordless absorption in the awesome reality of God. In the act of adoring we do not do anything else. But most people cannot sustain this for more than a few minutes at a time. So instead of adoration we pray the Rosary, read Scripture or other books, or say other familiar vocal prayers. These are all good things to do, but they are not what the church understands by adoration.

Before we can practice adoration, we need to know the heart we are to adore. So when we invite others to adoration of the Blessed Sacrament, we should teach them to prepare themselves for it by learning the mind and heart of Christ. We enter Christ's heart by letting his words abide in us: by reading and reflecting on Scripture and by making the connection constantly between what we learn and what we live.

True devotion to the Sacred Heart is not simply the repetition of certain acts; it is a profound change in consciousness that we acquire as a result of that repetition. St. Paul exhorts us, "Let the same mind be in you that was in Christ Jesus" (Phil. 2:5). This is a call to discipleship: a lifelong commitment to studying the mind and heart of Christ.

Why revive devotion to the Sacred Heart?

Devotion to the Sacred Heart is not a particular devotion that needs to be revived. Rather, it is the fundamental center of all Catholic spirituality that needs to be revitalized by a "new evangelization." If we revive devotion to the Sacred Heart in its authentic identity, we will have revived Christianity in the church. This would be a great way to celebrate the Year of Paul.

November 10, 2008

2008

Gateways to Prayer: The Enduring Spiritual Power of Icons

Stephen Bonian, SJ

Icons have been objects of faith, controversy and fascination for centuries. The popularity of icons, which are a rich resource for prayer, continues to this day as such artists as the Rev. William Hart McNichols and Robert Lentz, O.F.M., practice the art of modern iconography.

Praying with icons is an intuitive art gained with practice and experience. Henri Nouwen provides an enlightening introduction to the practice in his book *Behold the Beauty of the Lord: Praying with Icons*. Nouwen recounts the weeks he spent "gazing" at four Russian images and reflecting on select passages from Scripture. Christians interested in making use of icons in prayer can imitate Nouwen's method, but they need not do so. There is a freedom of engagement in the contemplation of art that varies from person to person and with time and place. Still, as one embarks on this journey of prayer, it is useful to keep in mind a few guiding principles and to reflect on the history of this holy art form.

An Incarnational Art Form

The Christian mysteries reflected in iconography are primarily the Incarnation and the Redemption. The primary power of icons lies in their physicality: they make the presence of the holy tangible. They rouse the imagination and generate emotions in the viewer.

Especially noteworthy among all icons are those of the Blessed Mother. Holding the infant Jesus in her arms, she radiates the light of Christ. Gazing upon her, the viewer is moved by her gestures, especially the movement of her hands and eyes. Like a mirror vessel, she reflects a profound mystery: that we, too, hold God within us and can touch the divine with our hands. Though the child may often be asleep in our earthen vessels, he is nevertheless a sign of the peace of the Father dwelling within us.

Two types of icons are most reflective of Mary's mystery: in the first, she is depicted holding the grown-up child Jesus in her arms; in the second, she gives praise with open arms as the child dwells in that perfect circle of her womb. In both representations Mary symbolizes the altar and the throne upon which and through which Christ is being fully transfigured to our world.

One is impressed by how often in the painting (or the writing, as it is called) of these icons, Mary appears larger than Jesus. Clearly the icon painter intends to show her great value before God. In such icons the emphasis is not so much on Mary's humility, but rather on her enormity as the mother of God. The icons of the annunciation to Mary by the Angel Gabriel vary in their depiction of the scene, though usually they emphasize the spiritual nature of the visit, with a special emphasis on Mary's discerning posture. Likewise the icons that represent the visitation of Mary to Elizabeth depict a holy kiss and a welcoming hug between the two joyful mothers. They seek to depict what Luke suggests in his Gospel account of these events, though more is left to the imagination.

The icons of the nativity of the Lord reflect moments of excitement, wonder and peace at the birth of the Lord Jesus in Bethlehem, expressed in narrative form in the Gospels of Matthew and Luke. (Since Luke emphasizes Mary's role in the Incarnation, he is often described as the first to have painted the icon of Mary—with words, of course, not paint.)

Painting the Life of Jesus

Many icons dramatize the life of Jesus. The traditional icons of the Baptism of Jesus in the River Jordan often show him sanctifying the river as he is immersed in it. The symbols of the Father and the Spirit are above him, while below he is flanked by the heavenly world of the angels on one side and by his human friends and followers on the other.

The Gospel accounts of the parables of Jesus are also filled with colorful and dynamic images. Gazing at icons of these parables can enliven the imagination, helping to flesh out what may be hidden behind the words of Scripture. The icons depicting the prodigal son and his loving father, for example, express in a gesture of embrace the longing of the two for each other, and of God's very longing to embrace us as well—perhaps even at that same moment of contemplation.

The miracles of Jesus, either of nature or healing, are also presented as dynamic events. Combined with Scripture passages, they can inspire us to contemplate the hidden powers of God. Consider the icon of the tempest on the lake: while Jesus sleeps in the boat, his disciples are pictured as fearful and anxious. This moment may call to mind various times of fear and anxiety in our lives, as we try to awaken the powers of Jesus dormant inside us. Another moving miracle often depicted in icons is the miracle at Cana, where the water turns to wine as it is poured into large jars. Here we witness Jesus' special relationship with his mother and the generosity he offers to the wedding couple.

Jesus' healing miracles also served to inspire many icon artists. The posture of women at miracles—whether it is the hemorrhaging woman holding fast to Jesus' garment, or Martha and Mary at the raising of Lazarus—stresses the human agony of separation as well as the human desire for healing and God's compassionate response to our needs.

A Rich Resource

Icons can be used in individual prayer or during retreats. They are especially suited to Ignatian forms of prayer, which by their nature seek to use the imagination to open doorways to mystical and spiritual realities. With time and careful attention, icons can reveal several layers of meaning. To make the best use of them, it is important to have a variety of images to choose from. As we have seen, it is natural to pair certain icons with specific scriptural passages. Other icons work well in conjunction with particular prayers. Images of Jesus and Mary, for example, can enhance the dialogue prayers in the Spiritual Exercises known as colloquies.

Here are a few other things to consider as you begin your prayer:

1. The choice of an icon should be based in part on the graces being asked for. If one seeks relief from anxiety, for example, the story of the calming of the storm (mentioned above) may be a good choice.

2. During prayer, one is likely to encounter moments of self-understanding, passion, zeal or conflict. Pay attention to these emotions, and what you were praying for when you experienced them. It is not uncommon for the image being gazed upon to change in affect as one continues to pray before it and through it.

3. After you finish your prayer, a reflective review can help to record the movements of the heart and of the Holy Spirit. Private reflection can be followed later by a conversation with a spiritual guide for guidance and discernment.

Praying with icons can help enrich our own spiritual lives, but the images can also help us to pray for family and friends, and even for an end to the maladies that plague our world. For example:

- Icons depicting God's love can be projected on loved ones, perhaps through the aid of a photograph. It is a way of putting on the love of Christ, to wrap our loved ones in the care of the heavenly mother and father. One might use an icon on the theme of Mary as Mother of Tenderness, which shows Mary and the child Jesus locked in a warm embrace.

- Icons expressing God's love for humanity can be used to pray for an end to war or relief from hunger and poverty. Icons of Christ's passion can be relevant here, as well as the genre known as Fountain of Healing, which pictures Mary and Jesus sitting atop a fountain of life-giving water.

- Icons of God's love can also be paired with images representing God's natural creation. By doing so one can achieve a sense of solidarity with God's world.

By using icons in prayer, we can transform our view of ourselves and of the natural world. Icons awaken us to a renewed reality—that we are living in a spirit-filled world, touched by the hidden redemptive powers of God's love through Christ. Our attitude toward the earth itself can become a matter of relating to a world redeemed. Likewise, we can no longer objectify our human brothers and sisters, for all people being redeemed by God's graces now reflect and radiate the loving traces of the beloved son's light.

In his treatise *On Holy Images*, St. John Damascene offers the important insight that God chose to become matter so that we can see, touch and be present with him through our material world. "When the Invisible One becomes visible to flesh," he wrote, "you may then draw a likeness of his form." All Christians are indebted to the icon artists, both past and present, who have heeded this call.

December 8, 2008

2010

The Quiet Space: Between the Lines of the Our Father

David Berry

In rugged mountains east of Seoul, Korea, in forests marked by wild streams, the footpaths of hardy hikers and the rooting spots of wild boar, Nature and Star Lodge nestles at the end of a road up a steep valley.

At a weekend retreat I led there, under images of galaxies and stars projected on a high ceiling, the retreatants and I paused to feel Earth's gravity pull us into our seats with a sense of awe arising as we found ourselves in the midst of the miraculous universe. The participants included a priest, a nun, and Koreans with Italian Christian names like Angelo and Maria, a custom in Korean churches. Mr. Kim, the founder and owner of Nature and Star Lodge, was also among us. He is a quiet, intuitive man sought out for counsel by friends and parishioners.

It was early December, so I included Christmas carols in the retreat program to encourage expression from throats and diaphragms as well as hearts and minds. Often a familiar practice or text, like a carol, offers a gateway to deeper feelings and perceptions.

The retreat was going well, but the people still seemed in a more intellectual frame of mind, perhaps because following my English and elementary Korean and then listening to a professional translator was primarily an intellectual exercise.

Nearing the end of our time together one day, as people shared with each other in pairs, I prayed quietly that we could deepen the experience and that participants would find a practice of prayer that would make a difference to them after the retreat. An idea came to me, reminiscent of a practice I encountered in a Jesuit retreat: to work with the most familiar practice of all. Calling the room back to order I invited them to share highlights of the previous exercise and then asked, "Who here has said the Our Father at least 1,000 times?"

The nun looked around the room and then back at me as if I had asked a foolish question, "Everyone," she said.

"Ten thousand times?" I asked.

They looked around at one another, all nodding, "Yes, everyone."

"One hundred thousand times?"

"Most, yes maybe all of us."

I looked slowly at each face then asked, "Did you pray like this? Our father, who art in heaven, *I have got to start supper before the kids get home*, Hallowed be thy name, *I hope I get this sales contract*, Thy kingdom come, *I wonder what time it is. . . .*"

They first looked surprised, then nudged one another, smiling in recognition.

"Do you think Jesus had something in mind when he gave us that particular prayer?" I asked. "Perhaps he is encouraging us to turn our attention in a different direction to realize something we did not previously notice. Perhaps Jesus gave us a key. But do we ever pause to wonder what that key is designed to open? Are we focused on the key or on the door?"

As interest sparked, I invited them to put themselves into a prayerful state and, when someone felt ready, to say slowly the first line of the Our Father in Korean. I suggested they listen to the phrase and rest in contemplation. Why would Christ ask us to say those words? After a few moments, when another person felt moved to speak, they should slowly say the next line of the prayer. Again we would remain silent for three breaths and consider the phrase.

As they entered silence and the priest said the first line, I began to pray an Our Father silently in English. The pauses they left between the lines were longer than I expected; the phrases of the familiar prayer were spoken in earnest and with focused attention. When the prayer was over, the intellectual frame had given way to a feeling of well-being and deep connection. We sat quietly for a few minutes reflecting on what had happened and then took a short break. The workshop closed at the appointed time an hour later.

A few days later, Mr. Kim told a participant that after the retreat, in a building he had erected with his own hands but in which for years he had a sense of the "energy not being right," something had shifted. He had a peaceful feeling there for the first time.

Since that weekend I have often prayed with silent pauses between the lines, and I am still startled by what sometimes happens during one heartfelt Our Father. What each of us finds there differs of course. For me, in the first two words I sometimes hear myself calling out, almost imploring the Lord to be present. Then I realize it is I who am less than fully present. Sometimes the spaces are filled with racing thoughts on unresolved issues. At those times I leave space for a few more slow breaths until the storm settles, until I realize that my prayers are answered by grace and blessings. When I forgive others, I feel a release of the judgments and unhappiness that were hurting me more than anyone else. I don't wish to bring unhappiness to anyone, I realize; if they were happy and aware they would rarely offend others. So I begin to pray for them, too.

More than a year later, while at a Christian service at an interfaith gathering on the National Mall next to the Washington Monument, I invited many participants from diverse traditions to pray one Our Father in that way. The spaces between the lines grew as peace moved through the crowd. Later that morning, a pair of eagles circled above the gathering followed by a rainbow around the sun in an otherwise clear sky. Silence between the lines can smile upon us in many ways.

March 1, 2010

2010

Sisters in Faith: Finding Renewal—and a Dose of Irreverence—in a Women's Prayer Group

Kaya Oakes

For months after I completed the Rite of Christian Initiation of Adults in my parish, I would often crane my head around during Mass, looking for the 15 or so other candidates who had become fully initiated Catholics along with me at Easter. But somehow they had all vanished. As a returning Catholic who had come bearing a lot of doubts and questions after a 20-plus-year ramble through the fields of punk rock and Berkeley politics, I was hungry for spiritual community, but I never quite found it in the RCIA. With five different Sunday services to choose from, perhaps my class partners were just scattered among them. A priest told me, "God will know when to send you companions." While he had been right about everything else so far, I suspected he might be wrong about that.

Every week I drifted to Mass in a bubble until the day I got an e-mail message from my confirmation sponsor, who is a feminist, a liberal and a social justice activist. We had been introduced by our parish priest and had hit it off in our short conversations. She asked if I'd like to join her prayer group—a once-a-month gathering of a few like-minded Catholic women. "We pray together," she wrote, "and complain about the church." It took me about five seconds to reply, "How soon can we meet?"

The prayer ladies may be a little irreverent, but they are also the best Catholics I know. Two are single, one is married with kids, one has a long-time partner, and they are all actively involved in ministries. From their work—from giving spiritual direction to teaching theology to running the parish monthly dinner for homeless guests—they are role models as modern Catholic women, especially to me. They are all feminists, and they are all liberals in the best sense. We often talk about the desire we share for social equality, a solution to poverty in our communities, more people to make a greater commitment to helping others.

Often we talk about our problems with the big-C church. It's not "blasphemy and a nice cup of tea," but it is a chance to hash out frustrations we feel as lay people, and particularly as lay women, in a church that too often fails to include our voices. My own decision to come back to the church was one fraught with difficulties about the patriarchal structure of Catholicism and the backpedaling from the reforms of the Second Vatican Council. I feared that the church was cultivating a culture of secrecy. The priests and nuns I met shared some of these doubts and concerns, but here is the funny thing: they believed anyway. So do my friends. Catholicism at its best allows us to think critically, to examine things from multiple angles. That is what we do together. Their faith helps me hold on to my own, however tenuous it might sometimes be.

Our small community harkens back to the oldest days of the Catholic Church. When the pastor of our sprawling parish recently asked people to give him feedback on what the parish could do to cultivate community, the answer came back clarion clear: more intimate connection with others, smaller group gatherings, a chance to finally learn the name of the person you have been sitting behind for 15 years. Most of the people who came to that meeting were women, and their desire to forge lasting relationships within the parish came from a very human need: the need to be recognized, the need to be heard, the need to be understood.

That is what Jesus did for his disciples, including the women who stood at the foot of the cross as he died and the women who went to the tomb when he rose to live again. At a time when the church often behaves as though it is combating its own death, it is not surprising that lay people are crying out for greater knowledge of one another. If Jesus taught us to recognize God in the poor and the outcast, it is up to us to learn to minister to one another's spiritual poverty and social rejection.

On the evenings when our group gathers, we learn what parts of our lives require nurturing and healing, then we read a short Scripture passage or prayer. We talk about whom we want to hold in prayer that evening, and we meditate together. It is in that time of silence that I most often sense the spiritual bond these women have cultivated for more than a decade. A Poor Clare nun I met last year explained her understanding of God as "relational energy"—the mutual exchange of compassion and love that our faith lives should provide. When our contemplative group concludes meditation and recites a psalm, that energy not only lingers in the room, but sustains us until we gather again.

I am the youngest member of the group. I feel I have gained not only four sisters but four spiritual directors, each of whom in her own way helps me to find my place in this faith, even if that place will always be on the fringes. Our ministry may be a tiny one in this vast, often impersonal church, but we try to carry the small light of our faith into our secular lives. Knowing my friends, I have no doubt that others can see it.

November 15, 2010

2010

On the Slope with Teilhard: Lessons on Spirit and Matter

Drew Christiansen, SJ

"Hymn to Matter" may be one of the oddest-seeming prayers ever penned by a priest. Christians pray to God, to the saints, to the angels perhaps, and sometimes to deceased loved ones. But a hymn to matter? To atoms and rocks, gases and plasma, minerals and stardust? It sounds like idolatry, and indeed as a boy the author of the hymn had such fascination with rocks that he referred to them as "my idols." He explained, "as far as my childish experience went, nothing in the world was harder, heavier, tougher, more durable than this marvelous substance." Soon, as he saw iron rust, he learned the impermanence of the hardest substance he then knew, and a spiritual hunger was born within him.

The prayer's author, Pierre Teilhard de Chardin (1881–1955), a renowned paleontologist and geologist during his lifetime, became better known after his death as a philosopher of evolution and a spiritual writer. But the Jesuit priest never left his rocks behind. Just as discovery of their flaws had initiated him on a mystic quest for a permanent and universal object worthy of his devotion, so Teilhard believed that without matter—without the resistance, disappointments and challenges matter offered humans—our intellectual and spiritual development as a species would be arrested.

Harsh Schoolmaster

Teilhard's "Hymn to Matter" praises the stuff of the universe as the harsh schoolmaster of the human spirit. "Without you, without your onslaughts, without your uprootings of us," he wrote, "we should remain all our lives inert, stagnant, puerile, ignorant both of ourselves and of God."

"By constantly shattering our mental categories, you force us to go ever further and further in our pursuit of truth," he wrote. "By overflowing and dissolving our narrow standards of measurement [you] reveal to us the dimensions of God." Matter, as Teilhard would write, is "'the matrix of spirit': that in which life emerges and is supported, not the active principle from which it takes its rise."

Drawing on his personal, intellectual and spiritual itinerary as a natural scientist and priest, Teilhard regarded the recalcitrance of matter and the need for human effort to uncover its secrets as the starting point for spiritual growth. Whereas other Jesuit giants of the 20th century, like Pierre Rousselot, Joseph Maréchal and Karl Rahner, built their philosophical theologies on the mind's inherent dynamism toward God, Teilhard found the hard effort of learning to be a privileged opening to the divine. The attention the scientist pays to the problem he or she studies is practice for the attention the mystic pays to God. In this discovery, Pierre Teilhard was like another French philosopher, Simone Weil, whose essay "Reflections on the Right Use of School Studies" argued that whether it was translating Homer or solving a problem in Euclidean geometry, study fostered the attention essential to prayer. The poised, energetic openness of the questioner possesses a kinship with the reverent, alert readiness of a person before God.

The Asceticism of Attention

In "Hymn to Matter," Teilhard offered this blessing:

> You who batter us and then dress our wounds, you who resist us and yield to us, you who wreck and build, you who shackle and liberate: it is you, matter, that I bless.

Unlike some who believe that once they enter the world of thought they can leave the physical world behind, Teilhard proposed that the human spirit matures in its effort to understand (master and respect) the natural world. That understanding of the physical world, however, comes through a discipline the scientist must endure. Whether nature or human nature is the subject, applying one's mind to a problem will involve hard effort (including, for a field scientist like Teilhard, physical effort), disappointment and disillusionment. Only then will one find joy in discovery and pleasure in the cumulative growth of understanding.

Insofar as the discipline of science helps us better appreciate God's creation, Teilhard proposed, it is a kind of asceticism, a spiritual practice with potential to deepen the spiritual life. Traditional spirituality stressed control of the body through simplicity, fasting, chastity and physical discipline. For his part, Teilhard pointed out the discipline inherent in the active life and especially in the application of the mind to learning, a discipline he practiced in fieldwork as well as in museum and laboratory research: identifying and analyzing distinctive facts, classifying and relating findings, posing hypotheses and verifying or disproving them. As we Christians practice the mechanics of learning, our spirits can grow as well. As the élan of the learning mind awakens its particular excitement in the learner, the process of inquiry holds the potential to whet our appetite for the infinite mystery of existence.

One problem that afflicts us today, as it did in Teilhard's time, is that there is often too little intellectual discipline on the part of those regarded as authorities in the spiritual life. They mistake the whole of faith with its most elementary expressions and regard question-and-answer catechizing as the equal of serious theology. No doubt, as Alfred North Whitehead wrote, religion takes place "at all temperatures" along a scale of human potentialities. Nonetheless, a richer intellectual life can often make for a richer spiritual experience and a profounder theology. Teilhard teaches us not only that the findings of science can add to our religious wonderment, but also that the scientific way of knowing can strengthen the mind's ascent to God.

An Eye for Rocks—and for God

As a field scientist, Teilhard was reputed to have an exceptional eye for rocks, quickly noting features that escaped the observation of his colleagues and understanding their implications. It is not surprising, then, that whereas the ancient masters of prayer taught about freeing the mind of preoccupation to better open it to the divine, Teilhard believed that the attention of science to the smallest detail of the physical world made the mind even more *capax dei*, "radically open to God." The secret to the spiritual life, as to science, he believed, lies in unremitting attention to details. As we come to appreciate the richness and complexity of the universe, so does our perception grow of the glory of God.

Of course, other spiritual masters also emphasized paying attention to details. St. Thérèse of Lisieux's "little way," for example, is about doing with devotion the small things of daily life. Teilhard's way differs from that of Thérèse or that of the desert fathers, however, in two ways. First, it is about the active life, in which humans exercise their creativity and inventiveness. The creativity of the artist, the problem-solving of the scientist, the inventiveness of the computer engineer, the diagnosis of the physician—all give opportunity to grow in holiness as much as attention to the routines of the monastery or the sacristy.

Second, the attention to details relates especially to intellectual activity and pre-eminently scientific research. Scholarship about the Bible and the classics had held a role in Benedictine spirituality and later in Christian humanism, but science involves active investigation and more than that, revision of earlier ideas. As the mind meets the resistance of the material universe—rocks and atoms, genes and galaxies—"our mental categories" dissolve and "our narrow standards of measurement" are shattered. Research in the natural world weans us from preconceptions to which we would otherwise cling; and as we discover the endless wonders of the universe, the mind opens up to the unimagined dimensions of God.

Asceticism comes in applying ourselves to the learning, letting go of prejudices and obsolete theories and acquiring new skills. At first the development of the students' minds involves rote learning, but the hope is that the atomic table and DNA become so natural that students can apply them in school exercises, design their own experiments, observe anomalies and finally verify their findings through replication. All stages—rote learning, application, experimentation, examining anomalies, verification—entail discipline. For the self-aware scientist or student, the effort it takes to prove a simple fact offers a hint of the dedication that growth in the spirit also requires. Likewise, for the believer and spiritual searcher, the practice of science should suggest the gradual growth of skills, including intellectual ones, that are entailed in the human cooperation with divine grace.

Moving Upward

In time Teilhard came to see matter in broad terms, not just as the object of physical science, but as everything in life that by giving us resistance helps us to move ahead, whether in knowledge, material progress or spiritual development. In *The Divine Milieu* he offered an illuminating analogy that is the key to the spiritual appreciation of matter. "It is the slope on which we can go up just as we can go down," he wrote, "the medium that can uphold or give way, the wind that can overthrow and lift up." Matter's proper role is to be the road of sanctification. "Created things are not exactly obstacles but rather footholds, intermediaries to be made use of, nourishment to be taken, sap to be purified and elements to be associated with us and borne along with us" on our journey into light.

Matter is not a static thing. It is the book just read, the hypothesis confirmed or falsified. It is landlines, fax machines, modems and the Apple computer. It is Gandhi's experiments with truth and it's the Tea Party movement. It is the past that has brought us forward and the past that has held us back. Matter is the toehold of the spirit in history. That toehold defines two zones:

> the zone already left behind or arrived at, to which we should not return, or at which we should not pause, lest we fall back—this is the zone of matter *in the material and carnal sense*; and the zone offered to our renewed efforts toward progress, search, conquest and "divinization," *the zone of matter taken in the spiritual sense*; and the frontier between the two is essentially relative and shifting.

We must lean on the things of this world to move us forward or when they give way, we will tumble back. The spiritual appreciation of matter involves both counting on its resistance to hold us as we press ahead and expecting the exertion demanded of us to move upward. Both forces are necessary.

Like mountaineering, the spiritual life requires steady movement upward, Teilhard reflected. Unless the rock climber poised on her toehold moves forward, she will slip and fall back. "That which is good, sanctifying and spiritual for my brother below or beside me on the mountainside, can be misleading or bad for me," Teilhard advises. "What I rightly allowed myself yesterday, I must perhaps deny myself today."

How matter functions depends on the route of each person's spiritual progress. What I make of the questions I face in my work, what I do with the events in my life, the opportunities I make of crises I encounter, all will determine how deeply I will participate (and the degree to which others share) in the divinization our world is undergoing in Christ. Like mountaineering, advance in the spiritual life depends on making upward progress, discovering, as Teilhard did, as we go that the matter of our life is "the sap of our souls, the hand of God, the flesh of Christ."

December 13, 2010

2011

How God Speaks: Parents Can Help Children Learn How to Listen to God

Edward McCormack

No parents want to receive an unexpected call from their child's school. When a guidance counselor called to report that our daughter Nina, who is in second grade, said some hurtful things to her friend Annie, my wife and I became concerned. That night, as we finished dinner, my wife turned to Nina: "Do you want to talk about what happened between you and Annie today?"

Nina sat straight up, her face turned ashen and her head dropped down. She slowly got up from her chair and made her way over to her mother, sat on her lap, placed her head on my wife's chest and whispered in her ear. My wife put her arms around Nina and pulled her close as she listened to her. The confession ended, and Nina looked up at her mother. My wife explained that Nina knew what she had said was wrong. She asked Nina to write a letter of apology, which she promptly did, to be delivered to her friend the next day.

Nina went downstairs to play with her sister until bedtime. As I listened to her laugh, shout and happily shriek, I knew she was back to her old self. At bedtime Nina said her prayers with me and told me how much better she felt after talking to us about what happened between her and Annie.

The Practice of Speaking to God

The next day, Nina came home from school with a pamphlet on prayer entitled *Catholic Prayer for Catholic Families*. It happily coincided with our desire to be a family of prayer. We say grace at meals and an Our Father or prayer of thanks at bedtime, but we want prayer to become a disposition that shapes how our family relates to the world. We want our children to develop a relationship with God and to become more attentive to God's presence throughout their day. In short, we want to cultivate a contemplative posture of finding God in all things.

During dinner, we read and discussed the introductory section of the pamphlet. It stressed that all prayer begins with the initiative of God, who invites us to know him in a personal manner. The triune mystery, the energizing presence in all things, is constantly reaching out to us through the indwelling Spirit. What appears to be our initiative is actually our response to God's Spirit prompting us to pray. Often we go about the day unaware of God's gracious presence calling us to new life. When we pray, we wake up to God's call and loving embrace. This is why St. Paul advises, "Pray without ceasing."

The pamphlet encouraged us to speak to God in prayer as one friend to another. I asked my kids what they could say to God in prayer. Much to my surprise, Julia, our 5-year-old, began to offer concrete examples: thanking God for food, our house, our teachers; asking God to bring Mommy safely home from work or saying sorry when we hurt each other. Her suggestions corresponded to those in the pamphlet: prayer of thanks, petition and forgiveness.

After dinner and a little violin practice, I read to Nina a chapter from a Harry Potter book. Julia asked me to read the Noah story from her children's Bible. After reading about the flood and the rainbow, Nina asked me, "Why doesn't God speak to us the way he spoke to Noah?" It was a profound question in light of our recent discussion about prayer. I assured my daughters that God does speak to us, especially when we pray.

Christian tradition teaches that God speaks to us in many ways, especially through Jesus Christ, but many struggle to hear God speak at all. The psalmist warns, "If today you hear God's voice, harden not your hearts." That is a big if. The psalmist thinks the problem is hard hearts, which is no doubt true, but we also have a hearing problem. Children are more direct about it, but adults, living in a fast-paced noisy world, struggle to hear the voice of

God. Many Christians do not know how to listen for God's voice because they do not know how God speaks. Many conclude, as my daughter did, that God does not speak to us as God spoke to Noah. If we do not expect God to speak to us, we will not listen for God's voice.

How Does God Speak to Us?

After what Nina had experienced the previous day with her mother, I was surprised that she did not believe God could speak to her "the way he spoke to Noah."

"Nina, I thought God spoke to you loudly and powerfully the other night," I said.

St. Ignatius Loyola teaches that parts of us have not been healed and freed by Christ. Sometimes we act against the work and mission of Christ and engage in destructive behavior. When these situations arise, the Holy Spirit works to change our behavior by filling us with remorse. Many Christians assume they only experience God in moments of peace and joy, but Ignatius reminds us that God speaks to us in other ways, particularly in experiences of remorse. This is an act of love on God's part because God desires to free us from our distorted attitudes and actions. I explained to Nina that God spoke to her through her feelings of regret and sorrow over how she treated Annie.

The Lord also spoke to Nina as she lay in her mother's arms and whispered her confession. Through my wife's embrace, Nina heard and experienced the Lord's mercy and compassion. After admitting what she did and agreeing to write an apology, she felt light, happy and filled with energy. She felt like herself again.

According to St. Ignatius, God encourages the person who seeks to do good by restoring relationships and by filling her with energy, courage, clarity and inspirations. God also gives spiritual consolation. The most common form is feelings of quiet and peace and experiences of interior joy that attract us to live like Christ. The Lord gave Nina a desire to write that letter, the courage to deliver it and the inspiration to act differently toward Annie in the future. Nina experienced how pleased God was with her decision, freeing her from guilt and filling her with joy. That was an experience of spiritual consolation, a result of her cooperation with the Lord.

Doubting Julia

Julia sat next to me listening as I explained to Nina how God had spoken to her in the last two days. "Dad, God doesn't speak to me the way God spoke to Nina," she said.

"But God speaks to you every day," I replied. Julia immediately tested my claim by getting on her knees in front of me, folding her little hands and bowing her head in prayer. When she sat back on the couch, she looked at me and said, "Dad, I just listened for God's voice, and he didn't speak to me as he did to Nina or Noah!"

St. Ignatius believed that all the good we receive in our lives comes from God, like light streaming toward us from the sun. I asked Julia, "What good things were you given today?" She immediately named her mom, her sister, one of her friends and our house. Of course, these were but a few of the many goods God gave her. I reminded her that all of them came from God to her. "Do you know what God is saying to you when he gives you such good things?"

"No," she answered.

I looked her in the eye and said, "God is telling you how much he likes you and cares for you." A big smile appeared on her face.

I paused for a moment and added: "Girls, there are many children who do not have all the good things you have. Many children around the world go hungry, live with violence and do not have a home." They nodded their heads as I spoke. "God is also with them and loves them very much, but the people God sent to care for them do not always listen to God."

"How is God with them?" asked Nina.

I thought for a moment and replied, "Remember Jesus was born poor and died a horrible death, showing us that God is with the poor and the suffering. Just as Jesus walked with the disciples on the road to Emmaus—and you know that story—he walks with all who suffer. He lives in their hearts, giving them courage, strength, peace and hope."

Does God Speak to Grown-ups?

Why doesn't God speak to me as he spoke to the prophets or the disciples of Jesus? This is a common question for many Christians, adults as well as children. Nina's experience, interpreted in the light of fundamental Ignatian principles, reminds me that the Lord Jesus is always speaking to us through our relationships and choices, through our feelings, desires, imagination and thoughts. He speaks through creation, through the gift of our lives, through other people and through our own abilities, opportunities and struggles. The Lord desires to be in a relationship with us, to free and transform us into his image. Our task is to listen and respond.

April 18, 2011

2012

The Art of Prayer

Timothy O'Brien, SJ

Some people, many of them Catholic, go to great lengths to learn about meditative and contemplative practices. For most of my life, I was not one of them. Rather, I came upon contemplation accidentally, almost despite myself.

As a first-year student at the College of the Holy Cross in Worcester, Mass., I registered for "Introduction to the History of Art," a course taught by Professor Joanna E. Ziegler. No great aesthete, I selected the class to fulfill the arts requirement for graduation. And as a novice in art history, my expectations were colored by hand-me-down wisdom from my contemporaries. I anticipated a steady diet of names and dates, with which one might catalogue everything from cave paintings to cathedrals. I remember uttering that dismissive (if common) question heard about the liberal arts: "When will I ever use *that*?"

My expectations were soon shattered. Certain things I remember vividly: Professor Ziegler's sly smile upon first entering the classroom; her hair, shocking in length and curl and whiteness; her gingerly held cup of tea, steam billowing over its top. Most of all, I remember my elation upon first looking at the "evaluation" section of the syllabus and finding none of the anticipated tests and quizzes. (Things were looking up for art history!)

Instead, we were given the names of three paintings and sent to the Worcester Art Museum. We were to look at each, identify which one most seized our attention and report back. Almost a decade later, I still remember my first viewing of Pieter Jansz Saenredam's *Interior of the Choir of St. Bavo's*

Church at Haarlem. There is no other way to put it: I was intrigued. The soaring, Spartan interior of the church had a subdued silence about it. And the painting fostered the same in me.

The purpose of this first museum trip was revealed at our next class. We would visit the museum for one hour each week, preferably at the same time of day, to look solely at our selected painting. Notebook in tow, we were to write down what we saw, beginning from scratch each week if necessary. No additional research about the painting or artist was permitted, not even dates. We were even discouraged from reading the work's identification placard.

For 13 weeks, I gazed at the austere choir of Saenredam's church. Though I later learned that this was one of his favorite subjects, I knew nothing about it at the time. Sitting before the painting early in the semester, I looked at my watch after what felt like an hour, ready to depart. Fifteen minutes had passed. Mumbling something uncharitable about art historians—or one particular art historian, at least—I stayed put.

To make time go faster, I wrote down everything I saw, noting colors and brush strokes. Was it painted on wood, not canvas? Several weeks later, I saw people in the painting that I had overlooked before. What were they doing? I noted features of the church different from any worship space I had ever visited. What kind of church was this? How did Saenredam convey the vastness of space and the intricate vaulted ceiling with mere paint? Gradually, I became more adept at "seeing" the work, letting it reveal itself over time. I grew quieter, writing less. And what I initially called "the painting" I now thought of, with all respect to the artist, as "my painting."

Back at Holy Cross, in class and conversation, I learned that this was precisely the point. Professor Ziegler was taken up not so much with names and dates as with how art intersected with contemplation, revelation and mystery. For her, introducing a class to art history involved our learning how to see, understood as both a spiritual and physical activity. We learned, or tried at least, to be attentive and heedful, to wonder at something beautiful.

Our teacher had asked us to become contemplatives.

In the Gospel of Luke, the disciples entreat Jesus, "Master, teach us to pray." He responds with the words of the Our Father. Many of us learned to pray with these or similar words, schooled by our parents and preachers before even thinking to ask for instruction. With time, these rote formulae can open the way to larger expanses of prayer, to meditation and contemplation, which are considerably harder to teach.

Professor Ziegler's class and Saenredam's church were essential for my schooling in prayer. I do not claim to have had some mystical experience in the Worcester Art Museum. Quite the opposite. My recorded concerns were distressingly terrestrial: uncomfortable seating and the stale air proper to art museums.

But like all good introductions, her course laid the groundwork for later growth. This project pointed to the virtues of routine and ritual. Repetition helped minimize the extent to which my own "baggage" in a given week colored how and what I saw. Most important, it underscored that contemplative practice hinges on one's disposition; that mystery—whether a painting's or God's—will be as apparent to us as our attentiveness allows.

Life after college took me into government service and then into the Society of Jesus. St. Ignatius wanted his followers to be "contemplatives in action," to see this world with different eyes. Most of the lessons I have learned as a pray-er cycle back in some way to Saenredam's work and my semester seated before it. After all, what is contemplation if not looking and seeing with care, awe and even love? As a Jesuit, I was heartened to encounter a definition of prayer by Walter Burghardt, SJ, as "a long, loving look at the real."

Professor Ziegler died last November, far too soon. My appreciation for what she was about continues to deepen, however. Since the cornerstone of her course was that our judgments develop with time, maturing as things are revealed to us, this seems entirely appropriate.

"Master, teach us to pray," the disciples asked. How fitting that some teachers and artists are called "masters." Both share Jesus' concern for people who have "eyes but do not see." And like him, they, too, can teach us to pray.

February 13, 2012

2012

Interrupting Grace: A Contemplative Learns to Let Go

T. B. Pasquale

Five minutes into my centering prayer practice—though it felt like 30—with a dedicated Thursday prayer group at the Sisters of the Cenacle, I sat fidgeting in a stackable chair with coarse fabric and a pin-straight metal back. The sound of the fan whooshed overhead adding a distracting rhythm to silence: *whoosh, pause, thump, whoosh, pause, thump.*

The woman next to me coughed; then the chair to the left of me, a rocker like the one my grandmother sat in to watch *Judge Judy*, began to creak. The symphony in my brain began to whir: *whoosh, pause, thump, creak, creak, cough, creak.*

I could almost feel the seconds ticking by on my watch, a slow-motion judgment of my inability to sit, be still and wait for God to do the heavy lifting. Its rhythm joined the sounds counting down to my failure to find bliss, peace and union: *Tick, tick, tick, whoosh, pause, thump, creak, creak, cough, creak.*

If only I could find a sacred image or word. But the search became a game of free association as my brain clamored for an anchor: God? No. Jesus? No. Joy? No. Peace? No. Fan? Um, really no.

"O.K." I told myself, "We're going to try *peace.*" That seemed like a reasonably sacred aspiration. Slowing my breath—inhale deeply, exhale completely—I used physical breathing to command my mental hyperactivity to calm down. *Peace, peace, peace.* The word called to my soul to lean forward through the psychological noise.

Then, rushing ahead of the word, a figure came into view—soft hair, bright eyes, gentle—the childhood image of Jesus I had always carried with me, like a postcard from another life. A scene unfolded, as in a guided meditation. "This is something I could use in teaching contemplative prayer next week," I thought, trying to nudge this distraction from my head so I could contemplate my sacred word. *Peace, peace, peace. Breath in, exhale.*

Then, like an impatient customer in line at the grocery store, another image pushed forward, this time of a figure sitting knee to knee before me, each of us on a chair staring lovingly into each other's eyes. I see my mother and feel a wave of unconditional love. I see the closeness between us grow in the shape of warm, white light radiating from her chest and mine.

"This will be a great meditation," I thought. "Now come on, brain, get back to silent prayer. Why can't I focus?" *Peace, peace, peace. Breath in, exhale.*

Again, the visualization rushed back, crisper than before: My mother and me, facing each other, knees almost touching, bright warm light moving together from the center of our chests into one larger light that encompasses us. The light grows with every breath, moving through us, then growing past us, around each side of us into the dark space beyond our chairs. With each breath the light grows, the warmth pulses, our bodies radiate with light and compassion.

"O.K." I began again, frustrated with my lack of concentration. "Everyone around me is probably ensconced in a sacred word or image, and here I am struggling to stay focused, planning this visualization for my own contemplative prayer students. I'm an awful contemplative." I sighed a deep sigh of self-inflicted judgment.

The visual came back fiercer than before, and I gave up trying to control it. "I guess this will just be a 'working' contemplation," I thought, giving in to it—the warmth of light, the love. Then as I gazed into my mother's eyes, her face became that of Jesus, like the postcard image, but more alive. I felt her loving me with the vividness of my mother, and I saw her eyes in Christ's gaze and her face in his.

This was not my mind intruding on my contemplation, I realized. This was God, trying to get some quality time in a prayer meant to be

God-centered. I smiled and let the warmth of the light wash over me, finally being quiet long enough to let God get a word in edgewise.

As a teacher of contemplation, I travel on daily pilgrimages of faith with others, acting as a road map or a tour guide, serving in whatever way God blesses me to be useful. Perpetually I am learning lessons in deeper and more humbling ways, trying to make my failings useful to other pilgrims.

I am surprised by the grace that regularly, softly shrouds the life I lead and the mistakes I make and by the God who helps me find the way when I stop interrupting. God calls us all to listen: "Be still and know that I am God." I am haltingly trying to learn that lesson.

July 16–23, 2012

2013

The Walking Cure

Michael Rossmann, SJ

There is a reason we don't talk about "sidewalk rage": It doesn't exist, at least where I've lived. Like many people, I often get frustrated while driving in traffic. I also get upset on my bike if drivers don't acknowledge the presence of bikers, even as drivers justifiably get frustrated with me on a bike if I do not follow the rules of the road. But the sidewalk? I honestly cannot remember a time when I was angry on the sidewalk. Even if I were frustrated before I started walking, the repetition of steps has a way of putting me at ease and clearing my mind.

Life is slower on the sidewalk—this is most definitely not "life in the fast lane"—but it's also far less stressful. You don't hear of someone complaining about how he was late because of sidewalk construction or a "sidewalk jam." I may know that walking will be slower than another means of transportation, but if it is a route with which I am familiar, I can know almost to the exact minute how long it will take me, whereas other methods of getting around are subject to many potentially delaying variables.

I'm far more open to pleasant surprises and simple beauties while walking and am able to change my plans completely. I can actually stop and smell the roses. While driving, I'm likely not even to notice the roses. Or if I happen to see them, I then may need to turn around—far more difficult if there is traffic or if I'm on a one-way street—look for and probably pay for a parking spot and then walk around looking for the roses that I saw from the car window.

There are also many more opportunities on the sidewalk for making the world a better, kinder place. It's impossible to strike up conversations with passing cars, and even if I try to smile at other drivers, they are unlikely to see me. These things, however, are normal on the sidewalk, at least in most of the places where I have lived. (I admit, however, that this isn't necessarily the case everywhere; my smiles and pleasantries on the sidewalk have been returned with very confused looks in a few cities I have visited.)

Additionally, walking has a surprising number of parallels with the spiritual life.

At an initial glance, walking seems rather unproductive, similar in many ways to spending time in prayer. There are usually far faster modes of transportation. Additionally, if one walks for exercise, it initially appears to be less efficient than other types of exercise that will raise your heart rate much faster.

Scientists, however, are starting to see how intense exercise is not necessarily the secret to losing weight; one may then be more likely to chow down and be lazy during the rest of the day, whereas simply incorporating more walking into one's daily routine might be more effective for reducing one's waistline.

Analogously, one can look around and see how there's a whole lot of work we need to do in the world—starting with ourselves and our families—and that prayer can initially seem like something that takes time away from the more important action.

Though I am not motivated by productivity in choosing to walk or pray, I might actually be far more productive when I do these things. Starting my day with a walk, rather than a traffic jam, even if the walk takes some time, is far more likely to put me in a relaxed state, ready to work. Prayer, while it might seem far less productive than active service, is likely the well that can sustain continued service over a long period of time.

More than this, walking, like prayer, makes me feel more like a human being, rather than a human doing. Sure, I could travel in a way that is far faster or spend my time producing more, but I often feel most liberated when I realize that I don't always have to produce. I don't always have to rush from place to place. I slowly learn with each step that life is not about efficiency or productivity.

People often ask me where I'm going during my evening stroll. "I'm just walking," I often respond, at times to perplexed looks. It can seem like wasted time. Similarly, one of my favorite definitions of prayer is "wasting" time with God. The truth is, however, that time with God, or time in the pedestrian lane during which I'm able to appreciate God's creation, is never really wasted time.

May 13, 2013

Contributors

George M. Anderson, SJ, a former editor of *America* and author of *Finding Christ in Prison*, works in pastoral ministry and resides at the St. Claude la Colombière Jesuit Community in Baltimore, Maryland.

William A. Barry, SJ, a longtime contributor to *America*, is a prolific author on a variety of topics concerning Catholicism and spirituality. Among his books are *Finding God in All Things: A Companion to the Spiritual Exercises of St. Ignatius* and *God and You: Prayer as a Personal Relationship*. He is a former Provincial and has been a coleader of part of the Jesuit formation program for the former New England Province of the Society of Jesus.

David Berry, an *America* contributor, is a consultant and speaker on sustainability and lives in Virginia.

Stephen Bonian, SJ, a Jesuit priest of the Eastern tradition, works in pastoral ministry among Iranian Catholics and resides at Bellarmine College Prep Jesuit Community in San Jose, California. He had previously been based in the Jesuit Center in Amman, Jordan.

Drew Christiansen, SJ, a former editor in chief of *America* and now senior fellow at the School of Foreign Service at Georgetown University, is known for his expertise in international relations, particularly on the Middle East, and also on questions pertaining to ecumenical issues.

Doris Donnelly, a contributor of articles and book reviews to *America*, is a professor of theology at John Carroll University in Cleveland, Ohio. She is also the director of the Cardinal Suenens Center at the university.

Cyril B. Egan was a Fordham graduate who taught mathematics for forty-four years at Regis High School in New York City. He also taught English and the classics at Fordham and Pace College. In 1959, he was awarded a medal by Pope John XXIII for distinguished service as a Catholic layman. A resident of Yonkers, New York, he died at the age of eighty-nine in the Bronx.

Karl Bjorn Erickson, a resident of the state of Oregon, is an *America* contributor and, in addition to being a prolific essayist, is the author of many books, including *Tristan's Travels* and *The Blood Cries Out.*

Gerard F. Giblin, SJ, at the time of his article's publication in *America*, had conducted extensive research on the service of the Jesuit chaplains in the Armed Forces of the United States from 1917 to 1960 and was the author of that study, which was published by Woodstock College Press in 1961.

Terrence W. Halloran, at the time of his article's publication in *America*, was an assistant pastor of St. Mary's Church in Los Angeles, California, and was an outspoken advocate for civil rights. Since that time, he has left the priesthood and is now married.

Dennis Hamm, SJ, is professor emeritus of theology at Creighton University in Omaha, Nebraska. He was a columnist for *America's* "The Word" column for several years.

Daniel J. Harrington, SJ, (1940–2014) was a noted professor of New Testament and chair of the Biblical Studies Department at Boston College School of Theology and Ministry (formerly known as the Weston Jesuit School of Theology). He was also the editor of New Testament Abstracts from 1972 until his death. Besides being a regular contributor to *America*, he was also the editor of the eighteen-volume *Sacra Pagina* New Testament series for Liturgical Press.

John C. Haughey, SJ, is the author of numerous books, including *Should Anyone Say Forever: On Making, Keeping, and Breaking Commitments* and *Housing Heaven's Fire: The Challenge of Holiness.* He resides at the St. Claude la Colombière Jesuit Community in Baltimore, Maryland. Among his other positions, he served as a professor of theology at Loyola University Chicago.

Richard J. Hauser, SJ, who has written articles and book reviews for *America*, is assistant to the president for mission and professor emeritus of theology at Creighton University in Omaha, Nebraska, as well as an associate director of Christian spirituality.

Rev. John B. Healey, a priest of the Diocese of Brooklyn, New York, has written frequently on the subject of charismatic prayer.

C. M. (Carlos Maria) de Heredia, SJ, came from an affluent Mexican family. From childhood on, he was intensely interested in magic and later became a friend of another magician, Harry Houdini. At the time of his writing for *America*, he was renowned for his studies in magic, philosophy, and religion; his studies culminated in a work he wrote as an adult, *Spiritism and Common Sense*.

George W. Hunt, SJ, (1937–2011) was the longest-serving editor in chief of *America* (1984–1998). His interests were in a wide variety of fields, from baseball to music to literature, as well as religion. His areas of interest provided the topics of much of his writing, particularly of his popular *America* column, "Of Many Things." He was also the author of studies on John Cheever and John Updike.

Robert Inchausti, editor of *Echoing Silence: Thomas Merton on the Vocation of Writing*, is a professor of English at California Polytechnic State University, San Luis Obispo. He is also the author of *Subversive Orthodoxy, The Ignorant Perfection of Ordinary People, Spitwad Sutras*, and *Thomas Merton's American Prophecy*.

Greg Kandra is a writer whose work has appeared not only in *America* but also in *U.S. Catholic, Catholic Digest,* and *The Brooklyn Tablet*. He has been a story producer for *60 Minutes II*, the CBS News program.

Thomas Keating, OCSO, is a Trappist monk noted for his writings on spirituality and contemplative prayer; his numerous books include *Invitation* *to Love, Centering Prayer* and *Intimacy with God*. He is noted for being a founder of the Centering Prayer movement. He lives at St. Benedict's Monastery in Snowmass, Colorado.

Rev. David M. Knight, a priest of the Diocese of Memphis, has authored more than 20 books and has taught at the Catholic University of America as well at Loyola University New Orleans.

Rev. Robert P. Maloney, CM, is a former superior general of the Congregation of the Mission and has served as an administrator for Dream, a joint project of the Community of Sant'Egidio and the Daughters of Charity for combatting AIDS in Africa.

James Martin, SJ, editor at large at *America* magazine, is the author of the recent best seller *Jesus: A Pilgrimage*. In addition to his novel *The Abbey: A Story of Discovery*, Father Martin is also the author of several books on spirituality, including *The Jesuit Guide to (Almost) Everything* and *My Life with the Saints*.

Stephen Martin, a writer who lives in Greensboro, North Carolina, has written for *Commonweal* and for *U.S. News & World Report*.

Edward McCormack, a specialist in Ignatian spirituality, is an associate professor of Christian spirituality and chair of the Christian Spirituality Department at Washington Theological Union.

Jacqueline McMakin had, at the time of her writing for *America*, been an active participant in grassroots ecumenical efforts and has written on the subject as well.

Frank Moan, SJ, an *America* contributor, is a member of the St. Claude la Colombière Jesuit Community in Baltimore, Maryland. He was also the founder and director of Refugee Voices.

Henri J. M. Nouwen (1932–1996) was a Dutch Catholic priest and renowned spiritual writer of his time, with many books to his credit, among them *Reaching Out, Clowning in Rome, The Wounded Healer, Can You Drink* *the Cup?, The Way of the Heart,* and *The Return of the Prodigal Son.* His teaching career led him from the University of Notre Dame in Indiana to Yale Divinity School as well as to Harvard Divinity School. He was also noted for his work with the mentally and physically handicapped at the L'Arche community in Richmond Hill, Ontario, Canada.

Kaya Oakes has taught writing at University of California, Berkeley since 1999. She is the author of the memoir *Radical Reinvention: An Unlikely Return to the Catholic Church,* in which she describes her transition back to her Catholic faith from atheism. She is also the author of *Slanted and Enchanted: The Evolution of Indie Culture* and was twice nominated for the Pushcart Prize for nonfiction. She is also a poet; her first book, a poetry collection called *Telegraph,* won the Transcontinental Poetry Award from Pavement Saw Press in 2008.

Timothy O'Brien, SJ, is a Jesuit scholastic preparing for ordination, and a graduate student at the University of Chicago Divinity School, as well as an associate editor of *The Jesuit Post.* In addition to contributing articles to *America,* he has also written for the magazine's online blogs.

William J. O'Malley, SJ, a frequent contributor to *America* over the years, has written extensively about prayer life and spirituality; he may be best known for being the first priest to play a priest in a film (Father Dyer in *The Exorcist*). An educator, he has published nearly 40 books, among which are *God: The Oldest Question, Daily Prayers for Busy People, Choosing to Be Catholic: For the First Time or Once Again, The Fifth Week,* and *Why Be Catholic?* His book *Help My Unbelief* was the winner of the Catholic Book Award in 2009.

T. B. Pasquale is a writer, trauma therapist, and educator on the contemplative dimension of faith.

M. Basil Pennington, OCSO, (1931–2005) was a noted spiritual writer. Among his books are *Centering Prayer: Renewing an Ancient Christian Prayer Form* and *A School of Love: The Cistercian Way to Holiness.* At the time his article was published in *America,* he was based at St. Joseph's Abbey, in Spencer,

Massachusetts. He also served as superior of the Assumption Abbey in Ava, Missouri, and was abbot of the Monastery of the Holy Spirit in Conyers, Georgia. He had returned to St. Joseph's when he retired; it was while being stationed there that he died from injuries sustained in a car accident in 2005.

Jane Redmont is the Northeastern Regional Director for the National Conference of Christians and Jews and is the author of *When in Doubt, Sing: Prayer in Daily Life* and *Generous Lives: American Catholic Women Today*. A retreat leader, pastoral minister, spiritual director, and theologian, she has also worked in campus, urban, and parish ministries. She is dedicated to ecumenical and interreligious dialogue as well as to social justice and is currently preparing for ordination as an Episcopal priest.

Michael Rossmann, SJ, a contributor to *America* and editor of *The Jesuit Post*, is a Jesuit scholastic who resides at the St. Peter Faber Jesuit Community in Boston, Massachusetts. He had previously taught at Loyola High School in Dar es Salaam, Tanzania.

Jerry Ryan, a freelance writer, lives in Chelsea, Massachusetts.

Evelyn Waugh (1903–1966), a noted English author, wrote 14 novels between 1928 and 1961 and was also known for his biographies and travel books. Perhaps his best-known book is *Brideshead Revisited*, published in 1945. Like Graham Greene, he was a convert to Catholicism. Waugh was once a mentor to the budding writer Thomas Merton, the noted Trappist monk.